A Survival Guide for Buying a Home

SECOND EDITION

Sid Davis

American Management Association

New York • Atlanta • Brussels • Chicago • Mexico City
San Francisco • Shanghai • Tokyo • Toronto • Washington, D. C.

Special discounts on bulk quantities of AMACOM books are available to corporations, professional associations, and other organizations. For details, contact Special Sales Department, AMACOM, a division of American Management Association, 1601 Broadway, New York, NY 10019.
Tel: 212-903-8316. Fax: 212-903-8083.
E-mail: specialsls@amanet.org
Website: www.amacombooks.org/go/specialsales
To view all AMACOM titles go to: www.amacombooks.org

Library of Congress Cataloging-in-Publication Data

Davis, Sid, 1944–
    A survival guide for buying a home / Sid Davis. — 2nd ed.
        p.   cm.
    ISBN 978-0-8144-1425-5
    1. House buying—United States.   2. Residential real estate—Purchasing—United States.   3. Mortgage loans—United States. I. Title.
    HD259.D38   2009
    643'.120973—dc22

                                                                2009004735

Printing number

10 9 8 7 6 5 4 3 2 1

Contents

Contents

Introduction to the Second Edition

When the first edition of *A Survival Guide for Buying a Home* was published in 2004, the housing market was well on its way to suborbit prices. The mind-set of buyers at that time was not how to buy a home they could afford and get the best deal, but how they could buy the biggest home possible with the lowest down payment.

Real estate agents grew skilled at finding lenders that would give buyers the biggest loans and be willing to ignore any egregious credit problems. And they learned how to handle multiple offers on homes that sometimes resulted in intense bidding frenzies. Each new round of homes built in a subdivision sported price tags higher than those listed previously. It was a one-way ticket up the economic ladder and no one thought about an eventual reentry, or even whether such a thing would ever happen. We now have our answer.

The first edition of this book covered subprime loans, high debt-to-income loans, buying conservatively or going for the max, and other concerns involved in buying a home. Those days, of course, are gone. There's now a new reality to home buying, the landscape has changed, and new home-buying skills are necessary in today's rapidly changing market.

This second edition of *A Survival Guide for Buying a Home* focuses on the new home-buying landscape that's still undergoing fast-paced changes. Gone are the sections on getting a loan with zero down and adjustable rate loans with interest-only payments. Instead, the emphasis is on how to build and maintain good credit and buy a home within your income.

Also covered is how to evaluate and compare good faith estimates from different mortgage lenders to find out which one is offering you the best deal. There should be no wondering at closing whether you got the best and cheapest loan possible. And coupled with the new information in Chapter 5 on how to make offers and negotiate the best deals, you're practically guaranteed to get the most house for your money.

Throughout the book, I've endeavored to explain in each chapter how that particular real estate topic affects your pocketbook and what you can do to save money. For easier navigation, each chapter begins with a list of the important concepts covered. Each chapter also concludes with a list of suggestions on how you can implement what you've learned in your efforts to buy and own a home.

Throughout the book you'll also find valuable up-to-date information on:

- How mortgage lenders now qualify you for a mortgage

- How to increase and maintain your credit score

- Why it's important to nail down a mortgage commitment before you start shopping

- How to shop for a mortgage lender and get the best deal

- How to streamline your home-shopping strategy to find your dream home fast

- How to present your offer and get it accepted

- How to find a competent home inspector, then how to use an inspection report to protect yourself and to negotiate with the sellers

- How to avoid common mistakes condo, co-op, and townhouse buyers make that cost money and happiness

- How to buy a manufactured home, whether modular, panel, precut, or mobile

- The insurance you need to protect yourself from floods, earthquakes, and other concerns

In addition, Chapter 10 distills over twenty-five years of real estate experience into a list of twenty common mistakes home buyers make and how to avoid making them yourself. Updated and expanded from the previous edition, this book is chockfull of tips on buying the best house at the best deal.

A new feature of this Second Edition is its wealth of "Survival Tips" that highlight critical points in the home-buying effort. Also, because single home buyers now account for nearly a fifth of all home sales, there's a new appendix for home-buying singles, with even more shopping and buying tips.

It's a great time to buy a home. Interest rates are down, sellers are flexible, and inventories are high. After reading this book, you'll have all the tools you need to go out and make it happen.

CHAPTER 1

Getting Started on Becoming a Homeowner

Becoming a homeowner can be a bittersweet experience. You look forward to getting out of your apartment and into your new home so you can do your own thing, decorating the interior and landscaping the exterior (if your home has a yard). But taking on a mortgage commitment for thirty years can be scary, and all the what-ifs can play like a horror movie in your imagination.

In reality, committing to a thirty-year fixed-rate mortgage with its predictable monthly payment is a lot less scary than waiting to hear how much your rent will increase next time it comes time to renew. However, both renting and buying have one thing in common: If you make your payment on time, the landlord won't appear on your doorstep and the lender won't send you threatening letters. The biggest difference between buying and renting is that, when you buy your home, you get the house free and clear after 360 payments, along with some attractive tax breaks, whereas when you rent your home, you may get a smile and a thank-you from your landlord for helping to ensure that his or her retirement will be a comfortable one.

To help you get started on becoming a homeowner, in this chapter I discuss some of the relative advantages of buying versus renting a home. I then guide you in taking those all-important first steps, advising you on what to do and what to avoid, and providing some real-life examples of homeowners who have blazed a path that you can follow.

In this chapter you'll learn how to:

- Recognize the financial advantages of buying over renting a home.

- Understand the real estate concepts of leverage, appreciation, and equity.

- Distinguish between a buyer's market and a seller's market.

- Determine how much money you may be able to get as a loan.

- Grasp the process of credit scoring and home-buying credit requirements.

- Determine how much home you can afford.

- Understand how automatic underwriting works and how it benefits you.

The Financial Advantages of Buying versus Renting

Gerald and Bonnie lived in a three-bedroom brick bungalow in an upscale neighborhood. In the years they were there, they raised their two children, were active in community affairs, and had a lifestyle just like other families on their tree-lined street, except for one factor. They were renters, and they rented from a homeowner who lived three houses up the street and who had built the home as an investment when he built his own home.

For twenty-five years, Gerald and Bonnie rented their home and treated it like their own. Then their landlord died suddenly of a heart attack, and one of his heirs decided she would remodel the rental home and move in. A couple of months later, Gerald and Bonnie were given a thirty-day notice to vacate the premises. This was a heartbreaking situation for Gerald and Bonnie, and one that happens all too often. When you're a tenant you have little control over your housing future.

Even more tragic in this case was that the tenants had, over the years, paid off the owner's mortgage with their rent and had given him a good tax deduction as well, while the home's value appreciated from $22,000 to over $268,000!

As the movers loaded Gerald and Bonnie's furniture, Bonnie came across a file box in which she had kept important papers. There, neatly stacked, were twenty-five years and four months of rent receipts, which was all they had to show for their 304 monthly rent payments in addition to a lot of good memories. By way of contrast, their neighbors Clyde and Heather bought a charming two-story frame home right after graduating from college, thirty years ago. When they upgraded to a new, larger home in the neighborhood, they kept their old home as a rental property. Over the years the tenants' rent had helped them pay off the mortgage on the property; currently the rental is generating over $900 a month in income and the home has appreciated from $23,000 to over $220,000.

> **HOME-BUYING TIP**
>
> **Most financial planners agree that it's best to buy a home as soon as possible in life so that you can begin building equity, get homeowner tax breaks, and create financial stability.**

The Financial Advantages of Renting

Becoming a homeowner is a dream that nearly 67 percent of Americans have achieved, according to the National Association of Realtors' 2007 numbers. (The term "Realtor," used in this book and in general conversation about real estate, is a trademark-protected name for a member of this group.) As for the other 33 percent, many of those Americans see renting or living with relatives as a temporary situation until they can qualify for a home of their own.

Renting can be a good short-term strategy. For example, if you're not sure how long you're going to be in an area, or your job future is uncertain, this route may be your best option. Renting can also be a good strategy for a few months while you get to know an unfamiliar area. Taking time to find the right neighborhood and the best home can save you an expensive move later. Renting can also be a smart move when it's a buyer's market (plentiful inventory and stable or declining prices) and you are able to shop around for the perfect home and the best deal.

> **HOME-BUYING TIP**
>
> **An effective alternative way to buy a home is with a lease option. If your credit or job history is weak, this strategy can often get you into a home. Tips and traps on lease options are detailed in Chapter 4.**

Incidentally, the flip side of a buyer's market is a seller's market. In this latter situation there are more buyers than homes for sale and prices are escalating, which increases the pressure to move quickly or lose the home to other buyers. A seller's market does have its downside, as we've seen from the downturn of 2006–2008, which has left many homeowners owing more on their mortgages than their homes are currently worth. (More about the seller's market later on in this chapter.)

The Financial Advantages of Buying

American society is based on what has been termed "family values," and for most people, getting married and raising a family is a major reason for buying a home. It gives family members a sense of belonging to a community, of putting down roots in an area and caring about its general welfare. Generally, renting doesn't provide these feelings. As one home-buying couple said as they filled out the paperwork to make an offer, "The reason we're buying right now is so our son will have memories of home, of the house he will grow up in."

Having a place of your own that you can improve on and use to express your decorating talents is another reason people give for buying a house. Never again will you consider renting after you've experienced the new-found freedom to paint rooms your favorite colors or experiment with carpets and wallpaper. Justin and Susan did just this when they bought their first home, a ten-year-old, three-bedroom, two-bath tri-level. After having rented a dreary basement apartment for the previous five years, Susan's pent-up creativity exploded. She and Justin painted every room a different, bright color and decorated with matching accessories. When they discovered that a baby was on the way, they were thrilled, not only by the addition but also by the opportunity to create a perfect nursery in Disney colors.

It's also no secret that home ownership is a good financial move. A few of home ownership's advantages are:

- It's a way many Americans build their net worth and add financial stability.

- It can be considered a forced savings plan, a way to save for retirement or pay for the kids' college. Overall, since the 1950s, land and home prices have steadily increased.

- A small down payment controls a much bigger investment, which grows as you pay down the loan and the house increases in value.

- If you choose a fixed-rate mortgage, the payments stay the same until the loan is paid off, while rents are unpredictable and can increase at the landlord's whim.

- If you choose your improvements wisely, you can increase the home's value and equity, sometimes dramatically.

How Leverage, Appreciation, and Equity Make You Money

The triad of leverage, appreciation, and equity powers real estate finance. These are important and powerful concepts that you need to become familiar with so you can put them to work for you.

Leverage

Leverage is a term used by people in finance to describe an investment that you make with little of your own money invested. Mortgages are typically highly leveraged investments. For example, you borrow $250,000 to buy a home with a $12,500 down payment. This means that your $12,500 investment controls a $250,000 asset. If the home increases in value to $300,000 over the next three years, your investment of $12,500 likewise has increased to $50,000—a 300 percent return—so your down payment has more than doubled in value each year you've owned the home. The financial power of leverage benefits you because the entire asset goes up in value, not just your down payment.

However, leverage also has its dark side. Buyers sometimes imprudently take out a mortgage that they can't make the payments on because of the easy terms they were offered. *Adjustable rate loans* (ARMs), which have low initial interest rates that can go up every year, or loans that start out with low teaser rates and then in six months or a year escalate hundreds of dollars a month, are notorious examples. It's important to look at leverage as a double-edged tool to be used with caution.

Appreciation

When a home increases in value, the difference between the purchase price and the current value is called *appreciation*. For example, if you bought a home for $250,000 and sold it two years later for $325,000, the home appreciated $75,000.

Factors that boost a home's appreciation include:

- The neighborhood has increased in value owing to local improvements or buyer demand for an area.

- There are now lower mortgage rates, which increases demand.

- You've made home improvements or added amenities, which can increase your home's overall value.

- Home values have inflated owing to monetary policy or currency inflation.

- A strong local economy has created more demand for homes in the area.

- The area has outstanding schools, which increases demand for homes within its boundaries.

Of course, there's a flip side to appreciation as well. If a home loses value, it's called *negative appreciation*. Conditions that may cause homes to lose value include:

- An increase in mortgage rates.

- Credit becomes tighter, making it more difficult for buyers to get loans.

- A slowing local economy, which reduces the number of buyers able to afford a home.

- Environmental changes such as a new freeway on/off ramp, rezoning, commercial building, or other factors that lower buyers' perceptions of the area.

- Overbuilding in the area, resulting in more homes for sale than the current market can absorb.

While there's no such animal as a sure thing, the long-term trend, recorded over the last fifty years, has been for real estate to appreciate. Although local conditions can sometimes cause a dip in the real estate market, those conditions eventually improve and values resume their upward trend.

Equity

Equity is the difference between a home's current value and any existing loan balances. It can go up or down, depending on the local real estate market. For example, if your mortgage balance is $189,000 and you have a home equity line for $46,000, then your total loan balances

---

HOME-BUYING TIP

Buy in the best neighborhood you can afford. It's better to buy a smaller home in a better area than a larger home in a less desirable area, because when the time comes to sell, your home's value will have increased more than the home in the less desirable neighborhood.

come to $235,000. Should you decide to sell or refinance, and you hire an appraiser who appraises your home at $339,500, your equity would be $339,500 minus $235,000, or $104,500.

However, equity can change because it is dependent on the value of your home, which can increase or decrease with market fluctuations. Value is usually established by an appraisal that is good for up to six months, depending on the market.

Equity can also come into play if you were to talk to a mortgage lender about a second mortgage, or home equity loan, and the lender may tell you that he or she is willing to loan you up to 90 percent of your equity. The bank hires an appraiser who determines that your home is worth $350,000. Subtracting that amount from your first mortgage of $180,000 leaves you $170,000 in equity, of which the bank is willing to loan you 90 percent, or $153,000.

Although the national economy strongly influences local real estate values, the equity you accrue is still dependent on local supply and demand. When you sell a home and move to another area, it's common to either suffer sticker shock or rejoice in how big a home you can qualify for. For instance, if you sold your 1,200-square-foot home in San Francisco's Sunset District and moved to Ogden, Utah, you could get basically the same home for about 70 percent less.

Whatever the Market, It's Always a Good Time to Buy

The real estate market is in constant motion. Like a giant pendulum, it swings

According to National Association of Realtors data on first-time homebuyers:

- 42 percent of home sales over the last twelve years were to first-time homebuyers.
- 70 percent bought a home because they wanted to own real estate and establish a household.
- 75 percent rented an apartment or home prior to buying a home, and 18 percent lived with their parents.
- 52 percent were twenty-four to thirty-five years old and 21 percent were thirty-five to forty-four years old.
- 28 percent plan to live in the home for at least five years.
- 51 percent were married couples, 11 percent unmarried couples, 25 percent were single females, and 11 percent were single males.
- 73 percent used their own savings as down payment, 22 percent received gift funds, 98 percent used a mortgage to finance their home, and 81 percent chose a fixed-rate mortgage.

> **HOME-BUYING TIP**
>
> **It's seldom a good financial strategy to wait for interest rates or home prices to drop before buying. Buy as soon as possible and begin building equity and qualifying for tax breaks that more than offset any gains from waiting.**

from a buyer's market to a seller's market and back again. Where the market is in the arc depends on many factors. Most common are interest rates and what direction they're heading, as well as local employment and the national economy. These factors in turn affect the number of homes on the market and ultimately the prices of these homes.

Both buyer's and seller's markets have their own sets of advantages and disadvantages. By following the right strategies, it's possible to make good buys in either market. These strategies are covered in the next few chapters.

The Advantages of a Buyer's Market

No matter what part of the country you're living in, the real estate market will be in flux. If there are more homes for sale than there are buyers, it's good for buying but not so good for selling. Finding good deals on homes to buy will be easier and there will be a lot more opportunity if you shop around.

> **HOME-BUYING TIP**
>
> **Always add concessions to your offer to buy, particularly asking for the payment of closing costs. It's amazing what sellers will agree to when they have a bird-in-the-hand offer on the table. This can often free up a few thousand dollars you can use to redecorate your new home.**

Looking at many homes and comparing areas and price-per-square foot increases your ability to spot the good deals and move decisively when you do find your dream home. Buyers who purchase when the real estate pendulum favors them and then wait until it favors sellers before selling can make big profits. Timing and luck are important in making this happen, but keeping a close eye on sales in your area can increase your odds considerably.

High interest rates, a recession, or a local employer's shutting down or cutting back on its workforce are some of the variables that can result in a buyer's market. In fact, anything that negatively or seasonally affects the local housing market can cause a short- or long-term buyer's market.

In a buyer's market, prices and terms soften. Sellers are more willing to pay *seller concessions* to give their house a competitive edge as more homes come on the market. Even sellers who may not be willing to lower their prices may, however, be willing to pay a few thousand dollars for the buyer's closing costs.

Seller concessions can be anything that entices a buyer to select one home over another. Typical seller concessions may be:

- Paying all or part of the buyer's closing costs.

- Including appliances or fixtures in the deal.

- Offering painting, carpeting, or other decorating allowances.

- Extending or shortening the closing dates.

- Replacing home components such as roofs, siding, and windows.

The Buying Challenges in a Seller's Market

A seller's market exists when there are more buyers than homes for sale. Because real estate is a function of supply and demand, when there are fewer homes for sale, a rising tide raises all the home prices in the area. Homes in the most desirable areas, however, increase in value faster and they top out higher before the pendulum starts to swing back in the other direction. This is why it's important to buy in the most desirable area you can afford.

In a seller's market, when home prices are increasing dramatically, starter and mid-level homes become especially hard to find. Since condo units and townhouses are less expensive to buy and tend to attract first-time buyers, the market for these homes can explode.

Homeowners who buy during a slow, buyer's market will see their investments skyrocket when the pendulum swings back into the seller's zone. If you've outgrown your condo or townhouse, this is a good time to cash in and move up. You'll find strategies for shopping and making offers in this type of market in Chapter 4.

■　■　■

Once you've decided to throw off the shackles of tenancy, your first step toward buying a home is to look at your financial situation and ask yourself two questions:

1. Is your job or career reasonably stable for the foreseeable future?

2. Can you handle a commitment to making monthly payments for long term?

If you can answer yes to both questions, then it's time to move on to the next step and find a mortgage lender you can work with. The following sections take the mystery out of the process by explaining how lenders evaluate your credit, how you can determine how much house you can afford, and how automatic underwriting can benefit you.

Qualifying for a Loan

Finding a mortgage with the best terms takes shopping around—much the same as you would shop for a car or major appliance. Lessons learned from the last few years have shown that lenders don't always offer you the best loan package. As a consequence, it's important to request and compare proposals from at least three lenders.

> **HOME-BUYING TIP**
>
> Don't assume that the bank where you have your checking or savings account will give you the best deal. Shop the credit unions and mortgage lenders as well as banks for the best rates and lowest closing costs.

Typically, the loan officer with whom you work takes your credit and income data and assembles it into a profile of you as a long-term borrower. Your loan application data are then entered on Fannie Mae or Freddie Mac software for approval, approval with conditions, or rejection.

Loan approval with conditions attached may require additional verification of income, credit explanations, tax documents, and other information. And rejection doesn't always mean no. Sometimes a lender can submit additional data or correct inaccurate data and get an approval. This is especially true when credit bureaus have inaccurate data or give you a lower credit score than you deserve.

How Credit Scores Affect Your Credit

Because most lending is Internet based today, a credit standard is needed to put everyone on the same page. As a result, a scoring system was developed and has become a universal, though sometimes controversial and misunderstood standard. *FICO scoring*, the industry standard, is named after Fair, Isaac and Company, the California-based

> ### Fannie Mae and Freddie Mac
>
> *Fannie Mae* is the shortened name for the Federal National Mortgage Association (FNMA) and *Freddie Mac* for the Federal Home Loan Mortgage Corporation (FHLMC). These are large publicly traded corporations created by Congress to purchase mortgages from lenders who originate loans that meet their guidelines. Often referred to as the secondary market, Fannie Mae and Freddie Mac's mission is to bring stability to the mortgage process and guarantee a continuing supply of funds for home buyers. Even though these two mortgage giants were taken over by the government in the current mortgage crisis, Fannie Mae's and Freddie Mac's mission still remains the same and they will continue to buy mortgages and make home buying possible.

firm that developed the software. From the person's financial data, it creates a computer-generated numerical number that predicts a lender's risk in loaning you money. Your FICO score can change from day to day, depending on what information is available from various credit sources.

When a mortgage lender orders a credit report, the credit bureaus evaluate and assign a numerical score to five different parts of your credit history. Two of the five factors, relating to your payment history and how much current debt you have, make up roughly 65 percent of the score. The length of your credit history, recent credit inquiries, and the type of credit you use make up the remaining 35 percent.

FICO scores range from 300 (very bad) to about 850 (you walk on water), and the better your track record of paying loans back promptly, the higher the score. Typically, scores of 680 plus get the best rates and terms, although some lenders are requiring 700 or above for conventional loans.

If you have a score lower than 680, it's not impossible to get a home loan, but your interest rates and down-payment requirements may go up substantially. Federal Housing Administration (FHA) and Veterans Administration (VA) guaranteed loans have programs for

> **HOME-BUYING TIP**
>
> Beware of scams that promise to "fix" bad credit scores for a fee. There's no magic bullet that can turn bad credit into good credit, although there are some things you can do to raise your score, covered later in this chapter.

For more info on credit
bureaus and FICO credit
scoring, check out:

www.myfico.com

www.creditexpert.com

www.experian.com

www.equifax.com

www.transunion.com

www.icreditreport.com

lower credit scores, but the interest rates and/or costs jump 1 to 3 percent higher.

For example, when Ron and Wendy applied for a $225,000 mortgage, they didn't think a couple of thirty-day late payments on their two maxed-out Visa cards would cause a problem. But when their lender called and told them she could get an approval only with an FHA mortgage owing to their credit score, their costs escalated. This meant, in real dollars and cents terms, that their low credit score would cost Ron and Wendy the following:

- Two discount points, or $4,500.

- $151.94 more a month in payments, or about $1,800 a year until they can improve their credit and refinance.

However, because interest rates may go up in the future, and the buyers might incur more costs in refinancing, their first-year costs of $6,300 might continue to balloon. The lesson here is that you should get your financial and credit ducks in a row before you shop for a mortgage.

Working with Credit Reporting Agencies

The three national credit-reporting agencies—Experian, TransUnion, and Equifax—are competing companies that assemble your credit in-formation into numerical scores. A mort-gage lender will usually get reports from one or more of these companies when you apply for a loan. Because each reporting agency gets its information in a slightly different way, it's not uncommon for your credit scores from each to differ by fifty or so points. That's not usually a problem. Mortgage lenders will typically update dis-crepancies or reconcile differences in your reports to get a current picture of your credit, for better or worse.

HOME-BUYING TIP

It's wise to work with your mortgage lender to clear up problems with credit scores. Your lender knows how the system works and can guide you through the maze. You'll learn how to pick a lender in Chapter 2.

Many people download a credit re-port from the Internet and later learn that the lender's score differs considerably from what they have received. For instance, an Internet report may show that you have a score of 720, but when a lender pulls your credit from all three credit sources and determines your real score, he or she may tell you that it's really 690. That's because many credit reports are frequently only estimates and may not reflect current data. If you want a more accurate picture of your credit history and rating, it's better to go to www.myfico.com and pay their fee or get a credit report through a mortgage lender.

The credit reports a lender pulls up usually include *reason codes*. These codes provide data that help you to identify problems, such as who gave you a thirty-day-late rating or a missed payment that you really didn't miss. Reason codes are an important tool for increasing your score by helping you correct inaccurate information.

Although FICO® credit scoring is by far the biggest player on the block, a few mortgage investors have developed similar scoring systems to fine-tune credit for their particular markets. Other criteria can be added to the mix to determine your mortgage eligibility as well. For example, FHA and VA programs give lenders some leeway to consider your individual situation, whereas Fannie Mae may not.

> **HOME-BUYING TIP**
>
> Get a copy of your credit report from your lender along with the reason codes. Ask the loan officer to go over the report with you and explain anything you don't understand.

Cleaning up or Maintaining Your Credit

Credit scams abound, whereby operators promise to fix your credit rating for a few hundred dollars. Quick fixes, magic potions, and silver bullets don't exist to transform bad credit ratings into good ones instantly. It's better to spend money paying down a credit card debt than to buy into a credit-fixing scam that in the end won't improve your score. However, there are easy and legitimate steps you can take to increase your numbers. These strategies can make a difference:

■ Ensure that you have accounts that have been open and active for several years and in good standing, because they are good evidence for a higher rating.

■ Avoid loans from low-quality lenders such as finance companies, payday companies, some auto lenders, and merchant or in-house financing because these will lower your score. Bank installment loans, mortgages, and active home equity lines are higher quality debts that can enhance your rating.

■ Avoid opening new accounts, especially those pushed by merchants offering you a big discount when you check out. Opening several accounts within a twelve-month period can drop your score.

■ Have a savings account or money reserve.

■ Make monthly payments on time. Watch those due dates and don't be late, if possible. Thirty-day late payments can really sink your credit rating.

■ Pay down loan balances to under 50 percent of your credit line, because high balances on credit cards and loan limits can cost you points. Maxed out credit cards and lines of credit make lenders wary that you're over-extended.

■ Eliminate small accounts and consolidate loans where feasible. Having a lot of small loans and accounts can hurt your score. Keep a few seasoned and active accounts with low balances as a point generator.

■ If you're shopping mortgage lenders and more than one does a credit inquiry, keep the requests within a 14-day period. Although credit bureaus often differentiate between types of inquiries, and two or three from mortgage lenders may not hurt, too many—especially from varied sources—can cost you points.

HOME-BUYING TIP

Consolidate or close small merchant accounts and finance company loans, and keep quality accounts that are two years old or older.

Do not follow Barry and Kelli's example. Their lender told them that with their 720 credit score and stable job history, they wouldn't have a problem qualifying for a mortgage on the new home they wanted. Excited by the news, they went furniture and appliance shopping, opening accounts at a Home Depot, two furniture stores, and an appliance outlet. Believing they were smart shoppers, they put their purchases on 90- and 180-day free-interest plans. A few days later when the mortgage lender updated the buyers' credit report before submitting it to the underwriter, she discovered that their FICA score had plummeted to 613. The lender had counseled them to avoid any credit applications or transactions until they closed on their mortgage, but in the excitement of buying their first home, Barry and Kelli got carried away; as a result, they were unable to buy their dream home anytime in the near future.

The Importance of Keeping Good Records

Occasionally, credit bureaus are slow to record paid-off loans, especially student loans. Since credit scoring is only as good as the data fed into the system, it's important to have backup paperwork.

Data on paid-off judgments, collections account, and other credit problems can take a long time to work through the system. It's especially important in these cases that you have the paperwork clearly showing the payoff along with your canceled checks.Too many loan approvals get held up at a critical time, jeopardizing purchase of that dream home because the buyers lost or didn't keep vital paperwork.

Keeping your finances on Quicken, Microsoft Money, or a similar software program is a great way to track your accounts. You can record your payments with dates and check numbers, and if a question arises, you can print out the payment histories and payoff dates along with the check numbers. Creating a paper trail can save you time, frustration, and bank research fees.

Correcting Credit Problems

Credit reporting is not an exact science, and errors and misreporting are all too common. Fortunately, you can usually clear up most errors and problems on your own, without paying hefty fees.

Should a dispute with a credit source or agency arise, you have remedies available through the Fair Credit Reporting Act (FCRA). This isn't a way to erase legitimate late pays on your report, nor is it a wizard to turn bad credit into good, but it is a legal avenue for you to remove errors.

Determining How Much Home You Can Afford

A big mistake that many first-time homeowners make is to not sit down and look realistically at their financial situation to determine how large a home payment they can comfortably handle. Not everyone lives the same lifestyle and has the same financial attitudes. For example, one family would go broke trying to make a $2,500 monthly house payment while another with the same income wouldn't have a problem.

For Fair Credit Reporting Act (FCRA) information on how to correct errors on your credit report, go to www.ftc.gov or call 877-382-4357.

What size monthly house payment you can afford is something only you can decide, and it should be decided before you complete a loan application. Letting a banker decide for you, based on your qualifying ratios, is akin to letting Colonel Sanders guard the henhouse. Suppose, for instance, that you decide that $2,100 would be the maximum monthly house payment you could afford comfortably and keep your current lifestyle. However, a mortgage loan officer tells you that, based on your income and debt ratios, they will make you a loan that comes with payments up to $2,900 a month. Do you get excited with the news that the bank is willing to loan you over $100,000 more than you requested, and do you then call up your Realtor to increase the price of homes you want to look at?

HOME-BUYING TIP

Determine the size of the home payment you are comfortable with. Then calculate how much home that amount will buy and stick with it, even though lenders may allow you go up to 55 percent debt. Happiness is *not* becoming a slave to your house payment.

If you answered yes to that question, and you increased your home-shopping price, you have put yourself into financial jeopardy even before your first payment is due. Be aware that lenders, agents, and home sellers all want you to buy to the max. *Resist their sales pitch.* You want to be more savvy than many other home buyers and simply say no to the additional money.

Avoid five common mistakes that many home buyers make and that they later regret:

1. Going with an adjustable rate loan (ARM) to boost your home-buying power.

2. Choosing a *stated income loan* (a loan in which the lender doesn't verify your income) so that you can get a larger loan, even if you have a large down payment.

3. Being sold an interest rate buydown that temporarily reduces your payments for the first few years. (Buydowns are covered in Chapter 2.)

4. Borrowing the money for a down payment if you know you will have a hard time paying it back.

5. Shopping for homes that cost more than your loan limit. Be firm with your agent about looking only at homes within your price range; many agents push the price ceiling, telling you it's only $30, $75, or a $100 a month more and you can afford it.

How Lenders Qualify You for a Mortgage

Once you've determined how much of a monthly payment you can comfortably afford, the next step is to talk to a mortgage lender and find out how much of a loan you can qualify for. A big mistake many home buyers make is to begin looking at homes before they know what kind of money they will have to work with and what their expenses will be. This often leads to frustration and discouragement, as they find out that their tastes are Mercedes but their incomes are Ford Focus. It's much better to go through the mortgage process first and get a loan pre-approval letter.

Although each lender can have a slightly different focus in making the calculations, most like to keep income-to-debt close to the following numbers:

- The total house payment (principal, interest, taxes, and insurance, or PITI) shouldn't exceed 34 percent of your gross monthly income, though in exceptional cases this ratio can go up. (Note: this is 34 percent of *gross* income, not take-home pay.)

- Typically, your total amount of debt plus the mortgage payment with PITI shouldn't exceed 42 percent of your monthly income before taxes. However, when a borrower has exceptional assets, high credit score, and/or other pluses, this ratio can go as high as 50 percent.

For most first-time home buyers, the 34/42 ratio is the one most lenders will use in working up the numbers, although with good credit the total debt can go up to 55 percent. For example, when Aaron and Rhonda decided to buy a home, they sat down and looked at their pay stubs for the last couple of months. Their combined monthly income totaled $7,240 before deductions. Adding up their monthly debt— $545 for a car payment, $150 for Visa, and $75 for Discover cards, and a $190 student loan—they found it totaled $960.

Taking their gross monthly income of $7,240 and multiplying it by the 0.42 total debt ratio yields $2,968 as their allowable debt, which includes the total house payment, or PITI, and their mortgage insurance premium (MIP).

Financial calculators are cheap, available from Staples, Office Max, Office Depot, and other office supply stores. Calculated Industries has an excellent series available online at www.calculated.com. These calculators are easy to use and indispensable when working up what-if scenarios.

HOME-BUYING TIP

Work with an experienced Realtor who knows your local market. He or she can advise you on when to offer less than the sellers are asking and how to negotiate the best deal.

Next, Aaron and Rhonda subtracted their monthly debt, $960, from $2,968, leaving them with $2,008 as their total mortgage payment, including principal, interest, taxes, and insurances. Monthly taxes, insurance, and MIP are determined by adding the yearly premiums and then dividing by twelve months. (Because property taxes vary considerably from state to state, you need to get that information on the home you are interested in from the owners, your agent, or the county assessor.) In Aaron and Rhonda's case, the monthly taxes and insurances totaled $402. Subtracting $402 from $2008 leaves $1,606 for principal and interest. Using a financial calculator and keying in a payment of $1,606, with 6 percent interest for thirty years (360 months), and solving for PV (present value), or loan amount, yields $267,867.

In addition, the buyers could add a 10 percent down payment, or $26,786, to the maximum loan of $267,867, for a home purchase price of $294,653 or less. Of course, depending on the area and how slow the local market is, they can possibly shop for homes priced at $350,000 or even more! But they can't offer to buy the home for more than $294,653 and be able to keep their total monthly house payments at $2,008.

Income from Second Jobs or Other Sources

Income from a second job may or may not help your chances of getting a loan. If you've been on a second job or a part-time job for less than two years, you may not be able to count it in your total income.

> ### The Mortgage Insurance Premium
>
> The *mortgage insurance premium* (MIP) is the cost of an insurance policy that the lender charges on loans that have less than 20 percent down. This policy insures the lender against default owing to the high risk involved with low down payments. When the loan is paid down to less than 80 percent, the policy cancels. Typically, the monthly premium is one-half to three-fourths of 1 percent.

However, that's not a hard-and-fast rule, and your lender may be able to shop investors to find one who will go less than two years.

Income from part-time sales and other sources that can't be verified on your tax return stands a slim chance of helping raise your ratios. Payments from child support and other verifiable income streams, such as royalties, settlements, and annuities, can, however, usually be counted. With child support, you will need to furnish the lender with a copy of the divorce decree and some bank statements that prove the money is coming in monthly.

HOME-BUYING TIP

It's important to create paper trails for any income you may want to use for qualifying for a loan in the future.

In one sale, when the buyer needed every dollar to qualify for a mortgage, he was able to furnish several years of tax returns showing $400 a month income from a rental home he sold, and carried the financing. But without this income paper trail, the buyer would not have qualified for the loan he needed.

The Role of Automated Underwriting in Getting a Loan

Most mortgage lending is through *automated underwriting*, or *desktop underwriting*, as it's sometimes called. The loan officer enters the borrower's application data into software developed by Fannie Mae and Freddie Mac (commonly referred to as the secondary market). The software evaluates the data and gives an approval, denial, or a request for more information.

This computerized approach streamlines the qualifying process and improves the quality of loans that Fannie Mae and Freddie Mac buy from banks, credit unions, mortgage brokers, and other entities.

This marriage of the Internet with a common loan-qualifying standard from the secondary market thus guarantees a plentiful supply of money for people to buy homes. True, it's not a perfect system, as we've experienced in recent years, but it's far better than any other method when used responsibly by both lenders and home buyers.

How the System Works

When you apply for a mortgage, the loan officer enters your employment, income, assets, and credit history into the Fannie Mae or Freddie Mac underwriting program. If all the data are within accepted guidelines, you'll get a quick approval. It's also possible to get a conditional approval if certain credit or income conditions are met. And, of course, you can get a rejection, too.

But the process can get more complicated in this tight credit market. Your lender may get Fannie Mae approval, which gives him or her a viable loan package to offer investors, but sometimes these investors have additional guidelines of their own. So lenders must go an extra step and match the loan package to investor criteria to get a commitment. Examples of additional criteria some wary investors may require are FICO scores over 720, down payments of 10 percent or more, or lower loan-to-income ratios.

Sometimes your application can be rejected, but with a little tweaking the loan officer can then get it approved. Paying off a credit card, closing out little-used accounts, or verifying ongoing overtime can make your application fly the second time around when it failed the first time. Not surprising, these qualifying programs appear to favor good credit scores. If you have a lower debt-to-income ratio and great credit, you'll most likely get approval.

How the System Benefits You

Once your loan officer has your application and has verified the data, he or she can request Fannie Mae or Freddie Mac approval. Most likely you'll get a phone call the same day with an approval, a rejection, or a "let's talk about it." This fast turnaround means that within a day or two you can start looking at homes and making plans.

Another advantage of this automated system is that once you have approval, your loan officer can shop your loan package to get you the best deal. Plus, he or she can give you a letter of loan approval that carries added credibility with sellers.

The key to making the system work for you is to have the best credit score you can and to present a stable employment history. If your income-to-debt ratio is a little high, the chances are you'll still get an approval at the best interest rate.

Seven Steps You Can Take to Make This Chapter Work for You

1. Get a copy of your credit report from FICO or a mortgage lender and make sure you understand the fine print.

2. If your score is on the low side, ask your lender to give you a list of things you can to do to bring it up.

3. Review your debts and income, and determine what mortgage payment would feel comfortable to you.

4. Don't let a lender or agent, or falling in love with a house, weaken your resolve to stay within your price range.

5. Buy a financial calculator and learn how to use it so you can work the numbers, too.

6. Get your paperwork in order so that the lender can verify income, payoffs, paid accounts, and so on for a quick approval.

7. Don't put off buying a home. Waiting for prices to fall can cost you more money if interest rates go up in the meantime. It's important to begin building equity and qualifying for tax breaks as soon as possible. Your landlord can find someone else to pay off his mortgage.

CHAPTER 2

Picking the Best Mortgage Loan

Many home buyers create huge problems for themselves by purchasing the wrong type of mortgage. This not only affects their ability to pay back the loan but also often adds thousands of dollars in loan costs and interest.

A bewildering array of loan options are often promoted by lenders who don't always act in a borrower's best interests and this creates a "buyer beware" situation. And if lenders don't explain clearly (in plain English) the pros and cons of a loan, consumers often settle for whatever program these lenders want to push—good, bad, or ugly. Of course, as a consumer you will want the best deal you can get, with the lowest interest rate and the lowest closing costs. The key to achieving this situation is to understand how the system works. That way you can compare the different loan options and pick the one that works best for you. It also doesn't hurt to acquire a working knowledge of "mortgage-speak"—those jargon-filled explanations that some lenders are so fond of using to muddy communication. In reality, mortgage hunting can be the Wild West of loan shopping, so this chapter will help by giving you quick and easy-to-use tools to compare loan options and pick the best deal.

In this chapter you'll learn how to:

- Find the best loan for you.

- Understand how the mortgage system works so you know what to expect from lenders.

- Become informed of other ways to finance your purchase of a home.

- Use points and buydowns to your advantage.

- Compare loans using good faith estimates and annual percentage rates.

- Distinguish the advantages and disadvantages of private mortgage insurance.

- Identify sources of down payments and develop strategies for their use.

- Recognize the mortgage payment options that might work for you.

HOME-BUYING TIP

Don't assume that the bank with whom you have a checking or savings account will give you the best mortgage deal. Ask the bank for a quote and then compare it to the deals offered by other mortgage lenders.

How the Mortgage System Works

The mortgage industry works much like the rest of the economy. It has wholesale and retail sectors that work together to create a plentiful supply of money for home buyers to use in purchasing a house. The system is so efficient that it has helped more than 60 percent of American households to own their own homes. Figure 2-1 shows you at a glance the most common home-buying financing options and their advantages and disadvantages.

The Wholesale Sector

On the wholesale level, the two biggest players are the publicly traded entities Fannie Mae and Freddie Mac, sometimes called *government-sponsored enterprises* (GSEs). Since Fannie Mae and Freddy Mac are the big elephants in the room and they buy close to 50 percent of all the mortgages written, their underwriting standards dominate the industry. You might say that this combo is to mortgage lending what Microsoft is to computing. Although these two giant corporations are similar in make-up, they do have some minor underwriting differences that can cause a lender to submit a loan package to one versus the

FIGURE 2-1

Ways you can buy a home.

Loan type	Advantages	Disadvantages
Conventional (conforming)	Wide range of lenders, payback options and low interest rates. PMI drops off when you pay down 22 percent. No prepayment penalities.	Must have reasonably good credit. Not as flexible as FHA for lower price ranges.
Conventional (non-conforming or jumbo loans)	More of a niche loan; if you have a special need there's probably a lender who does it.	Harder to qualify for, higher interest rates, and hard to find lenders who do jumbos.
Federal Housing Adminstration (FHA)	3 percent down; family can gift, help with costs, or co-sign. Seller can pay closing costs. Higher qualifying ratios, no prepayment penalties.	Lower loan limits that vary from county to county. PMI required regardless of down payment, but does drop off.
Department of Agriculture loans for rural areas	A good mix of programs for low-income, including subsidized payments.	Low loan limits may limit what you can buy in some areas.
Veterans Guaranteed loans (VA)	No down payment needed, flexible qualifying standards. No prepayment penalties. Sellers can pay closing costs.	Funding fees required and lower loan limits.
State Housing Authority	Many have zero-down programs. Qualifying follows FHA guidelines.	Cannot have owned a home in the last two years. Must live in the home and can't rent it out.
Seller financing	Can be the cheapest way to finance a home. Few closing costs and whatever interest rate you can negotiate.	You'll need a good broker or real estate attorney to make sure the paperwork is done right and you're protected.
Lease Options	A good way to live in a home while you repair credit or get established in an area. The option part gives you the right to buy the home.	If you don't follow through on the option to buy part you can lose your deposit.

other. For most home buyers, the differences between the two are negligible.

Both GSEs buy loans from lenders such as banks, credit unions, brokers, and others that originate them with individuals. However, some lenders don't sell their mortgages; rather, they keep them for their own portfolios or use them to create mortgage-backed securities. The Veterans Administration (VA) and the Federal Housing Administration (FHA) take yet a different approach by guaranteeing loans rather than buying them from lenders. Their underwriting is slightly different because of the buyer pool they seek to attract.

Fannie Mae and Freddy Mac package the loans they buy into mortgage-backed securities that are then sold to investors. The money from the sale of these securities enables them to continue buying mortgages from lenders. However since the federal government has taken over both of these entities, it appears this will guarantee stability and a continuing supply of mortgage funds.

Other entities such as banks and big investors also originate or buy mortgages and they also use them to back securities that they sell in the stock market. If these securities are backed by subprime or low-quality mortgages that subsequently default, the result is a credit meltdown and massive home foreclosures, such as we've recently experienced. In spite of this housing speed bump, it's the GSEs and VA- and FHA-guaranteed loans that help maintain a plentiful and consistent flow of mortgage money at reasonable interest rates. The track record of these organizations over the past few decades has been impressive in supplying funds for home buyers that otherwise wouldn't have been possible.

In mortgage-speak, the wholesale mortgage industry is often labeled the *secondary market*. Lenders who keep or buy loans for their own portfolios are said to *warehouse* their loans. The *primary market* includes banks, credit unions, and mortgage brokers.

Conventional Loans

Those mortgages that are not guaranteed by the FHA or VA are called *conventional loans*. They are purchased by Fannie Mae, Freddie Mac, or other financial institutions like banks, credit unions, retirement portfolio managers, and insurance funds. Because the secondary market is so big and so diverse, with a plentiful supply of funds to loan home buyers, conventional loans offer some important advantages:

■ They are available through a variety of financial sources throughout the country and via the Internet.

■ If you offer 20 percent or more as a down payment, you don't have to pay mortgage insurance (private mortgage insurance is covered later in this chapter) or the funding fees that the FHA and VA guaranteed loans require.

■ You have a sizable buffet of loan options and programs to choose from.

■ Loan limits on *conforming loans* (owner-occupied) are typically as follows:
—Single family homes, $417,000
—Duplexes, $533,850
—Tri-plexes, $645,300
—Four-plexes, $801,950

However, to support the federal government's stimulus package, loan limits have been temporarily increased to $729,750 in some areas of the country. Check with a local mortgage lender to see if your area qualifies for the increase.

For more information on the secondary loan market, check out www.fanniemae.com and www.freddiemac.com.

More Expensive Homes Need Jumbo Loans

A *jumbo loan* is a mortgage that exceeds $417,000, or $729,750 in selected areas. Because these loans are over the Fannie Mae/Freddie Mac lending limits, they are called *non-conforming loans,* and you have to find a niche lender that specializes in these higher end mortgages.

Because investors perceive that jumbo loans carry more risk, these loans demand higher interest rates, more loan fees, and *private mortgage insurance* (PMI) premiums if the down payment is less than 20 percent of the selling price. One strategy that some buyers use to cut these costs is to finance a first mortgage up to the Fannie Mae loan limit of $417,000 (or $729,750 in selected areas) and then take out a second mortgage to cover the balance of the purchase price less the down payment. This avoids the monthly PMI

HOME-BUYING TIP

The more money you put down on a jumbo loan, the better interest rate you'll get. If possible, put at least 20 percent down. Also, check on the feasibility of selling some of your low-performing securities and/or borrowing against your 401(k) if you're a first-time homebuyer.

fees and keeps the interest percentage under that charged for the higher interest jumbo loans. Even when the second mortgage has a higher interest rate, you can save money by not having to pay the PMI because the bulk of the loan is at the lower Fannie Mae interest rate. However, with current credit tightening by lenders, these loans may be harder to qualify for and may require a 700-plus credit score and a higher down payment.

FHA-Guaranteed Loan Programs

The federal government's FHA-guaranteed loans are one of the best ways for many first-time homeowners to finance a home. Their programs are more flexible than Fannie Mae or Freddie Mac programs because family members can give you the down payment and closing costs to help you buy a home. They just have to write a letter stating that the funds are a gift and their source of the money must be verifiable.

If you try to get a relative to loan you the money but declare that it is a gift, think again. Lying about this or other items on a mortgage application is federal loan fraud, and it comes with steep penalties.

For instance, if Aunt Josie wants to gift you the down payment on a home, she has to write and sign a letter to your lender stating that she is giving you $7,650 for a down payment. These funds need to be in a saving or checking account that the lender can easily verify. In other words, you need to create a paper trail that makes verification fast and easy.

There are two downsides to FHA loans, however. The first is the low loan limits, which vary from county to county in each state. Go to http://entp.hud.gov/idapp/html/hicostlook.cfm to check on the loan limits in your area. The second is that mortgage insurance of approximately one-half percent of the loan amount is added to the interest rate. This cost can drop off after five years, or when the remaining balance on the loan is 78 percent of the value of the property. In areas with high appreciation, this works; the homeowners start out with FHA loans and refinance with conventional loans when their homes' value increases enough to give them an 80 percent or lower loan.

One interesting FHA loan is the 203(k) program, which allows someone to buy a fixer-upper and combine the purchase and fix-up costs in one thirty-year loan. If you're in the building trades, are a do-it-yourselfer, or have relatives you can tap, this can be a great way to buy a home while saving yourself money. Check out www.hud.gov/offices/hsg/sfh/203k/203kabou.cfm for details.

Department of Agriculture Loans

The Department of Agriculture's Rural Housing Service (RHS) offers low-interest mortgages with no down payments required. Section 502 programs are designed for families buying a home in rural areas. To qualify, your income may not exceed 115 percent of the median income for the area, and you must not be able to qualify for a mortgage from other sources.

The RHS has two basic home-buying programs. One is similar to the FHA and VA loans, in that the RHS guarantees the loan written by other lenders. The other is a direct loan program aimed at very low-income rural buyers in the range of 50 to 100 percent of median income. Interest rates for these loans are set by the RHS and may include a subsidy that ensures a family does not pay more than 26 percent of its income for the total house payment. For more information on RHS programs, go to www.rurdev.usda.gov.

VA-Guaranteed Loans

Owing to the deployment of Reserve and National Guard units over the last few years, the number of VA-eligible buyers has increased dramatically. For first-time buyers especially, a VA-guaranteed mortgage is a good way to go. Some advantages are as follows:

- 100 percent financing up to $417,00 with no down payment required (some areas have higher limits)

- More relaxed credit standards than Fannie Mae

- No pre-payment penalties

- No mortgage insurance payments

- Other veterans can assume a VA loan, which is especially attractive if the loan's interest rate is lower than on the current market

> **HOME-BUYING TIP**
>
> The VA loan process will go smoother if you find a mortgage lender that is experienced with VA loans and is approved by the Lender Appraisal Processing Program (LAPP). These lenders can navigate the VA loan paperwork for you and close the deal quickly.

■ Sellers can pay up to 4 percent of the buyer's closing costs

■ Sellers can even pay off buyer debt to help the person qualify

The VA does charge a funding fee of 2.15 to 3.3 percent of the loan amount, which is added to the loan. These funding fees are reduced if the borrower puts 5 percent or more down. Go to www.homeloans.va .gov for more information on VA loans.

State and Local Housing Programs

All fifty states and many cities have housing agencies with programs designed to help first-time home buyers purchase a home. Typically, state agencies sell bonds to raise funds for their loan programs, which offer below-market interest rates.

The basics of state housing programs are:

■ Income limits and maximum house prices track federal U.S. Office of Housing and Urban Development (HUD) guidelines and vary from county-to-county.

■ There is 100 percent financing available.

■ Gift funds for down payment or closing costs are allowed.

■ Special incentives sometimes target special areas within a county or city.

■ State housing can be used with FHA or VA programs for no-down-payment financing.

■ First-time home buyers are defined as not having owned a home in the last three years.

■ The home must be owner occupied; you can't use it as a rental.

Go to www.hud.gov/local offices.cfm and key in your state for specific information and links to state finance and local grant programs.

In addition to state housing programs, some cities offer their own first-time home buyer programs tied to HUD grants. If you're interested in living in one of the targeted areas, the incentives can be enticing. For example, a city may offer a $4,000 grant to first-time home buyers who buy in certain areas that need rejuvenation. If the buyers stay in the home for five years, the loan is forgiven. Also, there are special incentives to entice police officers or teachers to buy in these areas.

Other Ways to Buy a Home

Although the loan programs we've discussed constitute the way the vast majority of homes are financed, there are other perfectly safe ways to buy a home that, in some cases, can allow you to avoid hefty bank fees and save thousands of dollars in closing costs and PMI fees.

Of course, paying cash would save a buyer lot of money, but few home buyers can afford that route. As an alternative, when you're house shopping, make an effort to talk to the sellers and find out what their needs and goals are. Sometimes you can create solutions that set up a money-saving win-win situation for both you and the seller. Two of the most common alternative arrangements are seller financing and lease options.

Seller Financing

Occasionally you'll find a seller who is willing to play banker and carry all or part of the financing on your purchase. Often called *carry-back financing*, this option creates a win-win opportunity for everyone if it's done right. The buyer saves thousands of dollars in bank closing costs and the seller gets a 6 percent (or current rate) return with a monthly cash flow.

From a paperwork standpoint, there's not much difference between a bank and an individual seller carrying the loan, as the investment is protected by a recorded trust deed. However, as a buyer you need to exercise some caution so you don't get scammed.

Some important do's are:

- Do keep the terms simple and make sure the monthly payment includes principal and interest, and that it pays off in a set number of years. In mortgage-speak, the loan amortizes.

- Do avoid balloon payments, whereby you make additional lump-sum payments, or other fine print that can cause you problems down the road.

- Do get a full title report and go over it with the title officer so you understand what encumbrances (such as taxes, loans, and liens) are on the property.

- Do make sure that the person in title (owner) is the same as the seller.

- Do use a state-approved purchase agreement and other paper-work to make your offer. Remember that everything must be in writing; accept nothing verbal.

- Do be wary if the seller wants to do something different from the accepted norm. In most states, the seller gives you a war-ranty deed that's recorded and you sign a trust deed and note that are also recorded to secure the loan.

- Do use an attorney or title company for the document prepara-tion and closing.

HOME-BUYING TIP

Make it easy for the seller to say yes. Get a loan-approval letter from a mortgage lender to show the seller that you are a good credit risk.

How do you find seller financing deals? If you're shopping for a home through newspaper ads, the owner will usually advertise "owner financing." You can also ask the owner when you call about the property to see if the individual is interested in carrying the financing. Also, properties listed on the Realtor's Multiple Listing Service (MLS) disclose whether an owner will consider playing the role of bank and do the financing.

Older homeowners who have paid off their mortgages and are going into an assisted living center, moving in with family, or downsiz-ing and don't need their equity in a lump sum are good candidates for seller financing. You or your agent may have to show the seller and the family or advisers the advantages of their carrying the loan. For exam-ple, a carry-back loan of $225,000 at 6 percent interest that pays off in thirty years creates a $1,348.99 monthly principal and interest pay-ment.

However, the seller may not want to or be able to carry a loan for thirty years, so you might have to agree to refinance the loan in x number of years. As a buyer, this arrangement is still in your best interest because you will be building equity and when you come to refinance, you may be able to get an 80 percent or better loan without PMI.

In one case, Troy and Angela were fortunate to find a retiring owner with a mortgage-free home who was moving in with family. A monthly cash flow was exactly what the owner needed, while the buyers needed a no-down-payment way to buy a home. Troy and Angela had previously pre-qualified with a mortgage lender, but coming up with a down payment and enough money for the closing costs was a problem. When they heard about the home for sale from a friend, they decided to talk to the owner. Because they had a pre-approval letter from the bank, the seller decided to take a chance on them and agreed to go with no down payment if the buyers would pay any closing costs except for the seller's title policy.

The sale closed two weeks later, and the buyer's costs and loan were:

- $350 for a certified appraisal that both parties agreed to use to determine the selling price

- $315 paid to the title company in closing and document preparation fees

- $180 in recording fees (warranty and trust deeds)

- A $217,000 loan at 6.15 percent with $1,322.03 as the monthly payments (thirty-year amortization)

In twelve years, or at the seller's request thereafter, the buyers would refinance and pay off the loan. In contrast, if the buyers had financed through a mortgage lender, the closing costs would have been between $5,000 and $6,500, and the monthly PMI payments would have been between $70 and $90. Should the buyers stay in the home for twelve years, they will easily have enough equity to get a lower cost mortgage or to sell and move up. As for the seller, he had a secured monthly cash flow of mostly interest. And at the end of the twelfth year, the loan balance would be paid down to about $172,446.

Another alternative for buyers to save serious money is to get the seller to take back a second mortgage for 20 percent (or whatever is needed) of the purchase price. This allows you to obtain an 80 percent loan at a lower interest rate, without having to pay PMI payments.

Buying a home with seller financing can be much simpler than dealing with a bank's paperwork—and saving thousands of dollars in closing costs and PMI doesn't hurt, either. However, be sure to hire an attorney to look over the deal before you commit. Spending a few hundred dollars in legal fees is a good investment in peace of mind.

Lease Options

In a slow market, with more homes for sale than buyers, the opportunities to creatively buy a home explode. Sellers who must move because of job relocation, to build a new home, or for whatever other reason are often faced with the prospect of double payments. They are desperate and open to ideas that can stop or reduce their financial hemorrhaging.

These situations are tailor made for *lease options*, which allow buyers to lease a home with the option to buy it sometime down the road. This can be a win-win situation for both buyers and sellers. For buyers with less than perfect credit, or who are new on the job, lease options make it possible to live in a home now, with the possibility of owning it in the future. Thus, sellers create a cash flow to make mortgage payments to stop or minimize a negative cash flow.

> **HOME-BUYING TIP**
>
> When negotiating a lease option in a buyer's market, insist on determining the selling price by a certified appraisal when you exercise the option. It's likely the value will have dropped during the lease period.

Typically, a seller leases a house to the potential buyer for a certain period of time—say, a year. At the end of the year, the buyer gets a mortgage and closes on the home. The buyer and seller can lock in the selling price at the beginning of the lease period or they can determine it at the end with a certified appraisal.

Five common reasons for buying with a lease option are as follows:

1. In a strong buyer's market, with lots of homes for sale, you may be able to rent for less than what would be a mortgage payment. But should you want to buy the home as soon as you feel the market has bottomed, try to negotiate an option to buy at the appraised value determined at the end of the lease.

2. Your credit prevents you from qualifying right now, but in a year you can clean it up and are likely to get a loan. You find a home you love and offer to lease it for a year, with an option to buy it at a certain price and with certain terms.

3. You're new to the area and find a home you may want to buy, but you aren't sure yet. A lease option may give you the time you need to decide.

4. If a career change, new job, or job probationary period prevents you from qualifying for a loan right now, a lease option can buy you time. When you do qualify, you can exercise the option and buy the home.

5. You are relocating and have found your dream home in the new area, but have a home to sell first. You can do a lease option on the new house until your old home sells and then close on the new one.

Although lease-option paperwork varies from state to state, it typically comprises two parts: the lease, which spells out the responsibilities of the owner and the tenant, the payment, the beginning and ending dates, any deposits, and so on; and the option to buy, which can either be a separate document attached to the lease or be included on one form. However it's done, the lease option spells out in detail the purchase terms.

Important items you want clearly indicated in any lease option are:

> The biggest reason many lease options fail or run into trouble is because the proper paperwork wasn't done in the beginning. Everything must be spelled out in writing. Take the same precautions as discussed in the section on seller financing, and hire an attorney to look over the paperwork.

- The time frame, with both beginning and ending dates

- What happens to the deposit if you don't buy the home

- If any of the monthly payments will be credited toward the purchase price

- How repairs and improvements to the house will be handled— who pays for what during the lease period

- Whether the selling price is set at the beginning of the option or is determined at the end by a certified appraisal

In most instances, if you don't buy the home within the option period, you lose the deposit and any money you have spent on home improvements.

No-Doc or Low-Doc Loans

No-doc loans are another casualty of the recent mortgage meltdown. Essentially, a *no-doc loan* is a mortgage for borrowers who have good credit and income, but who can't qualify using standard underwriting income rations. Originally intended for a small niche market, they were designed for people who have high assets or net worth but whose income doesn't fit the nine-to-five job pattern with a regular paycheck.

Their use was expanded by lenders in recent years and these loans were offered to anyone with reasonable credit. Now these loans are much harder to get and they require excellent credit, a substantial down payment, and strong assets. If you're a self-employed business person, in a new career, or have an irregular income stream, these loans can be a good way to go. For more information on no-doc loans check out www.bankrate.com/brm/news/mtg/19990624.asp.

Understanding Points and Buydowns

An important part of determining interest rates and putting together real estate mortgage deals involves loan points and interest buydowns. In fact, no understanding of mortgage interest is complete without knowing how these points and buydowns work—and most important, how you can use them to your advantage.

Essentially, *points* are prepaid interest on the loan. Each point is equal to a one-time fee of 1 percent of the loan amount. For example, if a lender charges you one point on a $200,000 loan, your cost is a flat $2,000. Typical examples of how points are used include the following:

■ If interest rates are fluctuating and lenders need to increase their yield (profit) to make a loan, they will charge points. For instance, a lender may quote you a 6 percent interest rate if you'll pay two points or a higher 6.36 percent with no points.

■ When a lender wants to sound more competitive and advertises one-quarter or one-half percent interest rate below what the other lenders are offering, the fine print explains that to get that rate you will have to pay a point or two.

■ New home builders often advertise lower interest rates to get buyers interested in their projects, so they pay the lender the designated points to give you the lower rate. Of course, ultimately you pay for these points because they are built into the cost of the home.

■ Home sellers can offer to pay a few points on behalf of the buyer so as to entice interested parties to buy their home.

Buydowns are mortgage programs whereby a third party pays some points to reduce the buyer's interest rate and thus help a home buyer qualify for the mortgage. For example, as a concession, a seller may pay four points to the lender, and the buyer gets a mortgage that is two percentage points lower than the standard rate for the first year, one percentage point lower for the second year, and then the full interest rate thereafter. This arrangement works best when the buyer anticipates that his or her income will increase over the next few years.

Paying points is not a practice limited to mortgage loans. Car dealers may advertise a lower (or zero) interest rate on new car loans as an incentive for sales. This means, as you probably guessed, that the dealer made an arrangement with the finance people, and you can be sure that the points have been built into the price. Actually, anytime financing is involved in a purchase, points are often used as a sales tool. The bottom line is that you can use points and buydowns advantageously or they can lure you into thinking you're getting a good deal when in fact you are not.

As mentioned previously, when you contact a mortgage lender and ask for a quote, likely you will get a buffet of rates and options. In addition to that day's rate (*par*), the lender may tell you that you can lower the rate if you want to pay a point or two. Typically, a point lowers the interest around one-eighth of 1 percent, depending on the market that day. However, in a competitive market, if you shop around, you may find point discounts as high as one-quarter of 1 percent. Plus, the length of time that you want to lock in the discounted rate is an important factor; a thirty-day lock will have better terms than a sixty-day lock.

That is, you usually face two choices when you begin the loan process: You can lock in the interest rate and points you are quoted for a period of thirty to sixty days, or you can float and take whatever the market throws at you on the day you close on the house. If you like to gamble and the interest rates are falling, this is a good way to go. But if you don't want to take the chance of getting caught by an upward spurt in interest rates, then locking in the rate can help you sleep at night.

Points

Points are normally charged by mortgage lenders as a way of increasing their up-front profit and of offsetting the uncertainty of a loan that would normally go fifteen to thirty years. However, since few mortgages go to their full term anymore, because owners sell their homes or refinance their mortgages much earlier, points can be a profitable way to attract investors looking to make money in mortgage securities.

In short, paying points results in an interest-rate buydown and a lower payment. As mentioned, some builders factor a few points into a home's price, so they buy down the rate and offer you a lower monthly house payment. As a consumer, you should ask the lender or salesperson how many points are built into the price of the financing when the interest-rate you are quoted is less than par. There's no free lunch in mortgages—points paid "on your behalf" are actually a cost for you.

HOME-BUYING TIP

Dividing the savings achieved by paying points into the cost of the points is the best way to tell if the results are worthwhile. Paying points may only make sense if the break-even is four years or less and you plan on living in the home a long time.

Is paying points worth the result? The answer is yes and no. It usually depends on how long you're going to live in the home before the savings in having a lower interest rate and the cost of the points comes out the same. For example, a $225,000 loan at 6 percent interest for thirty years costs $1,348.99 a month in principal and interest. If you pay $4,500, or two points, to buy the rate down to 5.75 percent, the monthly payment reduces to $1,313.04, a savings of $35.95 a month. Dividing the $35.95 into the $4,500 that you paid for the points yields almost 10.5 years to reach a break-even point. In this case, the buydown probably isn't worth it, especially if you move from that house in five years. The bottom line is that points are usually *not* a good investment, as you can see from the numbers above, *unless* you plan to live in the home for a few years or your qualifying ratios are razor thin.

Knowing About the Annual Percentage Rate Can Save You Money

How would you like a tool that gives you the ability to compare and pick the best loan? The good news is that such a tool exists, and it can save you thousands of dollars; the bad news is that few people take the time to understand or use it. This section shows you how to easily master the annual percentage rate (APR) and shop for mortgages with confidence.

How APR Works

When you look over the loan documents that a lender asks you to sign, you'll notice that there are two interest rates. The first is a rate quoted by the lender when you ask for a quote and read their ad. However, when you and the lender get serious about a loan, and the paperwork with disclosures starts to appear, a second, higher rate is introduced, called the *annual percentage rate,* or APR.

The APR is calculated by taking the quoted interest rate—say, 6.0 percent—and adding in all the loan charges that the lender tacks onto the loan. That's why the APR is always higher than the quoted or advertised rate. For example, suppose a thirty-year $200,000 loan with $1,199.10 in monthly payments is advertised at 6 percent. However, this lender charges $6,000 in loan costs. When the loan costs are added ($206,000 in actual costs) and the interest rate is recalculated, keeping the payment and thirty-year payback the same, the interest rate jumps to 6.27 percent APR.

Federal law requires that, within three days of receiving a borrower's loan application, all lenders disclose the loan's APR along with a breakdown of loan costs. This disclosure is called a *good faith estimate* (GFE), and it includes a list of all the loan charges a lender tacks onto the amount of money you will get.

How to Pick the Best Loan

In reality, the federal disclosure law creates a useful loan comparison tool. You can have two lenders, A and B, who quote the same interest rate—say, 6 percent. But when you get their good faith estimates, lender A's APR is 6.29 percent and lender

For more information on GFEs, go to:

www.hud.gov/offices/hsg/
    sfh/res/resappc.cfm
www.bankrate.com/brm/
    news/real-estate/good-
    faith1.asp
www.mortgagenewsdaily
    .com/wiki/Good_Faith_
    Estimate.asp

HOME-BUYING TIP

Once you compare several good faith estimates and become familiar with the different fees and their costs, don't be timid about challenging those you feel are "tacked on" or too high. Don't let a lender nickel and dime you the way some airlines do today. You're the consumer, and the lenders need your business, so sharpen the pencil and save some money.

B's is 6.39 percent. Obviously, lender A's loan will cost you less and is likely to be the better choice.

The best way to compare loans is to get good faith estimates from two or three lenders and compare the costs, line by line. Note where one lender is higher on one item but lower on another. Finally, compare the APRs, and the lowest percentage is the cheapest loan.

Private Mortgage Insurance: The Good, the Bad, and Good Riddance

Essentially, *private mortgage insurance* (PMI) is an insurance policy issued by private companies that insures mortgages against default. You might say it's similar to Lloyds of London insuring a BMW hole-in-one prize in a golf tournament. Chances are that the players won't even come close to the lucky hole, but occasionally it does happen. However, private mortgage insurance makes it possible for home buyers to purchase homes with zero to 20 percent down, and this is a big chunk of the nearly 65 percent of American households that currently own their own home. With more than 20 percent down, lenders don't require PMI.

For more information on PMI, check out www .gehomenow.com and www.privatemi.com.

The insurance world is all about risk. If buyers put 20 percent or more down on a home, statistics show that the chances of their skipping out on the mortgage shrink considerably. It's the zero to 20 percent down crowd that keeps investors up at night, so they require an insurance policy that covers them if the buyers don't make the monthly payments.

What Mortgage Insurance Costs You

Again, the mortgage industry is all about risk, and what determines your monthly premium is your down payment and your credit score. A 5 percent down payment carries more risk than a 10 or 15 percent down payment, so the mortgage will cost more. Likewise, good credit lowers the premium because a 750 credit score is less risky than a 680 score.

For example, the PMI on a $200,000 loan with 5 percent down might cost you $125 a month, while with 10 percent down the payment drops to $83. Putting 15 percent down drops the insurance payment ever further, to $50 a month. Of course, the best route is to put 20 percent down so you don't have to carry PMI at all.

Save Money by Getting Rid of Mortgage Insurance

In 1998, Congress passed the Homeowners Protection Act, which requires lenders to drop the PMI when a loan balance pays down to 78 percent of the original amount. This appears straightforward enough, but how long will it take to pay a $200,000 mortgage down to 78 percent? Well, 78 percent of $200,000 is $156,000, and an amortization schedule reveals that it will not happen until about the 178th payment, or in 14.8 years. That's a lot of money going to PMI company stockholders—approximately $14,770, if you put 10 percent down.

In reality, the best way to get rid of PMI is to keep a close watch on the house values in your neighborhood, and when your home appreciates about 22 percent, refinance with an 80 percent loan. For instance, a home purchased for $200,000 would need to appreciate to around $256,410. Depending on your local real estate market, this can happen fast or can take a few years, but certainly it will not take fourteen-plus years. Also, sometimes you can get the PMI company to drop its coverage if you can prove you have 22 percent equity. Check with your PMI insurer for their policy on this.

If you had an FHA loan and refinanced it, you may be entitled to a partial refund of your upfront mortgage insurance premium. To find out, go to www.hud.gov/offices/hsg/comp/refunds/index.cfm.

> **HOME-BUYING TIP**
>
> Keep in touch with your friendly neighborhood Realtor and ask him or her to check on what homes similar to yours are selling for. If you can prove that you have 20 percent or more equity in your home, call your lender and ask what paperwork is needed to drop your PMI coverage.

Sources of Down Payments

A common frustration for many would-be first-time home buyers is getting together the money for a down payment. Here are some down payment strategies:

- FHA and VA loans allow gift funds from family and even the seller.

■ If you have an asset like a boat or car the seller would like to have, you can sometimes use that for a down payment credit.

■ Your state housing authority may have zero-down programs.

■ Use your 401(k) or IRA for a down payment. Special provisions allow you withdraw up to 50 percent from your IRA to buy a principal residence for you, your child, or your grandchild. For details, go to www.investsafe.com/housefinancing.html.

■ You may be able to borrow from your insurance policies or employer programs.

■ Investors may be offering some zero-down programs; check with your lender.

Picking a Mortgage Payment that Works for You

Mortgage loans come with a menu of payment options, with the most popular being fixed and adjustable rate programs. Each option has its advantages and disadvantages, and the one that works best for you depends upon your financial situation.

Fixed Rate Mortgages

A *fixed rate mortgage* is one in which the loan is repaid in equal payments within a certain time frame. Most fixed rate mortgages have paybacks of fifteen or thirty years. The advantages of this type of mortgage are that you (1) know what the payment is from month to month, and (2) can track your growing equity by using an amortization schedule and see how much of your payment goes to interest and how much to principal. Fixed rate programs are still the most popular way to buy a home because of their predictability.

Adjustable Rate Mortgages

Adjustible rate mortgages (ARMs) are loans that start out with a low interest rate and then the payment goes up (or down) with fluctuations in the financial index to which the interest rate is linked. These interest rates are usually tied to regional cost-of-funds or Treasury bill rate indexes. As these indexes move up or down, so does the amount of your mortgage payment. This makes it difficult to anticipate your next mortgage payment when the adjustment period comes up.

Most mortgages with adjustable rates typically reset their payments every six months, every year, or even every two years. Some may give you an option convert to a fixed rate after a certain time. In reality, there are as many variations on this theme as bankers can dream up.

Some lenders have attempted to soften this uncertainty by placing a cap on rate increases. In mortgage-speak, a *cap* or *cap rate* is a guarantee that your interest rate won't increase more than 1 or 2 percent in any one adjustment period or 5 to 6 percent over the life of the loan. To put this in perspective, a 1 percent increase on a 6 percent, $200,000 loan will increase the payment by $131.50 a month.

Many home buyers start out with a low-payment ARM and then refinance to a fixed rate when the introductory rate ends. Unfortunately, this strategy can come back to bite you, as many homeowners found out in the last few years. When easy credit disappeared and home values dropped, many owners were unable to refinance and were stuck with painful escalating payments.

For most buyers, ARMs work best as short-term financing. For example, suppose you plan on living in the home for only a year or two; by having low initial payments you can save money if you sell before the loan payment is up for adjustment according to the index change and time period. Still, before you commit to an ARM, ask your lender to print you a payment schedule of the loan's worst-case scenario. The bottom line here is to go with a fixed rate if possible; the ARMs build too much uncertainty into your financial future. Especially you should avoid ARMs with teaser rates.

Loans with Balloon Payments

In mortgage-speak, a *balloon payment* is a payment that reduces the loan by other than the monthly payment. For example, say you structure a loan payment schedule of $1,400 a month, with a $5,000 additional payment due on March 15 of each year when you get your federal income tax refund. Another common balloon payment is when a seller carries the financing, with a balloon payment due for the outstanding balance at the end of the fifth year; in other words, you refinance the home at the end of the fifth year and pay off the mortgage holder. For instance, suppose you bought a home for $225,000 and the seller agrees to carry the financing at 6.25 percent, with monthly payments of $1,385.36 and a five-year balloon. This means that, at the end of five years, the entire balance of $210,009 is due and payable.

If interest rates are low and you qualify, no problem with this type of arrangement. But suppose interest rates have climbed in the interim to 9 percent and you can't qualify for a loan. The situation can then get sticky and the mortgage holder can foreclose. Therefore, if at all possible, avoid balloon payments. They often lock you into a refinance situation for the future, and you cannot know what the financial landscape will be then.

Bi-weekly Payment Options

With a bi-weekly payment schedule, you make two half-payments per month. For instance, if your pay period is every two weeks, you pay one-half of the payment on the first of the month and the other half on the fifteenth. Most lenders offering this service require an automatic deduction from a checking account.

One couple, Wes and Lynne, went with this option when they bought their townhouse and financed for $275,000. Since both of their paychecks were direct deposit and bi-monthly, they felt this was a way to put their mortgage payments on autopilot, save interest, and shorten their loan. This is how it worked out. Their monthly principal and interest payment totaled $1,692.22. The mortgage lender deducted one-half of the payment, or $846.61, on the first of the month and the other half on the fifteenth of the month. In effect, the owners make twenty-six half-payments of $846.61 each per year with this system. That reduces their loan payoff from thirty years to twenty-four and a third years and will end up saving them $74,329 in interest over the life of the loan.

For more information on bi-weekly payments, contact your mortgage company's customer service department. They usually have an 800 number or e-mail address on the monthly statement.

Eight Steps You Can Take to Make This Chapter Work for You

1. Study the different loan options and zero in on the one that works best for you.

2. Keep your eye open for seller financing opportunities.

3. Get a good faith estimate from a lender and become familiar with the different fees and how you can negotiate reductions.

4. Use APR quotes to reveal padded loan costs and pick the cheapest offer.

5. If possible, find a way to avoid PMI by putting more money down.

6. If it's a slow market, try to get the seller to pay the closing costs or points.

7. Don't assume that the lender where you have a savings or checking account will give you the best deal; shop around and compare fees.

8. If possible, avoid adjustable rate loans and balloon payments that can lock you into future commitments you may not like.

■ ■ ■

Now that you have a good idea of the many ways you can buy a home, Chapter 3 will show you how to shop for a lender and get the best deal.

Dealing with Mortgage Lenders

In the first two chapters I've covered the credit requirements that mortgage lenders look for and the buffet of loan options that they offer. The next step on the road to your dream home is to find a lender that can pull all this together for you so that you can get a loan approval.

Unfortunately, with the recent upheaval in the credit market, obtaining loan approval is getting tougher, though the situation is still far from discouraging. More home buyers are looking at FHA and VA loans, with their increased loan limits. Alternative financing is becoming more important as well, with seller carry-back loans, lease options, and property exchanges.

It's interesting to note that, in the later part of the 1970s and in the early 1980s, when the oil embargo caused a recession and mortgage rates soared to double digits, real estate sales didn't fold. Sellers still needed to sell and buyers still needed places to live. Someone needed to put these deals together, and it wasn't long until Realtors who refused to give in to the doom and gloom adapted to the market.

Likewise, the current market contains big opportunities because people still need to both buy and sell homes. It wasn't that long ago that home sellers had the upper hand, as the housing pendulum swung as far into their territory as possible. But nothing stays the same for long, and the pendulum has swung back into buyer territory, creating some great deals for home buyers.

However, one constant remains: regardless of how creative you get or how you slice and dice a real estate deal, sooner or later a mortgage becomes necessary to exercise an option, finance a balloon, or refinance. This means you need to shop for a lender either now or later, and you need to know the ropes so you can get the best deal. This chapter points the way.

In this chapter you'll learn how to:

- Avoid bad or predatory lenders.

- Assemble the paperwork you will need for loan approval.

- Find a good lender.

- Spot garbage fees that lenders often tack onto a loan.

- Be aware of the most common fees found in closing costs.

- Know which lender fees are negotiable.

- Find a lender on the Internet.

Avoiding Bad or Predatory Lenders

The mortgage industry shelters good, bad, and downright scary loan officers and companies, so you need to exercise vigilance and use the tools offered in this chapter to avoid pitfalls. Although there are plenty of good, honest, hard-working lenders in the business, too many buyers fall prey to slick advertising, unrealistic rate quotes, or going with a lender recommended by an agent without shopping around.

HOME-BUYING TIP

Always get three written loan quotes (good faith estimates) and compare them before you commit to a loan. If a lender tries to deceive you with smoke and mirrors, it will become obvious fast.

Unfortunately, bad lenders not only cost you time and money but also can cost you the deal itself when they don't have the resources or competence to follow through. Scary lenders focus on making as much money as they can by whatever means possible—without concern for matters such as fraud. Getting caught in their web usually costs you higher loan fees, overvalued appraisals, teaser rates that adjust steeply upward, and prepayment penalties.

In a nutshell, *predatory lending* takes advantage of borrowers by adding non-standard fees and by padding regular fees

Six Mortgage Fraud Warning Signs

1. A lender who advertises a much lower rate than makes sense in the current market, hoping you won't read the fine print.

2. A loan officer who qualifies you for a higher loan than the income ratios covered in the last chapter.

3. A lender, agent, or seller who suggests you sign two purchase contracts: one that represents the real intent of the buyer and seller and another higher priced one that is given to the lender. (Sometimes called *double-contracting*, this strategy results in a higher loan so the buyer can get cash back from the deal.)

4. A loan officer who suggests that you misrepresent earnings, debts, employment, or other information on the loan application. Walk away and find another lender fast.

5. An agent, loan officer, or anyone else who asks you to use your good credit rating to buy property that the two of you will resell for a higher price and split the profits. (Once you've signed loan documents, you're on the hook for the payments and, if property values drop, you're left holding the bag. This common scam snared a lot of naive would-be real estate investors in recent years.)

6. If the deal offers unusually high returns and appears too good to be true, it often is! This is an oldie but goodie.

for origination, document preparation, appraisal, credit reports, and so on. The most egregious of all bad-faith practices involves steering applicants to more expensive loans or to those with adjustable rates and prepayment penalties that the borrower doesn't understand. If you suspect a case of predatory lending, check out www.fanniemae.com/initiatives/lending/antipredatory.jhtml. You can also call Fannie Mae at 800–732–6643.

Manuel and Geri found out the hard way about bad lenders when a relative pressured them to use a friend in the mortgage business. They had found a cute bungalow close to their children's school and made an FHA offer with a four-week closing date. The loan officer took their application and explained that he would need a $450 credit and application fee to get started. Once he received their money, he said he would get back to them in a few days. Two weeks later, when Manuel and Geri hadn't heard from the lender, they tried calling him several times, getting a recorded message and the usual beep each time. He never returned their calls.

Finally, into the third week, Manuel got their lender's home number from their relative and called him. It came as a big shock when he told them that his company was not an FHA-approved lender so he could neither do a loan for them nor refund the fee they paid upfront. In the end, Manuel and Geri lost their home purchase because the seller accepted a backup offer the week before and refused to extend the closing date. Fortunately for them, they were able to get their deposit back owing to a clause in the purchase agreement that made the offer subject to financing approval.

The lessons Manual and Geri learned from this:

1. Never pay more than the credit report fee, normally $40 to $75, upfront. And only after credit and income ratios look good should you pay for the appraisal costs and small inspections that may be required in your area.

2. Be wary of application fees. Good lenders won't charge an application fee.

3. If a relative or friend is a lender, add their good faith estimate to a couple of others and compare the fees. The old saying about doing business with friends and relatives applies even more to mortgage lending, since it's such an emotionally charged situation.

4. Know the deadlines contained in your purchase agreement (such as for inspections, loan approval, and closing dates) and ensure the lender meets them.

5. Make sure the offer is subject to financing approval.

Getting a Loan Commitment

The next step is to assemble the paperwork you'll need to make a loan application. Lenders need documentation verifying your financial situation before they can give you a loan commitment. To make it easy, you can fax or e-mail all or most of the information the lender requires.

Assemble the following paperwork for all of those who will sign on the mortgage before you start talking to lenders:

■ A copy of birth certificates, Social Security cards or numbers, birth dates, current addresses, how long you've lived there, and the name and address of your landlord(s) for the past two years. Some lenders may also ask for a letter or printout from your landlord verifying that you've paid your rent on time and as agreed.

- Most recent pay stubs that show year-to-date earnings.

- W-2 tax forms along with tax returns for the past two years.

- Name, address, and contact information of current employers along with any previous employers for the past two years.

- Checking, savings, and other account balances and account numbers along with IRAs, CDs, stocks, bonds, insurance policies, and a list of other paper assets and their current values.

- A list of hard assets such as cars, RVs, boats, second homes, and recreational properties.

- A breakdown of money owed, account numbers and balances due on credit cards, student loans, auto loans, rent, child support, and any other debts.

- Tax returns from the past two years, along a year-to-date profit-and-loss statements, if you're self-employed or work on commission.

- Copies of any divorce decrees or separation agreements and documentation regarding any alimony or child support (paid or received), with cancelled checks or a court clerk's payments history for the past year.

- Income reports from sales, baby sitting, tips, or other hard-to-verify sources, all of which will need to be verified on your tax returns.

With all this information neatly assembled in a folder, it's time to go shopping for a good lender.

Prequalified vs. Preapproved Loans

Much confusion exists among real estate professionals concerning prequalified versus preapproved buyers. If you talked to a lender (or keyed the data into a mortgage lenders' Web site calculator), gave your income and listed your debts, and asked for an opinion as to what you could afford, the lender would come back with an approximate home price. Essentially, you know about what price range you are able to afford. The lender has *prequalified* you but has not verified anything or gotten any loan approvals.

On the other hand, *preapproval* entails a great deal more. To get a loan preapproval, you must meet with a lender and go through the following steps:

- Fill out a mortgage application.

- Pay for a credit check.

- Give the loan officer a pay stub with year-to-date earnings or other documentation of income.

- Verify the sources of your down payment and closing costs.

- Run the data on Fannie Mae or Freddie Macs software and receive an approval.

- Receive a letter from the lender verifying that you are good to go subject to an offer at or less than the amount you qualify for and the final underwriting approval.

- Avoid doing something dumb to mess up your credit or lose your job before closing on the sale.

When you find a home, a preapproval letter from the lender becomes an important part of your offer package. It gives the seller assurance that you are a real buyer and that the deal will close quickly. For an example of the type of letter you're likely to receive indicating preapproval, see Figure 3–1.

Shopping for a Good Lender

Start shopping for a good lender by creating a list of possible candidates and then narrow it down to a short list of lenders that you will talk to. Ask friends, relatives, or co-workers who have recently bought or refinanced a home how they liked their lender. If you get a positive response, add that lender to your list. Also check with Realtors, title people, real estate attorneys, and others in the real estate business.

Suppose your detective work yields seven possible lenders. That's a good starting number, so your next step is to pare your list down to three lenders from whom you will request good faith estimates. Chapter 1 explained how to calculate a rough estimate of the amount you can spend on a home. Run the numbers on your financial calculator or from the www.kiplinger.com/tools/ Web site so you have a good idea of your price range.

Next, call the loan officers on your list and ask for a ballpark figure based on your income and outstanding debts. The objective here is not

FIGURE 3-1
Typical preapproval letter.

ARBOR CAPITAL MORTGAGE INC.

July 24, 2008

RE: John and Jill Doe
Mortgage pre-approval letter

John and Jill Doe have applied for a mortgage loan with Arbor Capital Mortgage, Inc. We have evaluated their credit reports, verified incomes, employment history, sources of down payment and closing costs.

The Doe application has been reviewed by an underwriter and they are approved for a $267,500 mortgage subject to the following conditions:

1. Maximum purchase price of $267,500.
2. Home to appraise for at least the purchase price.
3. Interest rate at time of lock-in not to exceed 6.75 percent.
4. A clean title report on property by an accredited title company.
5. No significant change in assets or employment.
6. Final underwriting and quality control approval.

Blaine Rockford
President
Arbor Capital Mortgage Inc.

921 E. Executive Park Drive, Suite A, Salt Lake City, UT 84117 – 801-685-2505 – FAX 801-685-2509

to test the person, but to start a conversation to learn about his or her qualifications and experience, to decide whether you like the way you're treated, and so on. The second objective is to pare your list down to three lenders you feel comfortable with.

If you get voice mail when you call a lender, leave a message. A returned call within an hour or two is good. Drop anyone from your list who returns your call after the current business day. This may seem harsh, but waiting for a loan to close is an emotionally charged process and you don't want lax follow-up from your lender adding to your frustration.

Your homework should end with your having three possible candidates. The last step, then, in the paring-down process is to ask each of the three finalists to work up a good faith estimate based on your income and debts and to fax or e-mail the estimate to you. When you receive them, spread out the three estimates and compare the fees and APR (see Chapter 2 for specifics on APR and points). Then pick out the best loan package.

HOME-BUYING TIP

If you really like a lender, but he or she doesn't offer the lowest fees, you can always use the best quote you've gotten to negotiate a better deal. Don't be timid; it's your money you're saving, so beat 'em down shamelessly.

The final step is to call the lender you have decided on and set up an appointment to go in with your folder full of the paperwork discussed in the last section. Picking a lender to work with doesn't mean you should stop negotiating, however. After reading the next section on fees and closing costs, you may find it is possible to get a few of those costs reduced.

Being Smart About Garbage Fees and Closing Costs

Like any other business, banks, credit unions, and mortgage brokers can survive only if they are making a profit. And that profit comes from the fees they charge. Most of the loan fees are legitimate for a necessary service, but sometimes their services are padded with unnecessary costs. Your mission, if accepted, is to root out and eliminate these padded fees as early in the process as possible. If you wait until closing to spot any padded fees, you can either throw a tantrum and walk out (which could embroil you in a lawsuit or kill the deal) or swallow hard and sign the paperwork, vowing you'll be smarter next time.

Typical Closing Costs

The good faith estimate (see Figure 3–2) you got from your lender and the settlement statement (called HUDs) you will sign at closing are closely related. They both show a breakdown of the loan and closing costs and the numbered lines on both forms apply to the same costs. This allows you to compare your good faith estimate with the settlement statement to make sure no padded fees have sneaked in. Both forms are standardized and mandated by the federal government, and any loan closing involving a mortgage lender must use them.

Closing costs vary from state to state, but regardless of what state you live in, you'll likely find the following fees on the good faith estimate (GFE) and HUDs:

■ Appraisal fees can vary, depending on sale price and area. On the GFE you'll find this fee on line 803. Appraisal fees are competitive and should vary little from lender to lender. They are usually in the $300 to $500 range.

■ On line 804 of the GFE, you'll find a credit report fee of from $40 to $80. Credit reports are not transferable, so if you become unhappy with your lender and decide to go with another, you'll have to pay for a new report.

■ Discount points, as discussed in Chapter 2, are prepaid interest that a lender charges to buy down the interest rate. Each point is equal to 1 percent of the loan amount and lowers the interest a fraction of a percent. Look for these on line 802.

■ Document preparation and processing fees are undoubtedly the most abused fees on the statement. You'll often find them in two different places: the lender puts its "doc prep" fees in the 800 column, title or escrow companies put theirs on line 1105 or in the 1300 column. It appears that everyone involved in the transaction wants to add a document or processing fee.

■ Line 903 contains your first year's homeowners' insurance premium.

■ If your lender requires an escrow that you pay into monthly for property taxes and insurance when they come due, you'll find that in the 1000 column. Lenders typically charge you two or three payments

FIGURE 3-2
Good Faith Estimate form.

GOOD FAITH ESTIMATE
(Not a Loan Commitment)

This Good Faith Estimate is being provided by Arbor Capital Mortgage, Inc. a mortgage broker, and no lender has yet been obtained. A lender will provide you with an additional Good Faith Estimate within three business days of the receipt of your loan application.

Applicant(s):	Sales Price:
	Base Loan Amount:
Property Address	Total Loan Amount:
	Interest Rate:
	Type of Loan:
Preparation Date:	Loan Number:

The information provided below reflects estimates of the charges which you are likely to incur at the settlement of your loan. The fees listed are estimates—actual charges may be more or less. Your transaction may not involve a fee for every item listed. The numbers listed beside the estimates generally correspond to the numbered lines contained in the IIUD-1 or IIUD-1A settlement statement which you will be receiving at settlement. The HUD-1 or HUD-1A settlement statement will show you the actual cost of items paid at settlement.

"A ' designates those costs affecting APR.   "P" designates compensation to Broker not paid out of Loan Proceeds.

800		ITEMS PAYABLE IN CONNECTION WITH LOAN:		1000		RESERVES DEPOSITED WITH LENDER:	
801	A	Origination Due Lender @	$_____	1001		Hazard Insurance Impounds	$_____
802	A	Discount @	$_____	1002	A	Mortgage Insurance Impounds	$_____
803		Appraisal Fees	$_____	1004		Property Tax Impounds	$_____
804		Credit Report	$_____	1006		Flood Insurance Impounds	$_____
805	A	Lender's Inspection Fee	$_____	1007			$_____
808	A	Tax Service Contract	$_____	1008			$_____
809	A	Underwriting Review	$_____	1009		Aggregate Analysis Adjustment	$_____
810	A	Administration Fee	$_____				
811	A	Application Fee	$_____	1100		TITLE CHARGES:	
812	A	Commitment Fee	$_____	1101	A	Settlement or Closing Fee	$_____
813	A	Warehouse Fee / Interest Differential	$_____	1105		Document Preparation Fee	$_____
814	P	Yield Sprd. Prem _____% $		1106		Notary Fee	$_____
815	P	Serv. Rel. Prem. _____% $		1107	A	Attorney Fee	$_____
816	A	Origination Due Broker @	$_____	1108		Title Insurance Premium	$_____
817	A	FHA Upfront MIP / VA Funding Fee	$_____	1111		Endorsement Fee	$_____
818	A	MORTGAGE BROKER FEE 0–5%	$_____	1112			$_____
819	A		$_____				
820	A		$_____	1200		GOVERNMENT RECORDER AND TRANSFER CHARGES:	
821	A		$_____				
822	A		$_____	1201		Recording Fee	$_____
823	A		$_____	1201		City/County Tax / Stamps	$_____
824	A		$_____	1202		State Tax / Stamps	$_____
825	A		$_____	1204			
800		ITEMS REQUIRED BY LENDER TO BE PAID IN ADVANCE		1300		ADDITIONAL SETTLEMENT CHARGES:	
901	A	Prepaid Interest ___ days @ $	$_____	1301		Survey	$_____
902	A	Mortgage Insurance Premium	$_____	1302		Termite Inspection	$_____
903		Hazard Insurance Premium	$_____	1303		Property Inspection	$_____
904		Flood Insurance Premium	$_____	1304		Photo Fee	$_____
				1305			$_____
				1306			$_____
				1307			$_____
				1308			$_____

TOTAL ESTIMATED MONTHLY PAYMENT:		TOTAL ESTIMATED FUNDS NEEDED TO CLOSE:	
Principal and Interest	$_____	Total Purchase Price / Existing Payoff	$_____
Real Estate Taxes	$_____	Estimated Closing Costs	$_____
Hazard Insurance	$_____	Estimated Prepaid Items / Reserves	$_____
Mortgage Insurance	$_____	-Total Paid Items & Subordinate Financing	$_____
Homeowners Association Dues	$_____	-Seller Paid Closing Costs	$_____
Second Principal and Interest	$_____	FHA UFMIP/VA Funding Fee	$_____
Other	$_____	-Base Loan Amount	$_____
TOTAL MONTHLY PAYMENT		TOTAL ESTIMATED FUNDS NEEDED TO CLOSE	$_____

These estimates are provided pursuant to the Real Estate Settlement Procedures Act of 1974, as amended (RESPA). Additional information can be found in the HUD Special Information Booklet, which is to be provided to you by your Mortgage Broker or lender if your application is to purchase real property and the lender will take a rst lien on the property. The undersigned acknowledges receipt of a copy of the Special Information Booklet "Settlement Costs."

_____	_____	_____	_____
Applicant	Date	Applicant	Date

to put money into escrow so you'll have enough in reserve when these bills come due.

■ On Line 901, you'll find interest on your loan from the day of closing to the first of the coming month. Because mortgage payments are always due on the first of the month, and you get a full month before the first payment comes due, you may go nearly two months before you write your first mortgage payment check. For example, suppose you close on June 12 and interest on your loan is $1,200. It's eighteen days from June 12 to June 30, so you multiply those eighteen days by $40 ($1,200 divided by 30 days) and get $720, which goes on line 901. Your first payment is due on August 1, which includes interest for July. That's because during July you are accruing interest on your loan until August 1.

■ Lenders' title insurance is required by investors to protect their interest in the property. It guarantees that the property title is free and clear, with no problems. This is usually charged on line 1108.

■ Mortgage insurance, or MIP (covered in Chapter 2), is a monthly charge that protects the lender from the loan's going into default. You should see one or two months' payments on line 902.

■ On Line 801, you'll find the loan origination fee. This is what your lender charges you to put the loan together. Usually it's 1 percent of the loan amount, although it's not unusual to find some credit unions charging 0.5 percent. Is this fee negotiable? Sometimes.

■ The 800 column is where most of the junk fees are listed. These are the fees you want to review carefully because padding can flourish. Look closely at fees such as warehouse fees, commitment fee, processing fees, document or doc prep fees, courier fees, and lender's inspection fee.

The Fees and the Numbers

Be wary of lenders that create a loan package with low teaser rates and then make up for it with additional fees. The only way you can determine how good a deal you're getting is to compare the GFEs side by side. If the lender you're hoping to work with has higher fees on an item, question it. Once your loan officer knows you've done your homework, he or she will hesitate to add unnecessary fees, knowing you'll question them. In fact, your lender will probably develop a grudging respect for your attention to detail. Because few buyers take the time to understand these fees and are intimidated by the whole process, lenders sometimes pile them on. "Why not" is a common attitude with many bankers.

HOME-BUYING TIP

Many buyers are so intimidated by the loan process that they don't question the fees. Be a savvy consumer. Study this chapter and talk to loan officers until you understand the 800 line fees that are common in your area.

Question and negotiate fees as soon as possible after you get your good faith estimates. It's best to have everything settled a few days before closing in order to avoid a pressured situation that could cause a delay. And whenever you and the lender negotiate changes, get those changes in writing on a revised GFE. Remember that if it isn't in writing, it doesn't exist.

The last step before closing on the house is to ask the title company, or whoever closes the loan, to fax or e-mail you a copy of the HUDs a few hours before you go in to sign the paperwork. However, the closing people may not get the loan documents until just before you are scheduled to close. If that's the case, take a few minutes to sit down and go over the HUD statements alone before walking into the room. Take notes, and if you have questions, bring them up when you and the closing agent go over the statements.

If the HUDs contain fees different from your GFE, you want to take care of them before you get to the closing table, if possible. If you can't, then don't worry about it. Statements can be changed and reprinted easily.Don't let a closer tell you that the statements can't be changed. They may have to get on the phone to the lender and handle corrections by fax or e-mail, but that's okay. You're the consumer and you want the deal as agreed.

Blair and Letia went through this when they bought their second home. The first time around, they didn't know what was going on. This time, however, they did their homework and planned on making sure they paid not a dollar more than was necessary. After getting GFEs from their previous lender and two others, they found that another lender's fees came to $862 less than the other two. When their previous lender refused to meet the competition, Blair and Letia decided to work with the mortgage company with the lowest fees.

Everything went smoothly—until closing. When the title company faxed the closing documents to Blair at his office, he was out and didn't get them until an hour before they were to close on the property. Blair did a quick comparison of the HUDs and GFE and noticed the lender had added a $150 processing fee in the 800 column. Not quite sure whom to talk to, he called the title company and they referred him to the mortgage lender. Finally getting through to the loan processor, he had to do a little verbal arm twisting before she agreed to remove the fee and send a correction to the title company. The bottom line is that if Blair and Letia had not compared loans and had not compared their GFE to the HUDs before closing, it would have cost them almost $1,000 more for their mortgage.

Finding a Lender on the Internet

Sometimes you can save money by shopping for a lender on the Internet, but there are traps that can cost the unwary. Surfing the Web is a great way to get a feel for loan options and rates, and you can even get a good loan. However, watch out for teaser interest rates. The lender will try to make up the loss with padded fees or not be able to deliver when it's time to lock in the advertised rate.

For example, if most of the mortgage lenders are quoting an interest rate of 6 percent and a Web lender offers you 5.75 percent to get you to respond to its ad, you've encountered a teaser rate. You can be sure the mortgage company isn't going to lose money, so it will make up the difference in fees or discount points (see Chapter 2 regarding points).

Some Web lenders sites to check out include:

www. E-loan.com

www.getsmart.com

www.loanweb.com

www.quickenloans
.quicken.com

www.wellsfargo.com

If, in your surfing, you find a Web lender that's a national bank or mortgage company, the site may refer you to a loan officer at one of its branch offices closest to you. Other lenders may handle everything by overnight mail, phone, or e-mail, or use a local title company or attorney. Any of these ways can work out.

How to Compare Loans on the Web

Most mortgage Web sites have prequalifying worksheets on which you can fill in your debts, income, and other financial data and get instant maximum loan amounts, monthly payments, and other loan data. Some of these sites also have helpful calculators that compute buying versus renting, home-owner tax savings, and amortization schedules.

HOME-BUYING TIP

The same rules apply when shopping on the Web as they do when shopping in your home area. Get GFEs and compare the fees and APR.

If you want to go further with an Internet lender and complete a loan application, click the button that's usually labeled "Apply for a Loan." You fill out a detailed application along with a credit card number for a credit report, then hit "Submit." Within a few hours, a loan officer should contact you by phone or e-mail.

The first step in the www.eloans.com site, for example, is a prequalification questionnaire. You enter data about your income, debts, and down payment. The site calculates your ratios and tells you if your numbers look good. To continue, you can click "Apply" and fill out more detailed data, along with your Social Security number. Some Web sites make it more interesting by offering to take your information and forward it to several lenders that will compete for your business. Not a bad idea. But still, you know the routine—get it in writing and compare.

One disadvantage of using the Web is that it's hard to square off with a Web site eyeball to eyeball and negotiate the loan fees the way you can with a live loan officer. Remember also that if a lender offers you a lower rate if you will pay points, you know how to handle that; see Chapter 2. To recap, you subtract the loan payment without points from the lower payment if you were to pay points, and divide the difference into the cost of the points. That will tell you how many months or years it is until you break even. If the breakeven point is more than three or four years, it probably isn't worth paying the points. For example, if points cost $4,000 and your monthly savings are $73, dividing $73 into $4,000 yields slightly over fifty-three months before you break even.

Are Web Loans Cheaper?

Troy and Deborah went the Internet route when they bought their home through an online lender. Since both worked for a Web design company, they felt comfortable getting a mortgage through the Internet and they liked the simplicity of I-Mortgage's site. After talking to four lenders who e-mailed them good faith estimates, the one Troy and Deborah chose assigned them a personal loan representative who would handle their loan and answer any questions.

The loan representative mailed the paperwork that needed to be filled out and returned with the borrowers' W-2s, bank statement copies, and other verifications. Deborah paid the credit and appraisal fees by credit card. It all went smoothly and took about three weeks for the lender to complete and send the loan package to a local title company for closing.

It's interesting to note that some Web lenders advertise that they can save you about $1,500 in lender fees. In Troy and Deborah's case, they had a 750 credit score, were putting 10 percent down, and had good income-to-debt ratios—a slam dunk for any lender. And when they closed, they did save about $1,370. However, if Troy and Deborah's credit or income-to-debt ratios were not so good, Web lenders would likely have referred them to affiliate companies that would tack on fees and eliminate the savings.

The bottom line is yes—you can sometimes save money with a Web lender if you have good credit and ratios. These lenders are able to give you a good deal by streamlining the process and eliminating overhead. Passing these savings on to you eliminates many section 800 garbage fees. If you want to go with an FHA or VA guaranteed loan, however, or have credit problems, or need an off-the-beaten-path loan, the savings disappear. You are likely better off with an experienced local lender with the contacts and know-how to push the envelope and get you approved.

Six Steps You Can Take to Make This Chapter Work for You

1. Find a mortgage lender by putting together a list and then narrowing it down. Ask friends, co-workers, agents, and title people for referrals.

2. Contact the lenders on your list and, after speaking with them, narrow it down to two or three you feel most comfortable with and ask them work up a GFE.

3. Compare the GFEs side by side. Note the fees each lender is charging and the APR. Most likely, the lender with the lowest APR is offering the best deal.

4. Learn about closing costs and fees by talking to lenders, agents, and title people.

5. Get a copy of the closing statement before you close and check out the fees. Compare them against your GFE to make sure you're not paying too much.

6. If you have super credit, good ratios, and a good job history, check out Web lenders to see if you can get a better deal.

■ ■ ■

The next chapter tells you how to make shopping for your dream home fun and efficient. You'll learn little-known ways to narrow down the list so you only look at those homes that fit your criteria.

 CHAPTER 4

Shopping for Your Dream Home

After you've found a lender, waded through a mortgage preapproval process, and received a preapproval letter from the lender, you're ready to start shopping for your dream home.

The key to shopping efficiently and effectively for a home involves, first, deciding on a price range you feel you can afford, and then coming up with some strategies to help you find the property that meets your requirements. You then need to do some detective work to find a real estate agent who will assist you in your house hunting. Once you find one, the two of you will typically create a list of available homes in the area or areas that interest you, and you'll then begin eliminating listings until you've whittled them down to a manageable dozen or so. You may begin with only a few or as many as a hundred candidates, but if you're working with an experienced agent, you should have no trouble eliminating the "dogs"—those on busy streets, rentals, not-so-good neighborhoods, styles you don't like, and so on. Only those homes that make your short list will then require your walk-through and inspection.

To help you minimize any home-buying frustration, this chapter gives you the tools and know-how to develop a successful shopping strategy. Once you've found your dream home, the next chapter will show you how to get your offer accepted.

In this chapter you'll learn how to:

■ Determine whether you should go for the max or buy conservatively.

- Utilize some home-buying tools for finding your dream home.

- Find and work with a real estate agent.

- Narrow down a large list of homes into a manageable list to look at.

- Shop for a fixer-upper.

- Buy a newly constructed home.

Go for the Max or Buy Conservatively?

The first major decision you need to make in putting together your shopping list of homes to consider is to decide on the price range you can afford. Do you want to go for the maximum loan amount on your preapproval letter, or do you want to play it more conservatively? Most lenders will qualify a buyer for the maximum loan possible, which typically tops out at about 44 percent (but can go up to 50 percent or more) of their total debt level (house payment plus other debts), depending on credit score and assets.

Some homeowners can handle higher debt-to-income ratios than others. As a result, if a lender offers you a mortgage that eats up 50 percent of your income, it's your responsibility to decide whether you want and can handle that heavy a debt load for the long haul. Remember that you're likely looking at a thirty-year mortgage, so if you anticipate a change in your lifestyle that can negatively affect your income in the near future, you ought to factor that in. Other home buyers take a different tack and buy a slightly smaller home with a fifteen-year loan (see sidebar) that can channel a lot of bucks into a retirement or college fund. Which route you choose depends on your goals and lifestyle.

The Argument for Buying to the Max

One school of thought is to buy the most expensive home you can. Because most homeowners invest less than 20 percent down, you're using the lender's money to control a much larger amount than you've got invested, thus leveraging your investment. As the home increases in value, the return on your investment balloons because it's a percentage of the home's value, not of your low down payment.

In addition, with a thirty-year mortgage your monthly payment remains the same, but as your income goes up, the mortgage payment takes smaller bites out of your paycheck. In other words, a home pay-

---

Faster Payoff: Fiften-Year Loans

If you want a faster payoff with a big savings in interest, consider a fifteen- rather than a thirty-year loan. The payments on a fifteen-year loan are not double those of a thirty-year, but they are approximately 30 percent more. For example, on a $290,000, 6.75 percent, thirty-year mortgage, you'll pay monthly payments of $1,880.93. But if you go with a fifteen-year loan, the interest typically is half a percent less, or in this case 6.25 percent. A monthly payment for such a fifteen-year loan computes to $2,486.53, or an additional $605.59 a month—an increase of 32.2 percent. Thus, going this route saves you $229,559.40 in interest, as opposed to going with a thirty-year loan. Incidentally, your total cost, principal and interest on the 30-year loan paid to maturity, comes to $677,134.80 while the fifteen-year loan would cost you $447,575.40!

---

ment that begins by taking 28 percent of your income after a few years may take only 20 percent, 15 percent, or even less.

Home buyers who purchased their homes on thirty-year fixed rate loans in the 1980s and 1990s saw the value of both their homes and their incomes soar, while house payments stayed the same. Payments for most of these buyers dropped to 10 or 15 percent of their income, and many were able to pay off their mortgages early. In fact, according to the National Association of Realtors's figures, about 30 percent of Americans own their home free and clear.

Those who stretched and bought bigger homes in the best areas benefited because their homes appreciated the most. With the current federal tax rules, a husband and wife can sell their home and walk away with the first $500,000 tax free. For example, Wynn and Barbara took advantage of this situation when they sold the home they had bought in the late1970s for about $38,000. They chose a good area and kept their home in good shape. When they both retired, they sold their home for $462,000, bought a motor home, and banked the rest—all tax free, a gift from Uncle Sam for buying a home.

Proponents of this home-buying approach also point out that by buying to the max now, you're less likely to outgrow the home and need to buy a larger one later on. Since moving is disruptive, time-consuming, and costly, you'll not spend the $30,000 in selling, loan, and moving costs that occur each time you move.

The Argument for Buying Conservatively

On the flip side, the argument to buy conservatively is that you will not become a slave to your mortgage payments. This way, you keep your payment as low as possible, pay off the mortgage early, and can allocate funds for other needs.

In one case, Ron and Jenny, both freelance photographers, felt that they didn't want a large house payment keeping them from doing what they enjoyed most, which was traveling and taking pictures for their architectural photo business. They bought a small two-bedroom home in a good area and made the extra bedroom into a studio. That worked for a few years, until Jenny became pregnant and a larger home suddenly became a priority. They were able to sell their modest home and make enough money for a down payment on a larger home in a new subdivision.

Both Ron and Jenny felt that the five years they traveled and built their business wouldn't have been possible if they had been saddled with big house payments. While their small home did not appreciate as much as if they had purchased a larger home in a new area, for their situation this approach worked out well. Now, with the larger house, their increased house payments will necessitate scaling back their travel plans, but with the little one on the way, they would have to do that anyway.

> **HOME-BUYING TIP**
>
> Location is critical in real estate. If you buy well, you'll sell well. A good home-buying strategy is to buy in the best location you can afford, even if you must go with a slightly smaller home.

In the end, you must determine your priorities and decide how big a monthly payment you can comfortably handle, and not let an agent or lender talk you into going for a larger mortgage than you feel comfortable with. It's important to remember when house hunting that a home is more than just a roof and hearth. It's one of your most important long-term investments—one that will increase through appreciation and equity growth.

Home-Buying Hints for Finding Your Dream Home

Whether you go for the max or keep your mortgage payments comfortably low, you want to avoid costly mistakes that many home buyers make at this stage, as well as putting the sharpest focus on what to look for in your search. Here are some helpful hints you can use as you start putting together a home search strategy.

Buy Smart, Not Cheap

In less desirable locations, homes are cheaper and appear on the surface to be hot deals that are almost too good to pass up. Sometimes these "super deals" are in areas of older and smaller homes, which can have higher upkeep costs and bigger energy bills while you own them and that can offer a lower return when you sell.

Here are some tips on how to spot these situations and avoid getting taken:

▪ Avoid homes on busy streets, in high traffic areas, or where proposed changes may increase traffic flow. Check with city and county planning agencies for proposed changes that can negatively impact values, such as the rerouting of a freeway on or off ramp, making a zoning change from single-family to multi-family dwellings, or adding an airport runway that puts the home in the landing pattern.

▪ Inquire about the reputation of the area. Talk to neighbors and ask them what they like and don't like about living there.

▪ Be wary of fixer-uppers. Make a list of necessary repairs and needed upgrades, and get bids from contractors on the costs of bringing the house up to local codes or your standards. If the cost of rehabilitation plus the sale price is more than the cost of similar homes already upgraded, look elsewhere.

▪ If there are a lot of FOR SALE signs on the lawns of other homes in the area, that's a red flag. Find out why.

▪ Have your Realtor check the multiple listing services for records for the average listing prices and actual selling prices in the area; this ratio of list price to sales price indicates value; for example, a ratio of 90 percent means that homes are selling on average 10 percent below what they are listed for. Find out also how many days the homes stay on the market before selling.

▪ Good schools in the neighborhood add to a home's value. If the area schools have a bad reputation, consider looking elsewhere. You can get data on local schools by checking out www.schooldatedirect .org, www.schoolmatters.com, and www.greatschools.net.

A trap that first-time home buyers commonly fall into is the dream that they can buy on the cheap, fix the place up, and sell it for a profit. Fixing up a home for profit can work if you know what you're buying. Unfortunately, many would-be homeowners attend seminars or read books on getting rich quick in real estate and look for a cheap home they can fix up, without regard to the caveats listed above.

Other buyers select a small home and, when they outgrow it, they add on or remodel it so it becomes bigger and better than other homes in the neighborhood. When they decide to sell, they find that their home won't appraise for as much as they value it, and they won't be able to recover the money they have put into it. In real estate lingo, that's called a *white elephant*. As a prospective home buyer, it's tempting to sink your money into one of these white elephant deals. It appears you're getting a bigger home or one with more amenities for a good price. However, when you decide to sell, you may find it takes longer and requires deep discounts to move it.

On the whole, it's better to sell a home you've outgrown and buy a larger one in a neighborhood that will support the square footage you need. It's interesting to note that, when asked why they overimproved for the neighborhood, owners often say that they intended to live in the home forever, so it didn't matter. Then, however, a job loss, relocation, divorce, or similar problem forced them to sell—and "forever" suddenly became the present. Americans are a mobile society, and according to the National Association of Realtors, the average length of time people stay in a home is slightly over six years although that will probably change as the current home buying and selling economy plays out and owners stay put longer.

Make Location Your First Consideration

It's important to remember that location comes first, because better areas hold their value more than do less desirable areas.

So what clues should alert you that an area may be declining?

- Look at the schools. Falling ratings and districts that are consolidating schools may be the result of declining neighborhoods. Home values in these areas are likely to remain static or decrease.

- Zoning changes may allow big box stores or other businesses to change traffic patterns that can negatively impact a neighborhood's value.

- Check the local zoning master plan for proposed roads, offramps, power lines, or other improvements that can impact the area values.

- Before you make an offer, talk to several owners in the area. Ask them what they like and don't like about the neighborhood.

- If there are more than two or three rentals on the street, find out why. When owners move and can't sell, they often rent the homes. This may signal a problem with the neighborhood.

On the flip side, here are some suggestions on how to find neighborhoods on the upswing:

- Check out areas close to colleges, upscale shopping, cultural centers, and sporting events. You'll notice that, in trendy and improving neighborhoods, people are spending serious bucks remodeling and upgrading their homes.

- Find out what areas have the best schools and check out the homes within their boundaries.

- Research neighborhoods that are close to where young professionals work and where they are are moving into.

- Look for areas where prices have steadily increased over the past few years and where homes for sale may be hard to find.

- Visit new subdivisions and growing areas, because values tend to go up over the long term.

- Identify areas that may not be the best now, but where changes already in the works will make them more desirable. Examples include redevelopment areas, neighborhoods with new medical centers, college expansions, and other projects that add to a area's desirability as a place to live.

Small bungalows and cottages in older neighborhoods dotted throughout nearly every city can be good investments if they are near a university, downtown, or other desirable attractions. However, these same homes built near an airport or business park will go for many thousands of dollars less and be difficult to sell. It's all a matter of location.

Comparison Shopping

In researching a neighborhood, check out the values of comparable homes on: www.Realtor.com or www.[your state] realestate.com, www.zillow.com, www .trulia.com, or similar sites. But the best approach is to ask your agent for printouts from the Multiple Listing Service (MLS) of sold homes and those for sale in your price range. Note the list price/sale price, days on the market, and whether the seller paid buyer closing costs or other concessions.

In one instance, Andy and Rebecca found a 1960s split-level home near a small private college and close to an upscale shopping area. The owner had died and the two heirs, wanting a fast, trouble-free sale, were willing to discount if the buyers would buy "as is," with no concessions. Looking at similar houses in the neighborhood, Andy and Rebecca noticed that many owners had remodeled or upgraded them. By comparison, the home they were considering stood out as the neighborhood ugly duckling. This spelled opportunity, and they arranged for a fast closing.

> **HOME-BUYING TIP**
>
> If you're looking for a home to keep as a long-term investment, look for houses in areas that are on the rise owing to the development of shopping centers, medical complexes, new schools, and the like.

Over the next several months Andy and Rebecca painted the interior, upgraded the kitchen, changed the floor coverings, and replaced the furnace, as well as changed the unsafe aluminum wiring to copper. After three years they saved enough money to be able to replace the vinyl siding with sea foam green FiberCement textured planks and white trim. The ugly duckling became a swan.

Six years later, when they outgrew the home and needed to move up to more bedrooms and baths, values in the area had taken off, and Andy and Rebecca reluctantly put their home on the market. It sold quickly, and from their accumulated equity they could put a sizable down payment on their next home, thus avoiding private mortgage insurance.

So what did these home buyers do right? First, they looked for a neighborhood that would go up in value—one that was near a college, medical center, public transportation, and good schools. Second, they were careful about the money they put into the upgrades. Much of their effort involved elbow grease and paint. The money they did spend went where it would give them the best return—new furnace, new kitchen, and new wiring. It wasn't until later that they replaced the home's siding and exterior trim. Third, they realized that eventually the house would be too small for them and that they would need to sell and move to a bigger home. They planned on accumulating as much equity as possible by avoiding spending on items that wouldn't bring maximum return. And, fourth, they kept tabs on what homes in the neighborhood were selling for and which ones sold faster and for more money.

Look Closely at the Schools in the Neighborhood

Great schools make the homes around them more valuable. In fact, homes on one side of a street can sell for thousands of dollars less than those across the street that happen to fall in a more desirable school district. Parents want to send their kids to the best schools possible, and a school or district with an outstanding reputation can draw from a limited area. As a result, homes within that limited area become sought after and that boosts prices.

Most agents have worked with buyers who want to limit their search to a particular school district. In this case, it's just a matter of entering the school as an MLS search function; the computer prints out all the information on homes for sale in that area. For a small fee, you can go to www.schoolmatch.com and key in data for the school or district of interest, and find out how it compares. You can also talk to parents who have kids in the school to get a realistic picture.

> **HOME-BUYING TIP**
>
> If you have school-age children, talk to a couple of parents in the neighborhood regarding how they like the schools and teachers before you commit to buy.

When you combine a good area with desirable schools, you've got a powerful duet that ensures these homes will appreciate faster, for more money, and will hold their value better in a down market. So, the bottom line is to go for the best location you can afford. A bigger house in a less desirable area is not as good a deal as a smaller home in a better area. Be sure to factor in the school system as well, as it influences an area's resale value. Even if the dog or cat are all the family you'll ever have, it's still wise to buy in a good school district. You'll end up dollars ahead when you sell.

Working with an agent who knows the area and area schools can help you zero in on the best deals. And best of all, the Realtor's fees are paid by the seller (Actually, the listing agent splits with the selling agent part of the seller paid commission). As a buyer, this valuable knowledge pool is not only free for you to dip into but the agent later represents you in the transaction.

Finding and Working with a Real Estate Agent

An experienced agent can help you pull your house-hunting chores together and help you find your dream home. Realtors are the professionals you hire to help you handle this important event in your life—namely buying and selling a house. And like mortgage lenders, home inspectors, and brain surgeons, you want the best—someone with the experience to solve the problems that occur in just about all transactions, without costing you big bucks.

Entrusting Your Important Financial Decision to a Professional

Many prospective home buyers use Aunt Susan, Uncle Harry, or a neighbor who just got his or her real estate license. They don't realize how complex real estate transactions are and how easily a slip-up can cost you big bucks. The last thing you want to do is entrust one of the most important financial decisions in your life to an amateur. You're talking about hundreds of thousands of dollars and your family's happiness and future well-being. Just speak with any buyer who has made a bad decision on a home or mortgage that later resulted in escalating payments or foreclosure.

A typical example of this is when Aaron and Randi decided to buy their first home. They called Randi's Aunt Wendy, who the week before had passed her test and received her real estate license. Wendy was all enthusiasm and ready to show what properties she had. Wendy, Aaron, and Randi piled into her Honda Accord and started looking at homes in the price range of $190,000 to $375,000. All the houses they looked at, from one end of the county to the other, soon blended into a blur of images. The fun turned into frustration. After thirty days of looking, Aaron and Randi had made zero progress.

Clueless, Wendy thought that if she showed enough homes, they might get lucky and find one that clicked. This approach, sometimes called "throw-enough-mud-against-the-fence-and-some-may-stick," seldom works. This is why some buyers often go through several agents before they find a pro who can make finding their dream home a reality.

Finally, out of desperation, Wendy asked her broker to assign an experienced agent in the office to help. With professional help, things improved quickly. Aaron and Randi met with a lender, went through the loan-qualifying process, and got a preapproval letter for $295,000. Next, they met with the agent assigned to help, and she made a list of their areas of interest, home styles, and amenities. Keeping the price range between $290,000 and $315,000, the agent entered the buyer's preferences into the MLS database and came up with thirty-three possibilities.

After eliminating homes on busy streets, hard-to-show rentals, and other houses with obvious problems, twelve homes remained on the list, which the agent then gave to Aaron and Randi, She asked them to drive by these homes and pick out the best three. After their drive-bys Aaron and Randi were able to narrow their list down to two houses, and the agent made appointments to go through both. Although Aaron and Randi liked them both, they finally decided on one of the two—the three-year-old ranch with a big yard that listed for $310,950.

Their agent suggested that they offer $290,000 because it was a slow market and this home had been on the market for 105 days. The seller, anxious to get out of town and feeling he had a bird-in-the-hand deal because of the preapproval letter, eagerly accepted the offer. Fortunately, this situation worked out with only a few weeks of lost time and a little frustration. In the end, Aaron and Randi got a great deal on a home and Wendy learned a few hard lessons about working with clients.

> **HOME-BUYING TIP**
>
> An experienced agent in tune with the market can save you thousands of dollars. Agents look at days on the market and the ratio of list price to sales price of similar homes, and they gauge the seller's motivation to come up with a suggested offer.

Creating a List and Narrowing It Down

You find a good Realtor much the same as you would a good lender, builder, plumber, or pediatrician. Ask around for referrals, create a list, and then narrow it down to the best three or four. Good sources of information are people who have recently bought a home, and builders, mortgage lenders, title people, and real estate attorneys. Professionals in the business know the good agents because they work with them and are aware of the kind of job they're doing for their clients.

After you've got a list of three or four agents, give them a call and chat about their expertise in the areas you're interested in. Set up an appointment to meet

> **HOME-BUYING TIP**
>
> When interviewing agents, cross off the list those who spend most of the interview talking about themselves. Look for agents who focus on your needs and ask lots of questions about what you want in a home.

those you feel most comfortable with. And cross off your list those agents who take more than a couple of hours to get back to you. Of course, those who never return your call get crossed off the list, too.

Don't automatically assume that the area superstar agent will be your best choice. He or she may be so busy that you end up working with an assistant most of the time. An experienced agent from a small company who knows the area and you get along well with can be a good choice.

When selecting an agent, look for one who will listen to what you want to see and takes the time upfront to understand your needs rather than trying to sell what he or she wants you to buy. If an agent shows you homes outside your price range or area, or shows you only the company listings, get another agent fast. This one doesn't have your best interests at heart.

Understanding the Buyer's Agency

As mentioned previously, the buyer's agent usually gets paid by the seller through the listing agency commission split. This allows you to retain a buyer's agent to represent you in the transaction and it doesn't cost you anything. What commission percentage the seller and listing agency offers to buyers' agents is disclosed on the MLS listing data. Typically, it's 2 to 3 percent, although some agencies may offer more to entice buyers' agents to show the property.

You can also retain a buyer's agent to find properties and represent you where you negotiate and pay the fees. However, this arrangement is more common in specialty, high-end, and commercial properties,

Your chosen agent will likely explain *buyer's agency*, in which the agent represents you in the sale. Although an agent can sell his own listing and represent both buyer and seller, he would need to disclose this to both parties and get their agreement in writing. Otherwise, the agent would create a conflict of interest. Most states require that you complete a *buyers agency agreement*, which specifies who is representing you and the terms of your agreement. Typically, these agreements come in two types—exclusive and nonexclusive.

When you sign an *exclusive agency agreement*, you agree to work with the agent for a specific period of time—usually one to six months. In exchange for the agent's loyalty and best efforts, you agree to purchase a home through that agent only. For example, if you happen to drop in on an open house and fall in love with it, you are bound by the contract to go back to your agent to write up an offer.

Incidentally, one detail in the agreement you want to look at closely is how long after the agreement is terminated or expires can the agent still claim a fee if you reconsider a home you looked at previously. Sometimes this is part of the printed form; other times it's written in. Either way, you need to limit this condition to thirty days, rather than the six months some agents insist on. If you need to terminate the agreement, you want to make it a clean break and not have an obligation hanging over your search for the next six months.

An exclusive agreement usually motivates an agent to make your search a top priority, knowing that his or her efforts will likely produce a payday. Even so, it's a good idea to write in the agreement that you can cancel within ten days' (or whatever) written notice. You'll still be on the hook if you buy a home that the agent showed you, but if the relationship isn't working out, you can move on and find another agent.

The *nonexclusive agency agreement* option simply obligates you, if you want to buy a particular house, to use the agent who showed you that house. You can enter into as many nonexclusive agreements with as many agents as you want and are obligated only to the agent who shows you the home you decide to buy. Usually either party can terminate these agreements anytime.

> **HOME-BUYING TIP**
>
> Some buyers feel that working with several agents at the same time will give them better service. In reality, it's best to find one agent you like working with and give that person your loyalty. You'll likely get better service and the agent will be motivated to spend the time needed to find you a home.

When you insist on going with a nonexclusive agreement, few agents will take you seriously enough to spend their time looking for a home that fits your criteria. It's better to go exclusively with one experienced agent; loyalty works best when it's a two-way street.

Of course, an agency agreement does not permit the agent to misrepresent the buyer's financial condition or ability to perform when presenting an offer.

What If You Find Your Dream Home and Don't Have an Agent?

Suppose you stop by an open house or see a FOR SALE sign planted in the lawn of your dream home, and you aren't working with an agent.

Buyer Agency Forms

Buyer agency forms vary slightly from state to state, but the basics include the following:

- The agreement must be in writing and must detail the scope of the agency with beginning and ending dates.
- It must point out that the agent acts solely on behalf of the buyer.
- It must state that the agent cannot charge both buyer and seller without written disclosure to both parties.
- The agent must agree not to disclose any information that would weaken the buyer's bargaining position.
- It must disclose how a buyer's earnest money is handled. (Usually this money is deposited in a state-audited trust account, although some agencies deposit these funds with a title or escrow company.)
- It must agree to disclose to sellers and other agents upfront that an agency agreement exists.

What do you do? Well, you have three options. First, if you like the listing agent and wouldn't mind working with him or her, you can go ahead with a *limited or dual agency agreement,* whereby all parties agree to let the listing agent represent them in the transaction. The agent fills out a form that outlines the provisions of dual agency and the buyer, seller, and agent all sign it. Essentially, it discloses that the agent agrees not to say or do anything that would harm either party's negotiating position. The agent takes a neutral position and helps both sides reach an agreement.

Although it's controversial with many brokers, dual agency has advantages:

1. If the agent is an experienced professional, he or she can guide both parties toward a successful outcome because he or she knows what they both want. Yes, it can turn into a tricky rope walk, but it can work out great, too.

2. The sellers can be assured the agent isn't going to waste everyone's time with a buyer who can't qualify to buy the home and the deal will move forward in the capable hands of someone they trust.

3. The buyers feel comfortable working with an agent who is knowledgeable, knows the property, and whom they trust to be fair and impartial to both parties.

The downside of dual agency is the potential for the agent to not treat both sides of the transaction equally; indeed, the emotions involved in buying or selling a house make it difficult for a lone agent to keep everyone happy. Because of this, some real estate brokers don't allow dual agency and will assign another agent to represent the buyer. However, the biggest problem that state regulators find with dual agency is a failure of the agent to disclose in writing that he or she is representing both the buyer and the seller. This is a great way for agents to lose their real estate license.

Your second option, should you see your dream house and not yet be represented by an agent, is to shop around for a buyer's agent and have him or her show you the house and represent you in the sale. This can take some time, so if you don't want to risk someone else's buying the house first, consider the dual agency route if you feel comfortable with the agent.

In addition to the buyer's agent and dual agency, you have a third option: you can make an offer to the listing agent and opt not to use an agent to represent you. In fact, some agents insist on going this route rather than getting involved with representing both parties. However, there are some problems with this option.

To get around some of the sticky agency issues, a concept called *transaction brokerage* has recently been gaining momentum across the country. Without establishing an agency relationship, a transaction broker in effect becomes a facilitator, working with a buyer or seller to put the deal together. Those who use this system hope to limit the liability for agents and sellers and at the same time give consumers a choice of how they want to be represented.

If you're uncomfortable with one agent representing both sides of the transaction, consider talking to an *exclusive buyer agent* (EBA). Exclusive buyer agents specialize in working with buyers only and they don't get involved in listing homes for sale or in representing sellers. For more information, check out www.naeba.org or 800-986-2322.

HOME-BUYING TIP

Going with the same agent for both parties can work out great if the agent is experienced and professional. However, if the listing agent is new or you don't feel comfortable with the individual, find a buyer's agent to represent you.

From the consumer's point of view, putting the agents under the spotlight to disclose whom they represent is a plus. It discourages misrepresentation and it allows home buyers to legally tap the expertise of an agent through the buyer agency. That wasn't possible a few years ago, when all agents represented sellers and the legal framework for buyer agency didn't exist.

Developing and Working with a Home Shopping List

With a preapproval letter in your hand and your Realtor ready to go, your next mission, if you choose to accept it, is to develop a shopping checklist to help narrow your list of potential homes. To begin, you need to list what's important to you in a home. This process will focus your thinking and help you to create a template that your agent can use in entering your preferences into the MLS database. The more data you key in about what you like and dislike, the more detailed a search list will be generated.

HOME-BUYING TIP

Go through open houses and model homes in your price range and target ideas for your needs list. Avoid looking at homes way over your price range, because it creates unrealistic expectations—or, as they say in the industry, a champagne taste but a beer budget.

The Importance of a Wants and Needs List

It's helpful to divide your list into "must haves" and "would like to haves." This won't be easy, and may take some soul searching, but the more time you spend crystallizing your thinking, the less time you'll spend spinning your wheels looking at homes you don't like.

In one case, Randy and Jennifer looked at dozens of homes and spent a big chunk of their Saturdays driving by open houses. Whenever they walked through a home Jennifer liked, Randy didn't. What got Randy excited, Jennifer balked on. It had all the trappings of a power play. If she couldn't get her kitchen island and crafts room, he wasn't going to get his three-car garage. Their house hunting efforts were fast turning into a shipwreck

This deadlock resulted because Randy and Jennifer never sat down and worked out their priorities—the important things they both wanted in a home, in the order of their importance. They just started looking at homes, assuming that everything would fall into place—that their tastes and dreams would mesh into a cute cottage with a white picket fence. Reality, unfortunately, is sometimes much different.

Once Randy and Jennifer sat down with their agent and finally started talking about what they wanted in a house, they realized that their image of an ideal home differed considerably. Luckily they had an experienced agent and she skillfully guided them into working up a "wants and needs" worksheet. It took a couple of hours, but finally they started to compromise and that produced a workable list.

With Figure 4-1, I have provided a Home Shopping Checklist. To help you fill out the checklist, get everyone together who will live in the new house and make a list of six or more things you love about your present home and six things you don't like about it.

FIGURE 4-1
Home Shopping Checklist.

What You Dont L ike

1. _____
2. _____
3. _____
4. _____
5. _____
6. _____

What You Do Like

1. _____
2. _____
3. _____
4. _____
5. _____
6. _____

Once you've listed what you like and don't like in homes and areas, the next step is listing needs and wants.

Must Have

1. _____
2. _____
3. _____
4. _____
5. _____
6. _____

Wants

1. _____
2. _____
3. _____
4. _____
5. _____
6. _____

It's also important to ask yourself what kind of house will make a home. For example, if you have children, a family room next to the kitchen or a more open floor plan may be better than the formal floor plan found in many colonials. Crystallizing your thinking and making lists before you look will save a lot of time and frustration.

Many first-time home buyers think about the homes they grew up in as a template for their own home. This is good; use those memories along with what you like and don't like about friends' or relatives'

homes to get you started on your check-list. Also, it's important to ask yourself what kind of house will make a home for you and your family. For example, if you have children, a family room next to the kitchen or a more open floor plan may be better than the flormal floor plan flound in many colonials. Crystallizing your thinking and making lists before you look will save a lot of time and frustration, and perhaps a move later on.

It's an unfortunate fact of life that most buyers possess Lexus tastes but must live with a Kia Rio budget. That boils down to a lot of compromising and crossing off items in the "wants" column. Start by tackling area considerations first and asking yourself the following questions:

- How far are you willing to drive or spend time commuting to work? That determines the radius of your search area and sometimes your price range.

- How far away are the schools? If a certain school or district is a must, verify the boundaries because they can change.

- What style of home are you interested in and why? Newer homes and styles may require living farther from downtown.

- What type of floor plan do you envision most compatible with your lifestyle? That can influence home style and location.

- How important is proximity to shopping, houses of worship, recreational facilities, parks, and so on?

After you've circled the areas of interest, work up a checklist or use Figure 4-1 to narrow down your choices of what you want in a home. Go over this list with your agent so he or she develops a clear idea of what you want and can enter your preferences into the MLS database. Matching your criteria against the thousands of homes on the market takes only a few seconds, and the resulting printout should contain only homes in your price range, areas of interest, and with the amenities you selected.

Narrowing Down Your List

You're making progress! Now you have a list of houses that you can start paring down to a short list of houses that you will personally inspect. This is where an experienced agent becomes especially handy. He or she can help you eliminate homes on busy streets, in bad areas, with proximity to undesirable locations, and the like.

How many homes do you need to look at? Depending on the market and how many homes are on the market, narrow it down to between five and twelve. Still, it's possible that the first, second, or third home you see could be love at first sight. In that case, accelerate the search and make sure none of the remaining homes are preferable. You may be able to eliminate some by driving by and not liking what you see.

> **HOME-BUYING TIP**
>
> Never make an offer on a house until you talk to several neighbors on the street. If there's a problem you should know about, you'll hear about it from them.

Also, if you like the home, chances are other home hunters will, too, so you'll want to put together an offer fast. But before you submit that offer, do a quick reality check:

- Make sure that nearby businesses don't create nightly noises such as trucks unloading, loud equipment running, or other disturbing sounds that you don't notice during the day.

- Check out the traffic during the evening or early morning. Make sure your street isn't a shortcut to the freeway during commuter hours.

- Walk up and down the street and make sure a neighbor doesn't rebuild motorcycles, have a rock band, or isn't involved in some other disruption. Talk to several neighbors; if there are problems or irritating neighbors, you'll find out about them fast.

- Check the MLS database for home sales during the past six months or so. Note the days on the market and the gap between the list price and sold price. If both of these market indicators are increasing, the area may have problems you should check out.

■ Find out how many rentals are on the street you want to buy. If it's more than one or two, be wary because values in the area could be sliding.

Strategies for Targeting Your Preferred Neighborhood

It's a truism that the best areas go fast. You must be agile, so when a home comes on the market you can act quickly. There are two strategies that often prove successful for these situations:

1. Have your Realtor enter your preferences in the MLS database's prospect function. Your preferences will be matched automatically by the software to new listings as they come on the market each day. Of course, your agent can also check for new listings in the area or price range once or twice a day and call you if a home looks promising.

2. If you've ever wondered what it's like to play politician, you can take a page from their playbook, and either phone or knock on doors of homeowners in the area. Put together a simple flyer and leave it with everyone you talk to. When homeowners find out that there's a qualified buyer actively looking to buy, decisions to sell can happen quickly.

In one case, Ryan and Susan went this route when they wanted to buy a home in a certain school district and found none were for sale. They put together a flyer with a picture of their family and a couple of paragraphs of why they wanted to live in the area, and they asked anyone thinking of selling to call them.

A week later, after talking to about fifty owners in the area and passing out seventy-five flyers, Ryan and Susan got a call from a couple about to retire who wanted to talk to them. These homeowners didn't want to shovel snow another winter and were considering moving to a warmer climate. The flyer prompted the couple to seriously consider the sale of their home and decided that maybe now was the time.

On inspecting the home, Ryan and Susan found that it was exactly what they were looking for, and they and the sellers wrote up a deal on the spot. Of course,

---

HOME-BUYING TIP

The key to a successful flyer is to include a family photo (don't forget the dog or cat). Owners are often emotionally attached to their homes, and you want them to see you as the ideal family able to love their home as they did.

not all projects like this work out as well, but it's amazing how often potential sellers are galvanized into action when they hear a mortgage-approved buyer is interested in buying in their neighborhood.

Shopping for Fixer-Uppers

Sometimes home buyers want to find a fixer-upper and they are willing to build sweat equity. Indeed, buying a run-down house and fixing it up as a way to get in on the cheap is a dream of many. It can happen successfully, but bear in mind that the waters are shark infested. The key to not losing money is creating a step-by-step plan and following it.

It may by now sound like a cliché, but location is the key to finding a fixer-upper that will grow in value. Homes in good locations increase in value more quickly and hold their value when the market is down. Most important, you'll be able to build equity for a larger down payment when you move up.

Good sources for finding fixer-uppers are classified ads, referrals, the MLS, and foreclosure sales. And you must become an expert on home values in the areas you're interested in, so that you can move quickly when a deal pops up. So, networking in your areas of choice, especially with knowledgeable Realtors, is a great way to learn about estate sales or divorcing couples unloading homes they can no longer afford. Realtors can inform you instantly with text messaging, e-mail, or cell phone calls when homes come on the market through the MLS system.

> **HOME-BUYING TIP**
>
> The keys to successful fixer-uppers are to buy in the best area you can afford, to learn how to estimate upgrade costs, and to get bids on big items before you buy.

For instance, Ron and Ellen went the fixer-upper route when searching for their first home. For several months they had been seriously looking in an area near a small college when a Realtor told them about a new listing. The owner of a three-bedroom bungalow had died a few weeks earlier, and the out-of-town heirs wanted a quick "as is" sale. Although the home needed updating, considerable cleaning, a new paint job, and eventually a new furnace and roof, it was the opportunity Ron and Ellen were looking for. They made an offer of about $25,000 under what similar homes were selling for in the area, with a quick closing. The owners accepted right away.

Ron and Ellen's strategy paid off because:

- They lined up their financing by getting preapproved for a mortgage, so they could move quickly when opportunity arose.

- They zeroed in on areas with homes that, if fixed up, would appreciate in value.

- They let Realtors in the area know what they were looking for and were able to make a quick offer.

- They knew what homes in the area sold for and which ones were for sale.

- They learned how to estimate costs to replace or rehabilitate deteriorated conditions.

With the area becoming trendier, this home will appreciate over time, especially with the upgrades, and will yield a nice profit in a few years when Ron and Ellen are ready to move up.

Buying New Construction

Of course, not all home buyers want to become fixer-upper mavens or even like the idea of moving into a home that has previously been occupied. These buyers prefer to start fresh with new construction and the latest floor plans. Like buying a new car, there's something appealing about the smell, fresh paint, and new carpet that you find in a new home. Many buyers feel this is the way to go because they don't want to redo someone else's decorating and landscaping. If you're among them, here's how to find and buy a new home and avoid the pitfalls.

Homebuilder Web sites worth checking out include:

www.home-builders.com
www.nahb.com
www.homegain.com
www.newhomesource.com
www.eplans.com

Shopping New Subdivisions

The first step after you've got that loan commitment in hand is to make a list of the new communities in the area. You already know the price range you can afford. Before you waste a lot of time driving out to these new developments, find out the median price of their models. And don't go by the starting price shown in their advertising; builders rarely have homes or even sell them at that bottom of their price range.

From the builder's standpoint, the name of the game is to upgrade you to the maximum you can qualify for. But before that can happen, they need to get you out to the site and let the models work their magic on your emotions. Beware.

Shopping new constructions is similar to buying a car. The dealer attracts you with a low advertised price, but when you get there you find it's a stripped-down model. The salesperson then pressures you to upgrade with features no buyer can live without. The builders will give you a list of options and upgrades that you cannot live without, and then mention a final price that's nowhere near what you budgeted. For instance, you're likely to hear the salesperson tell you that the $15,000 in upgrades is only an extra $97 a month,

> ### HOME-BUYING TIP
>
> When buying new construction, it's prudent to budget an additional 10 to 15 percent for unforeseen changes or add-ons that often arise during construction.

and you wouldn't want $3.23 a day—the price of a Starbuck's latte—to stand between your family and its dream home. This is not to suggest that builders are dishonest. It's just that new home marketing (like most other marketing) pushes the envelope a little to get people to consider their models.

Do's and Don'ts for Signing a New Construction Contract

Before signing an agreement for the construction of a new home, keep the following tips in mind:

■ Builders often try to pressure you to use their lenders because they want financing control to minimize the possibility of deals falling through. And, frankly, builders' lenders can sometimes be more creative in solving problems to keep the loan from going south. Builders may also offer you upgrades or buydowns to go with their financing. Of course, the best way to find out if these incentives are really free is to get a good faith estimate from the builder's lender and compare it to a couple of others. The best deal becomes obvious when you lay the paperwork side by side and compare.

■ Get copies of the covenants, conditions, and restrictions that come with the construction. These are called *CC&Rs* in real estate lingo and are available from the builder, title company, or county recorder's office. If the subdivision has a *homeowners association* (HOA) an additional layer of restrictions could apply, so you need to get a copy of these as well. It's important that you read both CC&Rs and HOA rules carefully to make sure you can live with their restrictions on what you can do with your property. Typical restrictions include rules and restrictions on how or whether you can landscape, park an RV, leave your garage door up, have a rock band perform on your property, and install holiday lighting.

■ Research the builder by checking with the Better Business Bureau and state contractor's board. Check out not only the company but also the builder's name. You want to know whether any regulatory agency has had complaints filed against the company or builder. If a builder has several complaints or has filed bankruptcy, seriously consider shopping elsewhere.

■ Walk around the community and talk to at least three new homeowners. Ask them how they like the builder and how problems or complaints are handled. It's especially important to find out how many items on their *punch list* (list of problems found on final walkthrough to be fixed by builder ASAP) were promptly resolved. Should the new owners tell you that on their walkthrough they found a dozen or more items and the builder dragged his feet on repairs, that's a red flag.

■ Ask the salesperson or builder representative how close to the completion date homes are finished and ready to close. You might even ask for a copy of the construction schedule. If the builder is behind a month or two on projections, this may cause you problems if you have to close on your former home or move out of a rental by a certain date.

■ Should you find a model you absolutely can't live without and want to put a deal together, make sure you get all the upgrades, extras, and options itemized along with cost on an addendum. Not getting everything in writing is a painful lesson learned and relearned by professionals as well as buyers and sellers.

■ Don't ever sign any paperwork that doesn't have the exact cost specified. Never, ever allow "to be filled in later" on any paperwork. Also, never leave the sales office without copies of all the paperwork.

■ It's important to get copies of all the documents and to number the addendums 1/x, 2/x, and so on. Mortgage lenders and title companies get upset when addendums aren't numbered consecutively. Missing addendums often cause problems because this is where changes and contract modifications are written.

■ Make sure you understand the paragraphs in the contract regarding when you are supposed to close. Builders often pressure you to close before the house is finished or the punch items are completed. They do this so they can get paid sooner, but you don't want to close before all the work is completed and you've done a walkthrough. It's best to deal with this upfront and get it in writing that closing is on final completion of all items on the punch list.

■ Do your homework before going new home shopping. Read books and articles on home construction, take adult-ed classes at a local college. *Fine Homebuilding, Builder* and *This Old House* are excellent magazines on building information.

Seven Steps You Can Take to Make This Chapter Work for You

1. Before looking at homes, determine how much you can spend without becoming a slave to a house payment. Even though a lender may be willing to extend more credit, only you know your situation.

2. Get a mortgage preapproval letter. You'll need it when you find a home and make an offer.

3. Go for location first and house second. It's better to buy a smaller home in a good area than a bigger home in a less desirable area.

4. Interview several agents and go with the one who has experience and is familiar with your areas of interest. Don't go with an agent simply because he or she is a friend or relative. It'll cost you in the long run.

5. Determine what you want in a home, including style, number of bedrooms and baths, family room, and yard. Your agent will input this into the MLS and get a list of homes that fit your criteria. Whittle these down to a short list that you will visit and inspect.

6. If you want to go the fixer-upper route, know the home values in the area and have a sense of how much materials and labor will cost you to upgrade and correct problems.

7. If you decide that buying a new home is the way to go, learn
   about construction techniques and read the construction contract carefully. Make sure all changes and additions to the paperwork are in writing and that the addendums are numbered
   1/x, 2/x, etc.

■   ■   ■

Once you find your dream home, you need to understand the art of
the deal and how to get your offer accepted, which is covered in the
next chapter.

CHAPTER 5

Getting Your Offer Accepted

You've probably noticed that as you drive through neighborhoods and look at the properties on your shopping list, certain areas and styles of homes begin to stand out. This is good, because it helps you tweak your list and narrow your choices. Once this happens, it won't be long before you walk into a home and know immediately that you've found "the one."

It can be both exciting and stressful to stand in the entryway of a home and know it's the property you've been searching for. But while you want the home, you also want the best deal you can get. Some questions should begin zipping through your mind, such as:

- What should you offer?

- How low can you go without insulting the owners and losing the house?

- How can you protect yourself from hidden problems that can cost you money after you've closed?

These are critical concerns that nearly all buyers have, even professionals who buy homes to fix up and rent or flip. To tame these concerns, this chapter gives you the tools you'll need to make good decisions and get your offer accepted.

In this chapter you'll learn how to:

1. Determine what to offer for a house.

2. Handle making an offer on an overpriced home.

3. Use an emotional connection with the seller to enhance the appeal of your offer.

4. Get the seller to pay concessions in order to seal the deal.

5. Consider the advantages and disadvantages of making an offer on a foreclosure or a shortsale.

6. Hire a professional home inspector.

7. Shop for a home warranty.

Looking at Homes and Narrowing Down Your Choices

As you walk through the homes on your list of prospects, be sure to use the Home Inspection Checklist I've included as Figure 5-1. You'll find it useful in focusing your attention on vital things you need to be looking for.

What Is a House Really Worth?

What a home is worth is a complex question, because no two homes are exactly alike. Appraisers compare recent sales of similar properties and then add or subtract value to compensate for differences and amenities to arrive at an approximate value. While that approach can put you in the ballpark, it usually ignores important market and emotional factors that can influence what a home will ultimately sell for.

HOME-BUYING TIP

Some agents understand how powerful emotion is in the home-buying decision. They will redecorate and add furniture to push a buyer's emotional buttons. As a buyer, don't let the flash and tinsel of a staged home sway you.

Realtors approach value by going the *comparative market analysis* (CMA) route, in which an agent puts together a list of sold properties that are similar to the house in question. Realtors also add to the CMA similar homes that are for sale and those with sales pending. Because valuing a home isn't an exact science, different people look at the same data and come up with varying opinions as to what the house should sell for. Ultimately, the market decides what a home is really worth, despite its owners and agents wishing otherwise.

A home's emotional appeal plays a big part in determining the interest in and the selling price of a home. For instance, consider the home no bigger than others in an area that sold for nearly $8,000 more. What did this frame cottage-style house have

FIGURE 5-1
Home inspection checklist.

Home Inspection Checklist: Address _____

Item	Need fixing or replacing	Ok
Driveway: □ concrete □ Asphalt		
Landscaping: □ lawns □ trees		
Landscaping channels water away from home		
Fences and other outdoor structures		
Entryway: □ door □ porch □ stairs		
Carpets		
Kitchen flooring		
Kitchen counter tops		
Cabinets and range vent hood to outside		
Under-the-sink plumbing, look for mold		
faucets and sink working and draining		
Kitchen appliances		
Walls: □ damaged □ need painting		
Check ceilings for water damage or stains		
Fireplace(s)		
Check bathroom floors around toilet		
Flush toilets and check refill time		
Sink and faucet: □ check drain flow		
Plumbing under sink good and mold free		
Look around bathrooms for mold		
Check caulking around tub, shower and sinks		
Does bathroom fan vent to outside		
Check electrical outlets with an AC tester		
Look in electrical box for obvious problems		
Check laundry room for mold		
Check washer faucets and hose drain		
Check basement for water: □ stains □ smell		
Windows: look for fogging or broken panes		
Roof: look for brittle and worn shingles		
Rain gutters: □ down spouts □ extensions		
Do extensions route water away from walls		
Look for siding problems		

If the home fails this quick checklist, consider moving on and not wasting $350 on a professional inspection.

that others didn't? First, it had more curb appeal than other homes in the neighborhood. Outside, the owner had installed white vinyl siding with green shutters along with a new roof, and he kept the lawn and flower beds in top shape. White birch trees framed the house and contrasted with the dark green, well-manicured lawn. Driving by the home made you think of home and hearth, and you'd swear you smelled the aroma of fresh bread just out of the oven.

Inside, the owner used neutral colors to paint the walls and ceilings, and installed light-colored carpeting. The effect was nothing fancy, but it gave the interior a fresh, clean look. When you walked in, there was nothing to distract you from imagining your pictures, your furniture, and your ideas of how to decorate the house.

Three buyers looked at the home the first day it went on the market, and all three competed to see whose offer would prevail. To the seller's delight, the winning bid was nearly $8,000 more than the list price.

Most experienced real estate agents will agree that a home is really worth what someone is willing to pay for it. A home may appraise for $300,000, but if the colors or the way it sits on the lot, or the floor plan aren't appealing, it can languish on the market and end up selling for $250,000 or less. To add to the pricing confusion, many sellers get an inflated drive-by appraisal from a lender for a home equity line of credit or a real estate agent quotes them a high price in an effort to get the listing. And sometimes sellers just refuse to believe that the home they have lived in all those years is not worth more than its market value, leading to months of market buffeting and buyer rejection before reality sinks in.

In truth, the nicest homes in the best areas rarely experience a slow market. Even if the real estate market slows to half the number of home buyers, those remaining would zero in on the same homes for sale in desirable neighborhoods with attractive curb appeal. It's the homes in not such good condition, with bad decorating, and in less desirable areas that have rusting FOR SALE signs. Buyers don't have to settle for something they don't want, especially when there's an abundance of homes to choose from. And if you're a buyer who's looking for a good deal on a fixer-upper, life can be good.

What all of this means to you as a home buyer is that you have to sift through the chaff to find the nice homes, and when you find one you like, you need to move fast because other buyers will be out looking for the same gems.

Determining Your Offer

The thrill of knowing that all your efforts have finally paid off, and that you've finally found the house you've been looking for, can quickly turn into a high-wire balancing act between making an offer fast and getting the lowest price possible. If you take too long to submit your offer, another buyer with similar tastes to yours is liable to come along and submit an offer. In fact, many experienced agents can relate instances when homes have sat on the market for weeks with no activity, and then suddenly several offers were made on the same day. It's almost spooky!

The Neighborhood Statistics

Before making an offer, ask your agent to pull up on the MLS a list of homes that have sold in the area in the past three months. Look at the average list price to sold price. If, for instance, the difference between the two averages 5 percent or more, this gives you a starting point for determining how low you can make your offer and not insult the seller to the extent that he or she breaks off negotiations.

Then look at the average days on the market for houses in the area and compare that with the days on the market of the home you're interested in. For example, if the days on the market for the area average seventy-eight, and the home you're considering shows eighty-three, the seller may be feeling some stress and that could soften the price.

Let me add a note of caution on the MLS's days-on-market statistic. A home that's been on the market for two or three months doesn't mean that it's been sitting there with no action. Failed sales owing to a buyer's not qualifying, a questionable inspection result, poor appraisal, and so on can add to the days-on-market odometer. Your agent may want to casually ask the seller or his agent if there have been any offers that failed and, if so, probe for the reasons why. Other useful information you can pick up by talking to the seller or his agent may include:

> **HOME-BUYING TIP**
>
> Including a preapproval letter from your lender with your offer gives the seller a bird-in-the-hand feeling and makes it harder for them to counter your offer, knowing they're throwing away a sure thing.

- Why is the person selling? You probably don't want to put the seller on the defensive by asking directly, but with discretion you can solicit the reasons.

- Does the seller have any looming deadline from a job transfer, another home closing, or other pressure-creating situation?

- How soon does the seller want to close? Since you're preapproved for a loan, you can close quickly if this would enhance your offer.

- Would a week or two rent-back help out the seller? If the seller is in a pinch and needs the money from the closing to move or his new home's completion is behind schedule, you can offer to close and rent the house to the individual. This daily rent payment would equal what your mortgage payment would cost you.

The more you know about the seller's problems, the more you can structure your offer to solve them and increase your chances of getting your offer accepted, especially if it's low.

How One Couple Found a Home and Made an Offer

With a preapproval letter for $330,000 in hand, Russ and Linda scheduled a meeting with their agent to start the house-hunting process. Their agent used the MLS to print a list of twenty-seven homes in areas of interest priced between $320,000 and $360,000. Because the housing market was slow, they felt it was reasonable to believe they would be able to discount up to $30,000 off the list price of a home.

Going over the list with their agent, they quickly eliminated sixteen homes. They crossed off those on busy streets, those that had not been remodeled, or those whose styles Russ and Linda simply didn't care for. This left eleven homes to be personally inspected over the following two days. As it turned out, five of the eleven were disappointing. Number eight was a possibility, but it was the ninth home on the list that clicked. Priced on the high side at $356,900, it had everything they wanted, even the colors they loved.

HOME-BUYING TIP

If you end up with two or more homes that you can't decide between, revisit your choices two or even three times to eliminate two (the sellers won't mind). Don't be pressured to make a choice, because you have to live with your decision.

After hurrying through the other two homes on the list, they confirmed that their choice was the well-maintained multi-level on the cul-de-sac. Russ and Linda's agent, Andrea, swung into action and looked at what other homes had sold for in the area. She noticed that the average listing in the neighborhood sold for 94 percent of list, that the days-on-market averaged eighty-seven, and that this home had been on the market for ninety-eight days. They decided that their offer would be $26,900 under the list price, which was a considerable reduction, but considering these statistics they felt it was worth a try. Another factor influencing their offer was that when Andrea called the listing agent, she found out the seller's new home would be finished in about six weeks. Obviously, the sellers were feeling some pressure to get the house sold.

> Ask your agent to present your offer to the sellers in person, if possible. A skillful agent can present your offer in its best light and, when necessary, negotiate an acceptable counter. Your agent, who is getting paid to represent you, can't do that effectively by faxing or e-mailing it to the listing agent and letting him or her handle the task.

Russ and Linda decided to write an offer for $330,000, the maximum loan amount they could qualify for. Andrea then called the listing agent and set up an appointment to present the offer to him and the sellers that evening.

Note that when Andrea called the listing agent to set up the appointment she didn't disclose either their offer or the terms of the offer. She did this to prevent the listing office from calling other buyers they might be working with to try to use the incoming offer to motivate any fence-sitters into making an offer. As it turned out, no competing offers were forthcoming and the buyers were able to get their offer accepted. Their preapproval letter and short closing date convinced the sellers that they should not pass up this offer, especially with their new home nearing completion. That the owners talked with their builder a few moments before Andrea arrived to present the offer probably increased the pressure on them a notch or two to accept a lower offer than they may have taken otherwise.

Dealing with Overpriced Homes and Emotional Sellers

To some homeowners, their house becomes an extension of their egos. When they decide to sell, they overprice their home, reasoning that if the Adams home down the street sold for $280,000, then theirs must be worth at least $295,000. After all, they've added cool decorating and upgraded appliances.

How long it takes these homeowners to wake up depends on their level of motivation to sell, which is why it's important to find out why they are selling and when they must move. A good question to ask sellers tactfully after you develop a little rapport is why they would want to leave such a nice neighborhood. Avoid asking blunt questions such as "Why are you selling" or "When do you have to be out?" This puts sellers on the defensive and you're unlikely to get an honest answer.

What if Your Dream Home Is Overpriced?

Sometimes owners know deep down that their home is overpriced but they can't quite accept it. Greed, ego, and embarrassment can play a part in their refusal to accept reality. Some owners remain in denial all the way to foreclosure. In these extreme cases, the only thing you can do is walk away and find another property.

However, some approaches you can try if you really want a home are:

- Keep an eye on the house, hoping the price will come down to what you think is reasonable and then submit an offer. Of course, the home may sell in the meantime.

- Make an offer for what you think the house is worth. The sellers likely will counter, and you'll find out what their bottom line is (at least for that moment).

- If, based on your research, the home is overpriced for the neighborhood, offer to buy it for what an independent appraiser (one approved by both parties) values the home. This pricing agreement should be written into a purchase contract so you don't pay for an appraisal and then have the seller back out.

Joel and Penny experienced this problem when they wanted to buy a home near Penny's mom, who needed help recovering from a hip replacement. They felt the home was overpriced for the neighborhood, based on recent sales. The out-of-state owner priced the home on what he wanted to get out of it, hoping someone would pay his price.

The seller rejected their first offer, which put Joel and Penny back to square one. They didn't want to lose the house, but paying too much wasn't an attractive option, either. After talking over the situation with an appraiser, they decided to go back to the seller and offer the full price or the appraisal price, whichever was less.

With this approach, a neutral third party ends up setting the price. This allows the buyers to get the home at fair market value and gives sellers a way out without admitting they were unrealistic. Of course, the buyers have to know approximately what the home will appraise for so they can get their financial ducks in a row before making an offer. In Joel and Penny's case, they had already talked to an appraiser. After a few phone calls back and forth, the seller accepted Joel and Penny's offer, and the sale closed with both sides satisfied with the deal.

On the flip side, buyers can also sometimes be unrealistic as to market values and lose the home they wanted. Friends or relatives may say that they can remember when that house sold for $200,000 and insist they wouldn't pay a dime over $230,000 for it today, or they may bad-mouth the home's condition or location. It's best to ignore this kind of talk and either go with the advice of real estate professionals who know the market or speak with contractors who can pinpoint the costs of fixing problems.

Using an Emotional Connection to Boost Your Offer's Appeal

Important but too often ignored is the role that emotion plays in getting your offer accepted. Sellers sell on emotion, just as buyers buy on emotion. So, if possible, meet the sellers when you go through their home, especially when you are narrowing down your choices and going through the second time.

Don't gush and tell them they have the loveliest home on the planet or that you can't live without it. You don't want to come across as too eager and compromise your offer. Your objective is to get the seller to see you as real people who they would like to see live in their home and take care of it the way they did.

If you're faced with competing offers, you might write a letter to

HOME-BUYING TIP

When you go through a home the second time, don't be too chummy. Play it cool, and casually mention that it's a dead heat between their home and one or two others. You can also ask the sellers questions, such as when they believe they could be out. You just want to be able to boost their expectations a few notches.

HOME-BUYING TIP

Build rapport with sellers by looking for areas of common interest, such as work, hobbies, sports, and same schools. But don't talk about the loan you qualify for or provide details regarding what you would offer. Sales have been lost because buyers have said too much. An old World War II poster reads, "LOOSE LIPS SINK SHIPS." This thought also applies to real estate deals.

the sellers and attach it to the offer. Ryan and Susan did this when they presented an offer on an upscale home in a neighborhood where few listings came on the market and when one did, it sold within a week. In this case, three agents were presenting offers that evening, and Ryan and Susan's agent wasn't overly optimistic about their chances. To add sizzle to their offer, Susan decided to write a letter to the buyers expressing how they felt about the home and neighborhood. She felt they had nothing to lose, so she would give it a try.

Susan's two-page letter explained how they wanted their twin girls to go to the nearby elementary school and how much they liked the home and the effort the sellers had put into decorating and maintaining it. Their agent thought this was a little off the wall, but then orders are orders, and he clipped her letter to the paperwork. That evening, Ryan and Susan's agent presented their offer. It was the fourth the sellers' had received and pretty much the same as the other three with regard to price and terms. When the sellers read the attached letter, they looked at each other and didn't say anything for a few moments. Then the seller looked over at her agent and said, "These are the people we want to live in our home . . . this is the offer we're accepting."

As it turned out, the sellers were retired school teachers; they identified with the buyers through their letter, and they felt that they were the right people for their home. By following her intuition to connect with the sellers on an emotional level, Susan had made the difference. The other agents who presented offers simply emphasized their clients' abilities to buy and close quickly, all sounding similar with their dry nuts-and-bolts approach.

While this trick may not work all the time, it's important to note that making a connection with the sellers on an emotional or personal level can't hurt. Agents too often get caught up in the business aspects of real estate and forget that it's the human touch that frequently makes deals happen.

Sellers Are Not Always Rational

Determining what to offer is more an art form than a science. Sellers often don't even know what they'll accept until a signed offer with a deposit check is laid on the table in front of them. Sometimes they'll take offers they should counter and other times they'll reject offers they should grab. It all comes down to the ebb and flow of the seller's state of mind and what's happening in his or her life at the time.

In one situation, the sellers rejected an offer that came in $9,000 lower than the listed price. But the next day, when an offer they had made on a home in another state was accepted, everything changed. Money suddenly took a back seat to getting out of town as fast as possible. The sellers called their agent, told him they had changed their minds, and asked if he could retrieve the offer. They had pen in hand, ready to sign. So, it's best to stay flexible because you seldom know the motivating factors in sellers' lives or when and how they may change.

Getting Sellers to Pay Concessions

Concessions are anything a seller gives a buyer as an inducement to spark an offer. The slower the market, the more creative and desperate the inducements become. Concessions can include anything from paying all or part of the buyer's closing costs on the loan, to redecorating based on the buyer's wants or needs, replacing appliances, or throwing in existing appliances.

Before you write an offer, ask your agent to look at the sold listings in the area and see how many sellers paid con-

HOME-BUYING TIP

Most Realtor MLS systems allow agents to pull up sold listings that detail days-on-market, list price to sold price, how much the seller paid in concessions, and how the buyer financed the home. These are all good data that you can use to get a feel for how low you can go with your offer.

cessions and what their average costs were. In reality, when a seller pays concessions it should be subtracted from the sales price to get a true picture of the sale.

For example, if there were seventeen similar properties sold in the area in the last three months and the sellers of twelve of these homes paid buyer concessions, then you know this is common practice. Now, suppose the average concession was $3,600. You would then ask the seller to pay at minimum this amount toward your loan costs, redecoration expenses, or whatever else reduces the selling price.

Asking Sellers to Pay Loan Costs

Probably the most useful and common concession a seller can make is to pay all or part of the buyer's loan costs. From the seller's viewpoint, this is a good investment because it helps buyers purchase the houses they may otherwise not be able to afford.

Sometimes, when the seller is unwilling or unable to pay all of the buyer's loan costs (if, for example, the seller doesn't have any equity), a compromise can be worked out. For instance, if a home is priced at $257,000 and the buyer wants the seller to pay $7,000 of the loan costs, but the seller has little equity and can only afford $3,500, typically the buyer increases the offering price by $3,500. The seller would then pay the $7,000 so the buyer can get the loan.

Increasing the price to cover loan costs can sometimes be risky if the home doesn't appraise for the increased sales price. Sometimes the increase can be run by the appraiser to see whether it can be justified before the buyer spends a few hundred dollars. At other times the buyer just has to wait and hope until the appraisal comes back.

Asking Sellers for Redecorating or Repair Concessions

Sellers sometimes try to sidestep fixing up their homes by offering a cash kickback (called a *cash-back*) at closing to replace carpeting, to paint, to redecorate, or whatever. It's the lazy person's way to sell a home, and if you find one of these sellers, tread cautiously. If the seller has deferred maintenance on carpets, painting, or other home components, what else has the homeowner deferred on what you can't see? Still, there's opportunity in these properties if you know what you're buying and can get a good enough deal.

Mortgage lenders often take a dim view of seller cash-backs because they distort the true sales price and can border on fraud because the lender is led to believe the sales price is higher than it really is.

Federal and state regulators are getting really sensitive to anything that walks, talks, or smells like mortgage fraud nowadays. So, when a seller offers repairs or replacement concessions, it's better to list the problems and then get bids so you know the exact costs involved. Asking the seller to take care of the items on the list before you close is the best solution.

Repair items can also arise from a home inspection. In most states, real estate purchase contracts have a section that makes the sale contingent on the buyer's approval of a home inspection. In these cases, the repairs should be completed before closing or handled by a price reduction. More on home inspections is covered later in the chapter.

> **HOME-BUYING TIP**
>
> Ask your agent when he or she presents your offer to take along a printout showing the concessions that owners of recently sold properties have paid. If the sellers balk at paying your loan costs, your agent can show them that "everybody is paying them if they want to sell."

Combining Grants and Concessions

If you need help coming up with a down payment or loan, combining a community grant/loan program with a seller's contribution can be a great opportunity for a first-time home buyer. Goran and Nada took advantage of this combo when they wanted to buy their first home but didn't have much of a down payment. The community in which they lived offered a first-time homeowner program that paid up to $4,000 to help buyers in targeted areas. If they lived in the home for five years, the loan would be cancelled and become a grant.

The real estate market in the area had a good supply of homes to choose from and sellers were willing to pay concessions. Goran and Nada found a three-bedroom, two-bath home and made an offer asking the sellers to pay $3,600 in loan costs. Owing to a slow market and a job transfer, the sellers eagerly accepted the offer. With the $4,000 community grant program added to $3,600 in seller-paid loan costs, the buyers had $7,600 to put down and needed only $720 of their own funds to close.

The Opportunities and Challenges in Buying Foreclosures or Short Sales

In addition to homes on the MLS and those for sale by owners, bank foreclosures and short sales can be good opportunities for buyers.

Five Ways to Protect Yourself When Making an Offer

1. Make sure the offer is subject to loan approval. Even though you're preapproved, life is uncertain, as one buyer found out when he was laid off from his job three days before closing.

2. List all the items the sellers have agreed to include in the sale—such as appliances, swing sets, basketball standards—on an addendum. Do a walk-through on the day of closing to make sure the sellers didn't forget and load them in the moving truck.

3. Get copies of all documents, including addendums numbered 1/x, 2/x, etc. Having a complete set of documents upfront is the only way you can protect yourself from problems that may arise later on.

4. Make your offer subject to a professional home inspection. If you find problems, you can walk away or renegotiate the offer.

5. If you're not using a licensed Realtor, hire an attorney to do the paperwork. It's too easy to make mistakes that can cost you big bucks.

However, they come with a unique set of challenges when making offers.

HOME-BUYING TIP

Not all agents have the know-how or experience to work with REOs and short sales. You may have to interview several to find one with a track record. Ask title people or attorneys who close real estate transactions for their referrals; they know the agents who are doing these transactions.

Real estate owned (REO) is banker-speak for homes that lenders have foreclosed on and now own. *Short sales* refer to situations where the owners of a property are in default (behind in their payments) and, in order to avoid foreclosure, the bank is willing to accept less than the loan balance in order to sell the home.

The upside to REOs and short sales is that you may be able to get a good deal. The downside is that you'll probably end up dealing with an unmotivated bank's REO committee that takes its time responding to your offer. Still, putting up with some red tape and frustration can be a small price to pay for a good deal. If you do want to pursue a short sale or REO, shop around for a Realtor who has experience and a track record in these kinds of deals.

Making Offers on REOs

Banks spend in excess of $20,000 to foreclose on a property. If they have to fix it up to make it saleable, the costs can go up dramatically. So, when you make an offer on an REO home, the bank will look at the costs that have been incurred and weigh the chances of getting a better deal in the near future. However, they are more likely to discount homes they've had on their books for a while.

It's easy to get burned buying an REO, especially if the home needs work. Often, buyers get these homes at a great price, only to learn that the costs of restoration can equal or exceed the savings they hoped to realize. Before you write an offer on an REO, examine the home carefully and make a list of all needed repairs. If you plan on hiring a contractor to do some or all of the work, get a detailed bid, with labor and materials broken down. If you plan on making the repairs yourself, you'll have to do some legwork to get estimates on the costs involved. Then add the repair costs to the price you're planning on bidding for the home, and compare it with similar homes for sale in the area.

Let's say you find that an REO you're interested in has some damage left by the previous owners. It would be a great deal if you can get it for $230,000 because similar homes in the neighborhood are worth $290,000 to $320,000. However, the appliances are missing, including the hot water heater, three doors need replacing, the walls have extensive damage, and two windows are broken. In addition, the yard has gone native and needs restoring. After going through the home and making a list of what it would take to bring it up to neighborhood standards, you estimate the cost at about $25,000. Adding that to the sales price of $230,000 gives you $255,000. Not a bad deal, but you still have to decide on the maximum price you're willing to pay considering the time and effort you'll expend on the house. In this case, the suggested maximum price you should pay would be $240,000 if the bank counters your offer, making your total investment $265,000 when the fix-up costs are added in.

In one case, Shawn and Marie noticed an REO in a neighborhood they liked close to their daughter's elementary school. They called the agent, met him at the house for a walk-through, and found the home in bad condition. The carpets and appliances needed replacing, all the walls needed patching and painting, and at least five gallons of a strong cleaner would be needed for the rest of the home. The first thing Shawn and Marie did was to invest $350 for a professional home inspection. They knew spending the money was a gamble, but they needed to find out exactly what it would cost to put the house in livable condition before they wrote their offer.

A key to getting a REO committee to look at your offer seriously is to include supporting data, such as bids, repair lists, inspection reports, comparable sales, and a list of competing homes for sale in the area. Be sure to include a loan preapproval letter for the bid amount as well.

After the buyers got the inspection report back they shopped around for carpets, appliances, and materials, and they got bids for work they couldn't do themselves. Totaling all the costs, they came up with $23,578, including their inspection report. Shawn and Marie then met with their agent, who pulled up similar properties on the MLS that had sold in the area over the last sixty days. The data showed that similar homes had sold for about $275,000 in good condition. Homes currently for sale in the area confirmed the price range. Putting a sharp pencil to the numbers, they decided to offer the bank $225,000 for the home. Their agent wrote an offer and included copies of the bids and repair lists along with the inspection report and the buyer's loan preapproval letter. This was then overnighted to the bank's REO rep.

About five days later, the buyers' agent got a call from the REO representative saying that the bank had decided to accept the offer. It appears that REO committees like bird-in-the-hand offers, too.

Negotiating a Short Sale

When the real estate market slows and home values decline, owners with little equity find themselves owing more than the home will sell for. This is sometimes called negative or *upside down equity*, and if the homeowner needs to sell, it can get ugly real fast.

An alternative to sellers' letting buyers with low offers walk away, and seeing their homes go into foreclosure, is a possible short sale, whereby the lender discounts the loan balance enough to facilitate the sale. To do this, essentially the homeowner contacts the bank's customer service department (a toll-free number found on the monthly statement) and asks to speak to a representative. In most cases, the representative will mail the homeowner a questionnaire to complete and return. The bank may also ask for supporting documents to prove that the homeowner is eligible for short-sale consideration, such as proof of job loss, list of debts, and income verification. If the bank deems the situation worthy of a short sale, it will encourage the owner to put the home on the market and try to get an offer.

Short sales offers are handled similarly to REOs. Buyers have the burden of selling the bank on why they should discount their loans, and any offers buyers present must have supporting data to back up the offers. The downsides to short sales include the following:

- You usually have no idea what amount the bank will consider, so you have to submit an offer blind, without knowing whether you're even in the ballpark.

- Because lenders often try to reduce their commissions, buyers' agents are wary and often reluctant to give a project a quality effort.

- Listing agents are wary because they can't list a guaranteed sale price or buyer agent commission for the property.

- Some banks don't respond quickly, and it's not uncommon for them to sit on offers for a week or two, hoping for a better one to come in.

In spite of these drawbacks you can sometimes get a great deal with a short sale, but you should plan on spending extra time and have a great deal of patience.

Another wrinkle to factor in is that sometimes sellers are cooperative because they want to save their credit, while at other times they give up partway through and the sale fizzles because the bank can't deal with you as long as the sellers own the property. The bank doesn't become owner until the property goes through foreclosure.

Buying Peace of Mind with a Home Inspection

Before finalizing any type of deal on a home, a professional home inspection is critical. Although most states require sellers to disclose problems in writing to a buyer, in reality it's still "buyer beware." While a seller may fill out a multipage sellers' disclosure form, at the time there's no way to tell whether it's accurate. It boils down to the seller's opinion of the home's condition at the time the form is filled out, so it's best to use it as a starting point only.

The best protection from buying a problem home is to hire a professional home inspector to evaluate it before you commit. The advantages of getting a home inspection include the following:

- You can make your purchase offer subject to a satisfactory inspection. If the report comes back with serious problems, you can back out of the deal and get your deposit back.

- You can use the inspection as leverage to get the seller to repair problems or give you a credit on the sales price.

- The inspection report can reveal problems that are not serious enough to kill the sale, and that you can fix on your own afterward. This allows you to make an informed decision with no surprises when you move in.

- Some home inspectors will go over the home with you and point out potential problems and areas of concern. This can be a great learning experience as to how the different components of a house work.

One buyer, a handyman, told his agent he knew all about houses and didn't need an inspector who knew less than he did. Besides, he said, he could handle any problems a five-year-old house could throw at him. The sale closed, and a few days later the buyers moved in to a big surprise. The plumbing in the master bathroom was not hooked up and there were no water or waste lines to any of the fixtures or toilet. The buyer, on his walk-through, had looked in the bathroom, done a quick scan, had seen that everything looked normal, and moved on. Would an inspector catch that kind of chicanery? He would in a heartbeat.

Even if you're a contractor or are skilled in the building trades, it's still important to hire a professional home inspector because these individuals are trained and equipped to look for problems and they aren't emotionally involved in the sale. Having a neutral third-party report also gives you something concrete to go back to the seller with if problems are found and you must negotiate payment of the repairs or cancel the deal.

Hiring a Home Inspector

Home inspectors are not regulated in all states, and in some areas they don't even need a license. As a result, it's important to use caution and do some homework before making a hiring decision. The following tips will help you in your search for a professional:

Horror Stories

For informative and entertaining horror stories uncovered by the American Society of Home Inspectors (ASHI), go to *This Old House* magazine at www.thisoldhouse.com and key in "home inspections" in the search window. Undoubtedly, the home buyers in these cases appreciated getting their inspection reports back so they could start looking for another house.

- Use caution if a seller, real estate agent, or lender pressures you to use a particular inspector. It's important to choose an independent inspector who has no ties or conflicts of interest in the transaction.

- Ask around for referrals from agents or people who have recently bought a home and then assemble a short list of candidates to interview. Look for affiliation with the American Society of Home Inspectors (ASHI) or the National Institute of Building Inspectors (NIBI).

- Check out the experience of those on your short list. Retired contractors, architects, and those with other professional building skills are a plus. Also ask what accreditation classes the inspectors have taken and how long they've been in the business.

- Interview at least three inspectors, then select the one you believe will do the best job and that you feel you will get along with. In addition, ask if you can come along on the inspection and whether the inspector will be agreeable to explaining what he or she is looking for and why.

- Make sure a return visit is included in the price to verify that the seller corrects any problems found in the inspection.

Handling Repair Problems Found in a Home Inspection

Alan and Sandra found a twelve-year-old home in an upscale neighborhood that was exactly what they were looking for. They felt so lucky to find the home that they didn't want to jeopardize their offer by making it subject to a home inspection. Their agent insisted on it, though, emphasizing that an expense of a few hundred dollars is cheap insurance when you're investing more than $350,000.

A few days later, the inspector met the buyer's agent at the home,

---

HOME-BUYING TIP

It's not your fault when an inspection report reveals problems the sellers should have taken care of before they put the home on the market. Should you elect to deduct or handle the repairs, get bids and ask for 1.25 to 1.5 times the bid amount as a price concession or check at closing.

---

and it didn't take long for him to turn up some serious problems. Eight years earlier a major fire had damaged the home and the repairs made were less than professional, including fire-charred ceiling joists that were not replaced and many damaged wall studs that were simply covered over rather than replaced. The buyers quickly cancelled their offer, disappointed but also relieved that they had avoided a costly home-buying mistake.

In a slow market especially, few sellers want to lose a sale when preapproved buyers are involved. As a result, the threat of home inspections tied to an offer helps motivate sellers to repair problems rather than hope the buyers don't catch them. For example, Scott and Marissa's inspection report came back with several small but serious problems, such as an improperly installed furnace flue, no flex connectors or strapping securing the water heater to the wall, and no air vents in the door to the furnace room. Upon receipt of the inspection report, these buyers wrote up a repair addendum listing the problems that were found and sent it to the sellers' agent. It gave the sellers two options the buyer would accept in order to continue with the sale: either hire and pay for a heating contractor to correct the problems before closing or give the buyers $750 and let them take care of the problems on their own.

HOME-BUYING TIP

Always schedule a walk-through the day of or a day before closing to make sure all repairs are completed and no new damage has been caused by the sellers' moving out. Also make sure that if appliances and amenities are included in the sale, they are there as agreed.

In this particular case, the sellers elected to hire a contractor to fix the problems. Undoubtedly they decided to go this route because the bid totaled $497, which was less than the $750 the buyers asked to take care of it themselves.

Sellers who try to hide problems are finding out that with home inspections and disclosure laws, getting out of town before the problems are discovered doesn't work anymore. They're only costing themselves a lot more money trying to shortcut the sales process.

Minimizing Your Risk with a Home Warranty

When submitting an offer to buy a house, it's wise to have a home warranty included. Buying a home entails some risk, especially when you haven't lived in the home and don't know what needs repair and what doesn't. Sellers are not always forthcoming about problems.

One way to minimize this risk is to have a home warranty. For a one-time fee of $300 to $500, you can get a one-year insurance policy that covers electrical, heating, and plumbing problems. Sellers sometimes offer to buy a warranty for the buyers to make the home more saleable. If this is not offered upfront by the sellers, your offer should state that they include one as part of the deal. You can also buy a home warranty on your own before the deal closes, or anytime after. Regardless of who buys the policy, most home warranty policies cover:

> **HOME-BUYING TIP**
>
> You can ask that a seller include a home warranty in your deal. If the seller balks at paying for it, point out that a National Home Warranty Association survey of the California market found that 56 percent of the sellers paid for a home warranty to avoid potential lawsuits, complaints, and disclosure problems from buyers.

- Built-in appliances such as dishwashers, disposals, compactors, range/ovens are included. Refrigerators, air conditioners, washers and dryers, pools, and hot tubs are usually not included in basic coverage, but they can be covered at extra cost. If you want extended coverage, write that into your offer and list the additional items you want covered.

- Basic coverage is for one year, and most warranties can be extended at a reduced premium.

- Most policies require you to pay a small service fee of $35 to $50 for each call, so it pays to handle the small or inexpensive repairs yourself.

Confused Buyers and Irregular Regulations

Regulation of home warranties varies from state to state. In some states, the real estate commission is the regulator, while in others the

---

Appraisals Are Not Inspections

Appraisers are hired by the bank (usually paid for by the buyer) to make sure the value of the home is in line with the selling price. Many buyers believe that appraisers will uncover problems in a home. While it's true that appraisers will ag obvious problems, they are not trained home inspectors. However, common problems that an appraiser may flag are foundation damage, a roof that needs replacing, water damage or basement leaks, lack of insulation, or other problems that affect the value of the home. Any repair items an appraiser finds must be corrected before the sale can move forward.

To clear up this confusion, the Department of Housing and Urban Development (HUD) now requires FHA buyers to sign a form at closing affirming that they understand that the appraisal is not a property inspection or a home warranty. HUD had received many complaints from people who thought FHA appraisals should have found problems with the house that surfaced after they moved in.

---

department of insurance has jurisdiction. Also, the many different companies and policies have created confusion about what is and isn't covered. As a result, many consumers have the misconception that a home warranty covers everything, down to a leaky faucet. In reality, the only way to find out what you're getting is to read the policy carefully and verify the company's financial stability.

Four Things to Look for When Buying a Policy

Different parts of the country require different emphases on what is covered. In the Sunbelt, air conditioning and pool coverage are mandatory, but in the Northeast, furnaces and sprinkling systems are primary concerns. Regardless of the area you live in, there are four important things to look for in shopping for a home warranty:

1. Make sure the company has a long track record and is financially sound. The best policy is worthless if the company goes bankrupt. Look for agencies that are tied to national corporations that often advertise in your local yellow pages. Check with real estate agents for referrals. It also doesn't hurt to check with your state's agency that handles insurance licenses and financial filings.

2. Read the policy and its fine print. Be sure you understand what is covered and what is excluded, as well as what the service fees are. It's a good idea to compare two or three policies to determine which one best fits your situation.

3. Look carefully at the "preexisting conditions" part of the policy. Does the insurer require a pre-sale home inspection before the policy becomes effective, and is there a time period before certain items are covered after you move in?

4. Make sure the optional coverage you want—such as swimming pools, air conditioner, refrigerators—is included. If the seller is furnishing only a bare-bones policy, you may want to pay extra for the options you want. Also, read over the policy before closing, not when you're moving in and the air conditioner dies on the hottest day of the year.

> Check out these Web sites for more information on home warranties:
> www.nationalhome
> protection.com
> www.americanhomeshield
> .com
> www.nationwidehome
> warranty.com
> www.homewarranty
> .firstam.com.

Seven Steps You Can Take to Make This Chapter Work for You

1. Once you find the home you want to make an offer on, ask your agent to pull up a list of similar properties on the MLS that have recently sold. Compare list price to sold price, days-on-market, and whether the sellers paid concessions to the buyers. This gives you a starting point in determining what to offer.

2. When you've found your dream home, it's important to move quickly because other buyers may like the same property. If you have your financial ducks in a row, you can move fast to put the home under contract.

3. Determine the seller's motivation by tactfully asking why they are moving and what their timetable is. Sometimes a quick sale is more important than a full price offer. Ask questions and listen carefully for clues as to what the seller's hot buttons are.

4. When you write an offer, add an addendum that asks the sellers to pay for your loan and/or closing costs and any upgrades you feel the home needs. Buyers are more willing in a slow market

to pay a few thousand dollars in concessions rather than lose a sale.

5. If you find a foreclosure or short sale, get an agent who has experience and a track record with these types of deals. They often require savvy and patience to put together, but the results can be worth it.

6. Always get a professional home inspection before you buy a home. Make the offer subject to a satisfactory report, so if there are problems the owner won't correct you can walk away from the deal and get your deposit back.

7. Always write into your offer that the sellers will furnish a home warranty and pay the cost. Also, include that you (the buyers) get to pick out the policy. You may need to add a cap to the cost—say, $350 or whatever's common in your area.

■   ■   ■

If you're considering buying a condo, co-op, or townhouse, the next chapter details the special buying problems you may run into.

C H A P T E R **6**

Buying a Condo, Co-op, Townhouse, or Similar Home

Many people buy a condo, co-op, or townhouse when they don't want to mow the lawn, want to downsize from a home that's now too big for them, or want a home that's more affordable. Others, in response to the "empty nest syndrome" that occurs when the child or children leave home, want to shed square footage, move to a more downtown location, or be able to leave their home unattended while they travel.

Whatever your housing preference, you'll find that there are important differences between single-family homes and condos, co-ops, and townhouses.

Whether you're looking for a condo, co-op, townhouse, planned unit development (PUD), or twin home, this chapter will help you to navigate the obstacles to finding that dream home and getting the best deal.

In this chapter you'll learn how to:

■ Understand the similarities and differences among condos, co-ops, townhouses, planned unit developments, twin homes, and timeshares.

■ Be aware of the pros and cons of homeowner associations and how they can impact your decision to buy.

■ Understand the difference in how homeowners associations and co-op boards operate.

■ Know what paperwork to ask for and what to have made available before buying a condo, co-op, or townhouse.

■ Know what to look for in buying a PUD or a twin home.

■ Understand the pros and cons of timeshare ownership.

Buying a Condo or a Townhouse

Unlike single family homes, *condos* and *townhouses* are based on shared ownership and responsibility. When you buy either of these properties you normally get only the interior airspace. The grounds and buildings are owned in common with the rest of the owners of the project.

Some townhouses, however, also include a small yard, deck, or patio where owners can hang a hummingbird feeder and have a potted plant or two. Typically, townhouses are individual units built in a row—with or without a common wall while condos are multilevel, but their homeowner associations function in much the same way. By purchasing either dwelling, you automatically become a member of its association.

The first difference between a single-family home and either a co-op, condo, or townhouse project is the importance that homeowner associations (HOA) play in your life. Because the buildings and grounds are commonly owned by the community, HOAs are key not only to the enjoyment of where you live but also to maintaining your home's value.

The second difference is financing. A development needs to have FHA and/or conventional loan building and project approvals in place so that lenders can get fast loan approvals. Loan qualification is also more involved because homeowner association fees need to be figured into your debt-to-income ratios.

As a result, buying one of these properties is more complex than simply finding a home you like and making an offer. Getting financing and knowing how to evaluate the homeowner association becomes a critical part of the search process, and it ultimately influences your decision as to whether to make an offer. Of course, if you're not interested in a lifestyle that is inextricably involved with a homeowners association, there are alternatives, including planned unit developments and twin homes, which have similar amenities to the aforementioned styles of home ownership and are discussed later in this chapter.

How Homeowner Associations Work

A *homeowners association* (HOA) is typically a nonprofit corporation with articles of incorporation that define the association's purpose and powers. These articles of incorporation are filed with the state. The members of an HOA elect a board of directors to govern the affairs of the project subject to its bylaws, which contain the basic governing rules by which it operates. They lay out how the HOA functions, including how meetings are conducted, voting is handled, board members are selected, and assessments are determined. Ideally, the community is run like a small city government, with elected board members representing the will of the owners.

Federal laws as well as local ordinances, zoning, building codes, parking, traffic restrictions, resale regulations, and rent control provisions apply to HOAs. Another layer of restrictions are called *CC&Rs*, which stands for *covenants, conditions, and restrictions*. Created by developers when they plan a condo or townhouse community and get it approved by the local planning board, and recorded in the county recorder's office along with lot plans, CC&Rs are rules that govern what you can and can't do with your property. Common restrictions invoked to attempt to maintain the value and theme of the community involve landscaping, building additions, exterior colors, and whether

> **HOME-BUYING TIP**
>
> When looking at a condo for sale, ask the owners how they like the board members and if there have been any problems between board and owners. If there are ongoing problems, important decisions regarding the management and upkeep of the development can be at risk.

you can park an RV in your driveway. Most developers put a lot of thought into what restrictions they put in their CC&Rs. Get too restrictive and people may not buy their units; get too loose and a few slovenly homeowners can lower property values for all.

The final top layer of restrictions are the rules the HOA passes by the will of the majority of its members, such as how long you can keep your garage door up or leave your empty garbage can on the curb, what pets are allowed, and whether you can keep that rusty '49 Chevy body on your front lawn.

Condos and townhouses charge a monthly fee to maintain the infrastructure and amenities. Typically, these fees cover items such as grounds maintenance, insurance, garbage removal, snow removal, cable TV, and pool upkeep. The MLS listings usually disclose the total monthly fee, but do not give a breakdown of the fees themselves. That information you will likely have to get from the homeowners association secretary.

Since you'll be paying higher fees for amenities such as a clubhouse, a swimming pool, tennis courts, or a golf course, be sure these are the sorts of extras that fit your lifestyle before making a decision as to where you want to buy. Amenities such as these are great if you intend to use them, but if all you want is a quiet condo to get away from yard work, you'll soon resent the higher fees you'll be forced to pay for these extras.

Homeowner association boards are elected by the members who naturally want to keep the monthly fees as low as possible. No one likes to incur the wrath of their neighbors by increasing fees, so the pressure is intense to keep them low. As a result, a weak board will often not implement good financial policies in order to keep fees as low as possible in the short term. Additionally, HOAs can foreclose on your condo if you don't pay your monthly fees. How many months you can go in arrears before the association initiates a legal foreclosure process depends on the bylaws and the HOA's resolve. The association does have strong legal standing to enforce its bylaws, however.

HOME-BUYING TIP

Not surprisingly, the biggest HOA problem nationwide is the ability of condo and townhouse communities to manage their finances responsibly. Some hire professional firms to do this. It adds to your fees, but it's usually worth it.

Not surprisingly, one of the biggest areas of contention among homeowner association members is finances. If the board is responsible and runs the association professionally, it will accumulate a reserve to maintain buildings and grounds. However, this doesn't always happen, so it's important for you to find out before you buy how much money the development has in reserve. Otherwise, you may find yourself getting regular assessments (one-time fees to cover specific necessities, such as an increase in the price of heating oil) or hefty increases in your monthly maintenance fee.

A couple buying a condo in Seattle found this out the hard way two months after they moved in. The exterior on the fourteen-year-old property had weathered and deteriorated to the point that it needed replacement. Unfortunately, current and past association officers had failed to create a reserve, and each member got an assessment notice for $7,000. Owners who didn't happen to have the funds in their checking account had to pay the assessment off at $600 a month. The new owners had no choice but to pay the assessment. When they bought the condo, they assumed the

---

Know Your HOAs

Because HOAs are so important to your enjoyment of condominium living, make sure your agent goes over the rules and regulations, financial statements, and the last three or four months of board minutes with you before you commit. Also, make sure there are no long-term payments on assessed fees that you get stuck for. For example, a prior assessment for siding and roofing upgrades the current owner is paying off at $160 a month.

---

liabilities, and refusal to pay such assessments means the association can put a lien on the unit and sell it, if necessary, to collect that money.

What can you do if you don't like the way your fees are spent? You can exercise one of the basics of American democracy and get enough concerned neighbors together to vote in a new board or have a recall election.

The Politics of Living in a Condo or Townhouse

It's the board of directors' job to enact and enforce the rules that, in view of the majority, will make living in the project a pleasant and profitable experience. But here's the rub, and it's an important consideration before you think about buying a condo or townhouse: If you don't take part in HOA politics, the board may enact rules you don't like. Electing responsible officers is critical to your condo experience and your pocketbook. Even if the HOA hires a professional firm to handle day-to-day management, you and your neighbors are still ultimately responsible for your community's quality of living and financial management.

> The number of directors and their terms of office and duties are found in the association's declarations, articles, or bylaws. Most boards have three to five directors—usually an odd number to avoid voting deadlocks. Terms of office are usually for one to three years, but if there are five or more members, the terms are often staggered.

In reality, HOA politics are a microcosm of American politics. If you don't like certain rules, find enough fellow owners who agree with you and run for the board next time the elections come around. You can change or add rules by majority vote.

HOME-BUYING TIP

Economic Considerations in Buying a Condo or Townhouse

If you're graduating from downtrodden tenant to your first home by buying a condo or townhouse, there are three economic considerations that you should keep in mind as you shop around.

First, in a mixed area with single-family homes, condos and townhouses will not appreciate as fast as single-family homes will in a normal market. In slow economic times, the condo and townhouse markets often suffer first and are slower to recover. However, in urban areas competition with detached houses often doesn't exist, so normal supply-and-demand economics govern values.

HOME-BUYING TIP

Because you have such a large financial commitment as well as your happiness at stake, make sure you are willing to be active in HOA affairs. If this isn't something you're willing to do, you may want to consider something other than a condo or a townhouse.

Second, condos can be more area sensitive than detached homes. If a project becomes run down or the area suffers because a freeway off ramp or factory is built nearby, values can sink to the bottom and stay there longer than areas with single homes.

Think "sell" when you buy. Many first-time homebuyers visit new condo or townhouse developments that advertise a fun lifestyle and an owning-is-cheaper-than-rent sales pitch along with attractive financing packages. These homebuyers don't think about what will happen when all the units are sold, the developer moves on, and the project becomes part of real-world economics.

If you plan on moving within a few years, you'll want to consider the following questions:

- Will the property hold or increase its value in the short term?

- Are there similar projects in the area and, if so, have their values increased or decreased?

- What percentage of the units are owned vs. rented? If the ratio is creeping close to 50 percent, obtaining financing may become an issue and make your unit harder to sell.

- Does the HOA have future expenses coming due, such as lawsuits, infrastructure repairs, or improvements that will bump up owner fees?

Finally, it often happens that when you want to sell, several other owners will as well. A three- to five-year selling bubble appears to occur in new projects that attract mostly first-time homebuyers. So if you want to sell fast, keep in mind that price is all that sets you apart from the competition. An owner who is desperate to sell will bottom-out his or her sales price and that can hurt the whole community's values.

Lewis and Charlene faced this problem when they tried to sell the condo they bought four years earlier. Like most others in the development, they were first-time homeowners and couldn't afford the average $276,000 house prices in the area. Their condo with a gas fireplace, two baths, and two bedrooms appeared to be the perfect solution at $210,000. Monthly payments on a variable mortgage were on par with renting, even with the $97 condo fee added in.

The first two years of condo living was great for the couple. They loved the location, the pool, and the lifestyle. Then a baby came along and suddenly the future looked much different. After another two years they started to think about having a home with a yard. Since their increased income qualified them for a bigger loan, they decided to sell and look for a single-family home.

Before you commit to purchasing a property, walk through the neighborhood and ask three neighbors the following questions:

- How long have you lived here?
- What do you like best about the community?
- What do you like least about the community?
- Do you have a management company, and is it doing a good job?
- Do you attend the association's meetings?
- Do you feel the board is doing a good job?
- What do homeowner dues cover and how often have they been increased?
- Can you hear your neighbors? (This is the number one complaint of condo and townhouse owners.)

Around the same time, FOR SALE signs started appearing in windows around the community and few sold. And while Lewis and Charlene's mortgage payoff showed a high balance of about $205,000 because they had financed most of their loan costs, owners with more equity in their properties were able to discount their condos to $195,000, hoping to get a quick sale. As a result, prices of similar units for sale in the complex took a beating. When this happens, equity becomes the difference between an owner's loan balance and the lowest priced unit.

HOME-BUYING TIP

If there are a large number of FOR SALE signs in your community, find out why. It may just be a normal selling cycle, but it may also be an indicator of bigger problems, such as a freeway off-ramp nearby, rezoning for a big-box store, or even a large assessment due to deferred maintenance.

In this case, Lewis and Charlene had no choice but to stay in their condo and hope that prices would go up or that they would be able to pay down their mortgage so that they could sell. Their other option would have been to write a check for at least $10,000 at closing. In cases like this, when the loan balance is less than the sales price, it's called *negative* or *upside-down equity*.

Admittedly, an upside-down equity situation can also happen with single-family homes, but a condo or townhouse can take longer to sell, and with deeper discounting, because price is usually all that separates one unit from another. Once this spiral of cost cutting begins, it's hard to reverse. However, if you're retiring or plan on staying in your unit for a long time, selling bubbles and market ups and downs won't be as big a problem.

Condo and Loft Conversions

In many areas of the country, former rental apartments and even commercial buildings are being converted to condos. Close to downtown, with attractive prices and trendy architecture, these new condo units are popular with first-time buyers. Similarly, refurbished warehouses and old office buildings are getting a new lease on life by being broken up into small studios or one-bedroom units called loft conversions. These projects often attract buyers such as artists, young professionals, and employees of nearby businesses. The neighborhood shops and restaurants cater to these customers.

However, in buying one of these units you still have to consider what happens if you want to sell. As with other condo communities, you need to look at the realities and do your homework before committing.

Typically, one-bedroom condo units are at the bottom of the food chain and consequently are the most difficult to sell because most buyers want two bedroom as their first choice. If at all possible, go for at least two bedrooms so you'll have more room for yourself, and when you go to sell, you'll have a more desirable unit to offer buyers. Also, in an economic downturn, conversions are likely to lose more value faster than other types of housing. Financing for these types of projects tend to dry up first and lending standards tighten creating an oversupply because owners can't sell.

In one case, retired schoolteachers Joe and Sandy bought an upscale warehouse conversion in a great downtown location close to cultural and sports events. Unfortunately, this project didn't quite live up to their expectations. The real estate market cooled shortly thereafter, and two years later nearly a third of the units remained unsold. In desperation, the developer discounted the remaining units in an attempt to generate cash flow. That dropped the value on the units that had sold, and owners who wanted to sell found themselves competing with discounted new units and facing a substantial loss. The lesson learned here is to be

> ### HOME-BUYING TIP
>
> Remember that in condos, price is the main thing that differentiates one unit from another. If an owner discounts his unit to sell it quickly, all the other units' values will suffer accordingly. Not so great if you are the seller, but an opportunity for you as a buyer.

careful if you are one of the first buyers in a conversion or unusual project. Check out other similar projects in the area and find out how successful they have been, how many units have sold, and how long it took. Ask yourself what might happen if the project doesn't take off as the glossy sales literature promises.

When Joe and Sandy decided to move to another state, they found they had to steeply discount their condo unit and ended up losing $30,000, feeling lucky even to have gotten a sale, given the competition. Fortunately, they had bought one of the few three-bedroom units, and so their offer stood out among the competition.

Conversely, if a new condo project takes off and your values soar, the equity you hold in the unit will grow. Eventually, if you want to sell and move to a larger home, you'll have a good down payment available as a result. Real estate conditions are usually local, and home values depend on local supply and demand more than anything else. If you choose a location that has had a long history as an appealing place to live, and that promises to maintain that appeal, your purchase should be a secure one. But if you're not sure or the project doesn't have a track record, you'll need to do some homework to satisfy yourself that the project will increase in value over the long term. Also, you don't want to be swayed by a hot grab-it-or-lose-it bargain and skip due diligence.

The bottom line is that condos and townhouses can be a great investment and a great place to live, but you have to do some serious homework before you commit. The margin of error is slimmer than with single-family homes, where you can renovate to correct a layout problem or put up a fence to block out a pesky neighbor.

Tips and Traps to Avoid When Buying a Condo or Townhouse

Owing to the HOA and common ownership of the buildings and grounds, buying a condo or townhouse requires a few additional steps beyond those usually needed for a single-family home. The following ten tips and traps, along with Figure 6.1, will help you to make sure you cover all the critical bases when you evaluate such a property:

1. Look at several communities in your price range and average their monthly HOA fees to get an estimate of what your cost will be. Then make sure your mortgage lender adds in this estimate when he or she preapproves you for a mortgage.

2. Ask your agent to provide from the MLS a list of similar properties that have sold in the last thirty days; note how long they've been on the market and the difference between listing price and sales price. This gives you a starting point in deciding what to offer.

3. Find out how many properties in the development are owner-occupied, rented, and unsold. If rental units top 30 percent, find out why and whether the trend of rental units is increasing. When over 40 percent of the units in a development are rentals, financing becomes more difficult.

4. Get a copy of the bylaws, CC&Rs, and recent rule changes. Before you make an offer, you want to know if you can live with the current rules.

FIGURE 6-1
Comparison chart.

Home type	Ownership	Homeowners Association (HOA)	Fees
Condo	Your unit space only. All else in common.	Elected board of directors. Responsible for buildings, grounds, and amenities.	Monthly fee covers everything but your unit's interior and some utilities.
Co-op	You buy stock in a corporation that owns the building.	Elected board of directors. Can also have a say in who buys stock.	Monthly fee includes assessment, taxes, and most utilities.
Townhouse	You own the land and the unit it sits on.	HOA takes care of common areas only. Usually you take care of your unit's exterior.	Monthly fee for common areas.
Planned Unit Development (PUD)	You own home and land and interest ownership in amenities such as swimming pool, golf course, and riding paths.	HOA takes care of amenities only. Some developments have restrictive covenants similar to condos and townhouses.	Monthly fee for amenities upkeep.
Twin home	You own home and land.	Usually no HOA unless a group of twins are in a PUD.	Owners take care of their side.

5. In order to avoid a financial sinkhole, get a copy of the current HOA's financial statement. Note whether there's a fund set aside for repairs and replacements. Also, walk through the development and note the overall condition as well as what needs replacement in the near future. Will the fund take care of the repairs or will HOA fees likely go up? Finally, find out when the last fee increase happened and why.

6. Get copies of the minutes from the last ten meetings. If meetings are not held regularly or no one takes minutes, find out

why, because this is a red flag. If meeting minutes are available, look at what problems were discussed and whether they were resolved or allowed to continue.

7. Make sure the HOA is not involved in any lawsuits from past or present owners. You don't want to pay dues for past problems.

8. Talk to a least three residents of the community. Ask them how they like living there, what they don't like about the community, and whether they would buy there again. Listen carefully and you will find out all you want to know about what's going on.

9. Look closely at the community demographics. If you have kids and most of the residents are retired, you're likely better off looking for a development with owners of a similar age. Take some time to carefully look around to make sure you'll fit in and be happy with your neighbors.

10. If you don't have an opportunity to do the above homework before you make an offer, make it subject to your approval of the development's bylaws and financial statement. Then, if you find something you don't like, you can cancel the deal and get your deposit back.

Buying a Co-op

Unlike buying a condo or a townhouse, in which you own a percentage of the building, land, and improvements, when you buy a *co-op* you are actually buying shares in a corporation that owns the building. In effect, you are leasing a unit from the corporation, and your monthly fee or assessment depends on the number of shares you own. And like a condo or townhouse, monthly fees can go up if the revenue needed to maintain the building falls short. As a shareholder you have a vote in co-op matters and, depending on the bylaws, you need a two-thirds or three-fourths majority to enact or change rules.

Typically, co-ops are in older urban areas, such as New York City, San Francisco, or Chicago. Often they were formerly rental apartment complexes. At some point, the landlord decided to sell the building, offering the current renters an insider's price for their units, which can be a very good deal, depending on the location and condition of the building. Some tenants buy their units and then sell them at the market price; others stay on in the building, either as tenants or now as owners. Gradually, the building converts to a total co-op, but that can take years. The co-op is an older housing arrangement; most new apartment houses in these cities are built as condos now. Nevertheless, there is a healthy real estate market in co-ops, and in some cities like New York, they remain the primary type of purchasable apartments. In fact, people debate the virtues of co-ops versus condos regarding rules of operation and real estate values.

How a Co-op Board Works

Because co-ops are corporations, a co-op board, or board of directors, runs the show. It sets the rules and can determine who is allowed to buy shares and what improvements can be made to the units. For some people, that's an attractive feature; they feel the units hold their value better. In reality, who gets to live in the building can be tightly controlled, and contrasts greatly with a condo, where whoever has the money to buy a unit is in. Likewise, condo rules often allow for the owners to sublet, or rent out their units to others, whereas those situations are rarely allowed in a co-op. However, this co-op exclusiveness can make selling the unit difficult and more time consuming than with a condo, because any new ownership is subject to lengthy and extensive review.

Although a co-op board can't discriminate based on race, sex, or religion, it can reject your application if your income level indicates that you won't fit in. They also often reject applicants who won't be using it as their primary residence, as they want true stakeholders in the building's welfare. Also, be aware that if you want to buy a co-op, the board will want as much financial information on its application as a mortgage lender.

One caveat is that, in some areas, the seller of a co-op doesn't have to provide a disclosure form detailing the condition of the unit. That's

---

Look for Realtors Who Specialize

When looking for a Realtor to help you buy a co-op, select an agent who specializes in the neighborhood and price range youre considering. These agents often know the buildings and the quirks and preferences of their boards, and they can help you get approved. If you are eyeing a particular building or buildings, ask the superintendent which agents most often show that building.

because the seller is selling stock, not real estate, so disclosure rules don't apply. This presents a special challenge in verifying the co-op's condition, as well as the unit's. If the co-op board is keeping costs down by deferring maintenance, you may want to look elsewhere.

It's important as well to find out if the board imposes a *flip tax*—a fee levied when a shareholder decides to sell; depending on the market, this is paid by the buyer or seller. The fee can be a percentage of the sale price (commonly 1 to 3 percent) or a set cost per share. It can also be based on the profit from the sale or on how long the person has lived there. The formula boils down to what the board and members agree on. Whether a flip tax will hurt you when you sell depends on the co-op and the current demand for units in the building. You may have to do some homework to find out if it has created sales problems in the past.

How a Co-op Is Financed

Financing a co-op can pose special financial challenges. Some boards require a 30 to 50 percent down payment and allow financing for the balance, while others don't. Every board is different and the practices differ depending on the area.

For instance, when Anita sold her small New York co-op apartment that she had lived in for four years and moved to the West Coast, she had only enough money from her sale to afford a condo or co-op, rather than the three or four bedroom, two bath house she had hoped for. After a month of house shopping, she finally found a co-op that she could put 50 percent down on to keep her payments low and filled out the application. A couple of days later she got word that the board had accepted her offer.

"It was amazing," Anita said. "When I bought my New York co-op the board ran a credit check, employment check, and called my references. Here in San Francisco the board seems almost indifferent, and the financing was up to me, with no minimum down required."

Like condo and townhouses, co-ops can be a good investment if you do your homework and buy wisely. A knowledgeable agent who knows the market and the buildings is the best way to start. This is a niche market, and you want to find an agent who knows the co-ops. In New York City, for example, there are real estate brokers who specialize, not just in co-ops but in specific buildings and neighborhoods. They know the market and the board preferences, so they can help you assess your possibilities of getting past their requirements. They also know the gossip on the buildings—on their maintenance reputations, code violations, and resident turnover.

Tips and Traps for Buying a Co-op

Much of the advice that goes with purchasing a condo also applies to buying a co-op, but there are some other key points to keep in mind as well.

1. Ask co-op members and supers which agents are most active in selling the co-op you're interested in. Create a short list of possible agents and interview them to find one you feel most comfortable with.

2. Sign a buyer's agency agreement with the agent you've selected. You want the agent to take you seriously and work to find what you're looking for. However, add a clause that if you're unhappy you can cancel the agreement. Also, make sure the clause that says the agent is entitled to a commission if you buy a unit that agent showed you is one month or less.

3. Get a copy of the co-ops by-laws, rules, and financial statements. Do some homework and make sure there is no deferred maintenance or other items what will cost you in the near future.

4. Talk to several neighbors around the unit you're interested in; get a lay of the land to make sure there are no sound problems or other issues you wouldn't like to live with.

5. Consider getting a professional home inspection to find out if there are expensive problems lurking in dark places that can affect your investment.

6. Finally, do your homework on the current sales statistics of the building so if you decide to sell, you won't have to take a loss or spend months finding a buyer.

Buying a Planned Unit Development or Twin Home

Planned unit developments (*PUDs*) typically are detached homes with small yards or patios. Sometimes only a few feet separate the homes. Though privacy is at a premium, their biggest selling feature is their competitive pricing. Simply put, the developer can fit more homes on an acre of land, so the price per home is lower. Common areas such as a clubhouse, swimming pool, and golf course are offered as lures, and often the yard care is included in the monthly fee for upkeep of the neighborhood and the amenities.

Twin homes can be a single part of a duplex where you own only one side or a unit of a PUD with clusters of twin homes. Depending on the size of the development and the number of its amenities, you will have a large HOA to manage all the affairs or a minimal one that is responsible only for street maintenance, snow removal, and perhaps a small park.

What to Look for in Buying a PUD

Where land is expensive and scarce, PUDs are a way to provide homes for less than it would cost to build on standard lot sizes. For example, lot sizes may average a quarter of an acre in the area, but the developer gets the city to approve a PUD with ten homes to an acre, which makes homes a lot more affordable, though somewhat cramped. So, in buying a property in a PUD, be wary of developments that have too many look-alike homes jammed together on small lots. This gives the homes a sterile, cookie-cutter look and is not the type of community that creates homeowner pride. Keep in mind that homeowner pride is a key component in maintaining and increasing your property values.

For homebuyers who don't want the restrictions of a condo or the yard work of a single family home, PUDs are a good compromise. The units often are detached, giving the feel of a house with a small yard or private patio.

Because many PUDs have market economics that are similar to condos, read the earlier section on condos and townhouses. The monthly HOA fees are often less than for condos and townhouses, however, because you are responsible for your entire dwelling rather than just the inside. Although you have more control over your surroundings, you still need a strong HOA to keep the area looking attractive and inviting to homebuyers, so owner-to-rental ratios are still important here. Having lots of rentals in the development will depress the neighborhood's value—in a standard subdivision, that means more than 20 percent rentals.

Financing to purchase a PUD is the same as financing a single-family home, since you own both the dwelling and the land. However, you have to factor the HOA fees into your qualifying ratios. Additionally, you may run into problems if the percentage of rentals in the complex is large or if the complex is new and you're one of the first buyers.

Because FHA, VA, and conventional financing rules frequently change, make any offer subject to receiving financing, even though you're preapproved for a mortgage. The lender may look at the community and ask for a higher down payment or may even decline your deal if the ownership to rentals ratio changes or credit standards tighten.

Lastly, in a PUD, it's important to stay active in HOA affairs and realize that changes in your community will happen as owners sell and new buyers move in with different ideas. You may find that you have to make a few adjustments as the community evolves. This can be a positive experience or a negative one depending on your outlook.

For example, Loren and Dora found this out when they retired and downsized to a smaller home in an upscale PUD with a golf course. It was a new development and they enjoyed making friends as more people their age moved in as well. Soon phase one of the complex sold out and the homeowner association assumed management of the community.

The first four years were fun. Dora was active in the HOA, while Loren improved his golf swing. But when new people were voted into the homeowners association, things began to change. New, more restrictive rules were passed by the new administration: RVs were now prohibited from being parked next to houses. Christmas decorations on the exterior of a home had to be taken down no later than two weeks after the holiday. Owners had to cut their grass twice a week. These rules were an attempt by the HOA board to maintain the image and value of their community, but Loren and Dora had a small motor home that they had parked next to their unit on a concrete pad. Since they were one of the first to buy into the complex, adding the RV pad at that time didn't pose a problem. But now the rules had changed and they were given notice by the association that their RV and the pad had to go. Also, the association's enthusiasm for the new rules grew some more, and soon maintenance personnel were instructed to knock on doors or leave notes on those who were slow to comply with the new rules.

For most of the homeowners, these changes weren't a big deal, but for Loren and Dora, the restrictions and their deteriorating relationship with the association were too much and they decided to sell. It wasn't long before they found a buyer, and they ended up making a good profit, which, ironically, was due in part to the association's working hard to maintain the community's image as a quality place to live.

Lesson learned here is that it's important to stay active in the HOA and realize that changes (often for the better) are going to happen in condo and PUD communities—more so than in single family neighborhoods—as people move in with new ideas.

What to Look for in Buying a Twin Home

A twin home is basically a duplex with each side owned separately, or two single-family homes connected by a common wall. Financing is the same as for a detached single-family home because the homeowner owns both the dwelling and the land.

You'll find twin homes in PUDs, subdivisions, and occasionally duplexes converted into these kind of properties. They attract mostly first-time homebuyers and retirees scaling down. Developers build twin home projects when land costs are so high that the higher density is the only way to build a home that people can afford. You'll find these projects near newer single-family subdivisions as a way for the builder to satisfy federal or local housing regulations that require a certain number of affordable units be available in the area.

Twin homes exist in both subdivisions like those with single-family homes with no HOAs and in PUD communities with strong, active HOAs. If you are considering buying a twin that is not part of an HOA, extra caution is needed. For example, buying a well-maintained twin with great landscaping and then having a new owner who is a slob move in next to you will likely lower the value of your home. Andy and Pat found this out when they bought a twin home on a street with eighteen other twins sandwiched between two mid-priced subdivisions. Their neighbors, also first-time homebuyers, were great, and everything went smoothly for a couple of years. Then a slowdown in the local economy forced several large businesses to lay off people, and Pat and Andy's neighbor was one of the unlucky ones let go.

A FOR SALE sign followed, but after several months of no action, the bank foreclosed and an investor bought the twin for a rental. The tenants didn't take care of their side of the yard, the grass died, and it soon became an eyesore. Although the small twin subdivision had CC&Rs requiring owners to maintain their yards, the city lacked the manpower and will to enforce the rules. Had these twin homes been part of a PUD with a strong homeowners association, they could have pressured the new owner with foreclosure to keep the yard up.

Buying a Timeshare

Another type of condo ownership, a *timeshare* is primarily associated with resort or vacation properties rather than home ownership. Instead of purchasing a home to live in full time, essentially you are buying a fraction of a condo, and that fractional ownership entitles you to use the unit a certain number of weeks in a year. Additionally, some urban areas have apartment buildings or hotels that offer "club memberships" that are essentially fractional ownership arrangements. These are popular with people who visit the same city repeatedly or who come regularly for business. Whether the fractional ownership is at a resort or a business hotel, there usually are many amenities. Timeshares give people the chance to own a property in a great location that they wouldn't otherwise be able to afford. But timeshares and fractional ownerships also have their drawbacks.

The Advantages and Disadvantages of Timeshare Ownership

The economics of timeshares is simple. Suppose a developer builds a 2,600-square-foot, four-bedroom, three-bath condo on the Oregon coast; normally that unit would cost someone $700,000. However, the developer decides to market the property as fractional ownership and sells each of eight people a one-eighth deeded share for $125,000. That allows each of them to use the condo six and a half weeks per year. These shares can either be fixed weeks or can be set up so that the time periods rotate by one month each year. As an alternative, if someone wants more time in the condo, a one-quarter share could be purchased for $225,000, which allows a thirteen-week stay per year.

A big advantage of timeshares, or fractional ownership, is that you get a vacation property without having to worry about taxes or upkeep. Of course, you have HOA fees that typically run $100 to $300 a month, depending on location and amenities. Also, these condo projects usually allow you the option to rent or trade your weeks, and they handle these arrangements through their management company for a small fee. You may also be able to trade your weeks through a professional exchange company for other timeshare projects around the world.

It's not hard to see why timeshare sales have gone through periods when they are quite popular and other times when their market has imploded. The ups and downs are a reflection of economic times. One advantage to timeshares is that you don't have to work through a developer to buy one. There are brokers who specialize in timeshare sales, as well as a brisk Internet market for the units and advertisements in local classifieds.

Know What You're Buying

Before you go very far toward buying a timeshare, exercise due diligence and know exactly what you're getting. The following are some tips to keep in mind:

- Know the type of ownership you're buying, such as deeded real estate, in which you receive a deed to real property; right to use, in which you don't own the real estate; lease-hold, in which you buy the right to occupy land or a building for a specific length of time; or points in a membership club.

- Make sure you understand how your weeks are calculated. For example, a *fixed week* allows you access to the property on week twenty-six every year. A *floating system*, or first-come, first-served system, enables you to request first, second, or third choices on the week taken. A *rotation program* gives you a week that is rotated through the calendar year and gives all members a chance to use prime weeks on an equal basis.

- If you're buying into a vacation club, make sure you know what resorts are part of the system and how weeks are allocated.

- *Points programs* give members so many points equal to their level of membership. Members then use these points to book a resort in their system. Not all destinations "cost" the same number of points; high-demand locations require more points. Be-

Timeshares

It's unfortunate that timeshares have gotten a bad rap because of promoters who have used high-pressure tactics to push their projects, usually via free dinners, luxury trips, and publicity events. If you want to buy a timeshare, don't sign up at a presentation. If you're pressured to commit on the spot, leave. Also, check with a Realtor because the MLS may have timeshares listed as well. Check out these Web sites for more information:

www.scambusters.org/timeshare.html

www.c21flamingo.com/timeshare/

www.homebuying.about.com/cs/timesharebasics/a/ownership.htm

fore you commit, be sure you understand how many points you're buying and where they can be used; get a list of resorts and how many points are needed for each one.

■ Financing timeshares and fractional ownership is limited to a few lenders and there is no secondary market. If the developer or timeshare offers financing, look over the disclosures carefully, especially the terms and APR. Many people use home equity loans to finance these programs because the rates and terms are often better.

Seven Steps You Can Take to Make This Chapter Work for You

1. When you find a condo or townhouse complex you like, look at the ratio of rentals or unsold units to those that are owner occupied.

2. Check out similar developments in the area. Have they held their value or are owners discounting to get out?

3. Get HOA financial statements, bylaws, and minutes and read them carefully before you sign a purchase agreement.

4. Talk to neighbors and get the real scoop on what's happening in the community and with the HOA.

5. Don't buy a condo, co-op, townhouse, or PUD if the HOA has financial problems or you don't feel comfortable with the owner demographics.

6. Make sure the owners don't have unpaid assessments they are making payments on or assessments that are pending and could come due before closing.

7. It's better to buy a time-share through a reputable broker than at a high-pressure sales promotion. You can often get discounts that you can't get at a free sales event.

■   ■   ■

Two more up-and-coming ways to get into a quality home are to look at manufactured and modular units. Chapter 7 gives you their pros and cons.

Buying a Manufactured Home

For many buyers, the best route to owning a home is buying a new manufactured home because they're often more economical, not every area of the country has many building contractors available, and a manufactured home can be completed faster than a *stick-built home*, or home assembled on the building site.

Typically, manufactured homes fall into three broad categories: (1) modular homes that are shipped to the site in sections and assembled, (2) mobile (also called manufactured) homes that are build on an undercarriage and towed to the site and assembled, and (3) kit or precut homes that are assembled on site. Many homebuyers have the attitude that if it's not stick built, or constructed completely at the building site, it's not a quality home. That may have been true decades ago, but with current building materials and techniques you can get a manufactured home that has advantages rivaling or even surpassing a conventionally constructed home.

There are a number of advantages to buying a manufactured home. One advantage is that the completion times are fast and the quality control is high. For instance, a typical stick-built home takes three to six months to construct, depending on weather, labor, and site preparation. A manufactured home can be scheduled to arrive on site within a day or two of when it's ready to install on the foundation, pad, or crawl space.

Another advantage is the cost savings. Quality control and lower labor costs of these homes translate into serious savings when compared to on-site construction. Typically, you can save 15 to 25 percent per square foot on a manufactured home versus one built on-site.

In rural or remote areas, where it's difficult to find good contractors and subcontractors, a manufactured home can be the best way to get the home you want with all the amenities. Plus, these homes meet all state and federal building codes, and financing is available through FHA/VA guaranteed loans and conventional 30-year mortgages.

However, like any other housing option, there are minuses and pitfalls to look out for that can cost you big time. This chapter shows you how to avoid those pitfalls and get the best deal when buying a modular, manufactured, or mobile home.

In this chapter you'll learn how to:

■ Determine the pros and cons of the four types of manufactured homes.

■ Understand how to finance a manufactured home.

■ Know how to shop for a manufactured home.

■ Be able to find the right building lot for your home.

■ Go about buying the necessary permits and site fees.

■ Understand what influences the resale value of a manufactured home.

The Pros and Cons of Manufactured Homes

Four types of manufactured houses essentially dominate the market. The first three—modular, panel, and precut homes—vary by how much of the home is built at the factory and how much is completed on-site. The fourth, mobile homes, are typically finished at the factory and shipped to the site in two or more sections that are then joined and anchored to a pad or foundation.

Manufactured homes are built to meet the federal building code, the Manufactured Home Construction and Safety Standards (HUD) code, and they display a red certification label on each section. In addition, each state has its own building codes that usually follow the Uniform Building Code (UBC) or the International Building Code (IBC).

Regardless of construction type, these homes are also subject to local building codes that can exceed federal codes. This ensures that the home meets the quality and safety standards of all residential construction in the area, as judged by local building inspectors.

Modular Homes

Modular homes, sometimes called *sectional houses*, are almost completely built in sections, in a quality-controlled assembly plant. Each step of the process is inspected and the final sections are tagged, certifying that the home complies with all state and federal building codes.

As the building sections come off the assembly line, they are loaded onto carriers for transport to the home site. Owing to federal and/or state highway wide-load restrictions, sections are limited to a width of fourteen feet by a length of sixty feet. These sections are then transported to the building site and joined together by local contractors.

At the site, a crane lifts the sections onto the foundation, where they are connected and permanently anchored. Utilities are connected as well, the finish crew completes the interior work, and the home is ready for occupancy in a week or two. Once assembled, local building inspectors check to make sure the home's structure meets code requirements.

Modular homes are usually less expensive per square foot than site-built houses and should have the same longevity as their site-built counterparts, increasing in value over time. This can be a big plus when you consider the months it would take to stick-build a home of the same size. It's also a big advantage knowing upfront exactly how much the home will cost, when it will be done, and when it will be delivered.

Another big plus of modular homes is that home styles are limited only by your imagination. Stack a couple of sections and create a Cape Cod, modern two-story, or a multilevel. Connect them horizontally for an L-shaped ranch-style home. You can even build condominium projects and duplexes made from modular sections.

HOME-BUYING TIP

Two great books on modular homes are *Modular Homes: The Future Has Arrived,* by Michael Zenga and Attila Javor, and *The Modular Home,* by Andrew Gianino.

Web sites you'll want to check out include:

www.modularcenter.com

www.skylinehomes.com

www.mobilehome.com

www.factorybuilthousing .com

www.modularhomesnet work.com

www.hud.gov/offices/hsg/ sfh/mhs/prod01.cfm

www.modulartoday.com/

Not sure what you want? Most manufacturers have design departments that can help you customize a floor plan to fit your dream, with vaulted ceilings, upgraded kitchen islands, cabinets, and so on.

Panel Homes

Panel homes, like modular homes, come in a wide variety of styles, sizes, and plans. They, too, are built under controlled factory conditions with the same quality control. Unlike modular construction, however, panel homes are shipped to their home sites in panels that typically are eight feet high and up to forty feet long, with doors, windows, and wiring factory-installed, and then the panels are assembled and the finish work completed in about a week or two on-site. Panel homes are built to federal and state building codes, so they qualify for FHA/VA and conventional thirty-year financing.

You can also order a panel home in kit form, with everything included, and finish it yourself. If you or Uncle Joe is a finish carpenter, you can save some bucks and time by going this route. Otherwise, you can have factory site crews complete the assembly and interior finish as part of the package.

The advantages of panel homes are that:

■ The structure can be up and weather-tight in a day or so.

■ You can create a custom package that allows you to do as much of the work as you can handle.

■ In areas where contractors and subcontractors are hard to find, panel homes can give you a quality home for less money and construction time than a stick-built home.

■ In areas of natural disasters, when good contractors are hard to find, panel homes can give you quality construction much faster than a rebuilt home.

Precut Homes

As the name suggests, *precut homes*, also known as *kit homes*, are just that: all the components of the home are precut at the factory and shipped to the site, ready to be used. These kit homes are like model airplane kits or automobile kits in that all you have to do is put them together and they will look like the picture on the box.

Typically, log, timber frame, and specialty homes (round, hexagon, etc.) come precut and the owner or contractor assembles the home on site. These homes require specialized know-how to assemble, owing to the unique materials involved and the hardware needed.

Precut or kit home packages offer a lot of flexibility. You can buy a precut home in just about any size or style from your plans or theirs, along with the quality and upgrades you want and can afford. You can also choose how complete you want the kit, from the structure only to a complete house, with nails included and ready for you to start pounding. For a do-it-your-selfer with some experienced help, this can be a ticket to the most house for the least money because there's little waste.

For the site work, if you're acting as your own general contractor, you'll need to schedule local building inspections for each construction phase. You'll also need to line up subcontractors for installations you might not want to tackle, such as the foundation and concrete work, plumbing, electrical hookups, tying into the sewer main, or the installation of a septic system.

> To find out how much you would save with a precut home, contact a manufacturer and get a list of materials for the home you want. Take the list to your favorite lumber yard and compare costs. While you're at it, compare the appliances and hardware offered with the kit to what you can by locally.

Mobile Homes

Forget everything you've ever heard about mobile homes, especially the old Hollywood image of cheap trailer and seedy mobile home parks. New technology and improved materials are making *mobile homes* an attractive housing option again. Built under factory conditions and using quality materials to meet federal and state codes, mobile homes are surprisingly attractive. Once placed on a pad or foundation, seldom are they moved.

Unlike modular homes, mobile homes are built on a steel undercarriage. The wheels are used to transport the sections to the site, where they are slid off the carriage onto a foundation or concrete pad. Typically, you can configure one of these homes with one to three sections, with each section twelve or fourteen feet wide and up to sixty feet in length. With each fourteen-foot section comprising about 840 square feet, you can order a 1,680-square-foot home with two sections, or 2,520 square feet using three sections.

Anchoring and Tie-Down Systems

When considering a mobile home, factor in an anchoring or tie-down system as part of the cost. Contact the local building inspector for regulations regarding anchoring and blocking installation in your community. In some states, tie-downs aren't required, but they should be. In other states, tie-downs are stringently regulated and inspected. The cost of installing additional tie-downs and anchors is small compared to the potential cost of wind damage to a manufactured home that was not properly tied down.

Today, the terms *mobile* and *manufactured home* are almost interchangeable, since both are transported in sections with their own undercarriages and joined at the site. Siding, decks, and interior finish work are usually added at the site.

Factors to Consider Before Buying a Manufactured Home

When buying a new or existing manufactured home, you need to know what the costs are before you start signing the paperwork. And unless you stay on top of the process and ask lots of questions, the costs will creep up until you get a final bill and go into sticker shock.

To prevent these unpleasant surprises, fill out the worksheet in Figure 7-1 as the different costs become available from bids, cost of materials, and labor. If you have to cut corners somewhere to keep costs down, this activity will help you determine where to shave a few dollars.

You'll also need this worksheet to show your banker as you go over the final costs in relation to how much of a loan you qualify for. This also helps you accurately pinpoint what your monthly payments will be.

Putting the Home on Your Own Land

Many buyers purchase a manufactured home to put on their own lot or a piece of land in a semi-rural area, or in a subdivision specifically created for these types of homes. You'll need to do some research; don't assume you can just place the home anywhere you want.

Often, semi-rural or rural areas have lax or no zoning restrictions. You buy a piece of land and find someone to do the site work, without

FIGURE 7-1
What your manufactured home will cost worksheet.

Your Expenses

Total cost of home, including taxes, processing and options	$_____
Cost of building lot	$_____
Building permit and application fees	$_____
Utility hookups: water, power, gas, sewer, etc.	$_____
Foundations, footings or concrete pad	$_____
Basement excavation if you have a full basement	$_____
Concrete flat work: sidewalks, driveway, stairs, etc.	$_____
Excavation and trenching	$_____
Laterals: sewer, water, gas, etc.	$_____
Septic system (best bid of three)	$_____
Well: drilling costs, pump, pressure tank and lines	$_____
Air-conditioning	$_____
Crane and roll on costs	$_____
Misc. site prep costs	$_____

Mortgage Data from Lender

1. Down payment needed	$_____
2. Interest rate	$_____
3. Mortgage loan amount	$_____
4. Monthly payment with taxes and insurance (PITI)	$_____

inspections or red tape. Though this may seem like a good idea, in reality this lack of oversight puts the burden on you to take precautions and do the proper work. Some of the things you need to do are:

- Get a copy of the most recent flood map, if available, and make sure you're not in a flood zone.

- Check with the county for other hazards common to your area, such as earthquake zones, unstable hillsides, seasonal flooding from runoff, or unstable soil conditions on or near your building site; look also into prior land use, such as a dump site, or presence of radon or hazardous materials.

- Look at the surrounding area for possible problems. For instance, is your building site below a canal that can burst and flood your home, or are there earthen dams above you that can do the same, or are you in a brush-choked canyon that can be a fire hazard?

■ Assess the location and transportation routes. Do you have good access to the nearest town, or is there only one way in and out that can be blocked to prevent you from getting out in an emergency?

■ Determine your source of water and method of sewerage disposal. Does your site have a reliable well or city water source? Is there good drainage for a septic system or site for a septic tank, and a contractor reasonably close by who can maintain it?

Remember that semi-rural and rural areas often lack the services that you may be accustomed to having if you have lived in urban or suburban areas, such as garbage pickup, a municipal water supply, or local sewers and water treatment plants.

Buying a Site in a Developed Park

Throughout the country there are attractive manufactured-home developments where you buy the lot and install your mobile home or buy one already installed. In many mobile-home parks a homeowners association similar to those of a condo or townhouse project takes care of the grounds and amenities. In the Southeast and Sunbelt areas of the United States, some mobile-home developments are so fine that they approach the stature of expensive gated communities with high-end amenities such as golf courses, clubhouses, and equestrian trails. If you do buy a lot in a development, find one that's well managed and has a strong homeowners association. This ensures that your investment will increase in value as other home buyers perceive the park as a desirable place to live.

Dan and Ashley found this out the hard way, when they bought a three-bedroom manufactured home and lot in a new subdivision. Impressed by the models and the promise of having their own home and of building equity, they took advantage of the zero down financing offered by their state's housing authority. It wasn't long before all the lots sold and the community was an enjoyable, fun place to live. But after about three years, several owners moved and their homes became rentals. As more people moved, some selling and other keeping their homes as rentals, the development began to lose its charm. Several tenants and owners failed to take care of their yards and values started to drop.

Although the development had a homeowners association, the association lacked the will to pass and enforce rules that keep yards and homes in good condition, so people living there found it more difficult to sell their homes for what they owed on them. In Dan and Ashley's case, they wanted to move to a bigger home, but they had financed the mobile home and their original closing costs with a zero down program. When the mobile home's value didn't go as high as the developers had promised, they ended up owing more than their home was worth. As a result, they had to stay in their mobile home and hope they could eventually pay their mortgage down to a point where they could at least break even when they sold.

> **HOME-BUYING TIP**
>
> Many families start out with a manufactured home and then move up to a larger traditional home later on. If this is your plan, shop carefully for a quality park or lot that will be conducive to selling your home when the time comes. Typically, existing communities with a track record are the best place to start looking.

If, instead of buying a lot in a mobile-home park, you decide to place it on a rented pad, be aware that you become subject to all the reasons you didn't want to be a tenant in the first place:

- The landlord can raise the rent and there's little you can do. Moving a manufactured home to another lot can cost you thousands of dollars.

- You have no control over the lot and the rules the landlord imposes.

- You're financially marking time and not building equity. Why pay a monthly pad fee when you could be building equity in your own lot?

- If the landlord decides to sell the property to, say, a developer who wants to build an apartment complex, you will be required to leave, possibly receiving a below-market offer for your home or having to abandon it completely.

The bottom line is that whether you buy the lot or rent a pad, if the community or area deteriorates, you may not be able to sell. If you've financed the purchase price and loan costs of your mobile home and the values drop, you could end up owing more than the house is worth. This isn't to say that taking advantage of these finance programs is bad;

it's just that you have to be more location conscious and do your homework before committing.

Buying the Manufactured Home

Once you have considered all the factors involved in buying a manufactured home, and determined its site location, it's time to focus on financing the home as well as shopping for the home itself.

Financing Your Purchase

Financing for a manufactured home that is to be mounted permanently on your lot is available through FHA/VA or conventional loans, much the same as a stick-built home. (Note that a home sited on a rental pad may command a higher interest rate and shorter payback time.) Typically, dealers or manufacturers have lenders they work with that can finance the home and the site work, as well as, in some cases, the lot.

It's important to shop around and compare loans. Dealer loan packages are convenient but not always the best deal. In fact, you should be wary whenever a dealer or builder offers extras to go with the financing. Somebody is paying for those extras, and that person is usually you. Instead, you may save money by getting a construction loan through your bank or credit union and a thirty-year loan through a mortgage company. As covered in Chapters 1 to 3 on financing and finding a lender, the only way to know if you're getting the best deal is to talk to several lenders and compare their good faith estimates.

From Chapters 1 and 2, you'll recall that mortgage lending is now primarily risk-based financing, in that your interest rate will depend on:

- Your FICO or credit score, which preferably will be 680 plus.

- Your down payment, which may be 10 percent or more.

- Your assets, and whether you have enough money in reserve for three or more payments.

Obtaining loans for all types of housing is getting tougher, so it's important to maintain a good credit score so you can get the lowest interest rates and the lowest payments. One advantage of a manufactured home that can decrease your loan costs is the shorter length of a construction loan, if you take one out for site work. You pay interest for a week or two versus months on a stick-built home.

For example, suppose you take out a construction loan; the interest clock starts ticking the moment you draw money from the account. As different stages of the home are completed and you pay from the account, the amount you're paying interest on grows. If the home takes six months to build, you end up paying a few thousand dollars in accumulated interest. With a manufactured home, however, the only construction loan you would need would be for the site work, which is usually completed just before the home sections are scheduled to arrive.

Shopping for the Manufactured Home

After you've talked to two or three lenders and gotten their good faith estimates, compare them side by side and select the best deal. Then fill out a loan application and get preapproved for the loan. The lender should give you a preapproval letter for the amount you qualify for. Only then do you go shopping.

Many homebuyers drop into a dealership, fall in love with a certain model, and the salesperson ushers them into the office and signs them up for financing that may not be the best deal. If you have financing lined up before you go shopping, you can compare what the dealer offers to what you've previously lined up and pick the best deal. Also, a mortgage lender that is knowledgeable about manufactured homes can help you narrow down your dealer list. He or she probably knows which dealers have the best reputations.

Many dealers have model homes set up on-site, where you can go through them and get ideas. Others have subdivisions with both model homes and lots for sale. Since you'll have about the same options as a stick-built home, it's a good idea to work up a list of wants and needs so that you can determine what style and floor plan will work best for you. See Chapter 4 for tips on how to do this.

Dealing with Tighter Credit Standards

Owing to tighter credit standards today, FHA/VA and farm home loans in rural areas are likely to be the most economical and buyer-friendly financing available. If a dealer offers financing, look the terms over carefully and read the fine print. If possible, avoid adjustable rate loans because those payments can go up dramatically and you have no control over them. Avoid balloon payment options as well, as these force you to refinance in five to ten years.

Deciding on the right home for you can be confusing and frustrating. What follows are ten tips to help you make your decision, whether you're buying a mobile (manufactured), modular, or kit home:

1. Like most other things, higher quality costs more in the beginning but not in the long run, so go for the best home you can qualify for. A top-of-the-line model or one with upgrades will hold its value better when the time comes to sell.

2. Shop around for a model that doesn't have the mobile home silhouette—in other words, a rectangle with a flat roof. Many manufacturers have models with steeper pitched roofs, porches, and additional sections that create an L shape.

3. Look closely at the furnishings and appliances that often come with the home. Many times they're low-end. Do some comparison shopping, because you might get a better deal elsewhere.

4. To get a good idea of what types of manufactured homes are available, go to regional trade shows, where you can see the latest innovations from many manufacturers at one time. Any dealer can tell when and where these shows are in your area. Modular home dealers sometimes have model homes or past customers who may be willing to show you through their homes.

5. Visit several dealers and price similar homes. Look out for the models loaded with options that you may not want or need—options that are included in the price. Get a breakdown of all the costs so you can tell what items you don't want and may be able to eliminate or trade for something you do want.

6. Check on the dealer as you would a builder. Call the Better Business Bureau and see if there have been any complaints against the dealer. The bank that does the financing is another good source of information. Also talk to several past customers and see if they've had any problems, and if they would use the dealer again.

7. Manufactured and modular home builders will usually quote you the base model price with the cheapest appliances, finishes, and fixtures. The molding, windows, floor coverings, and fixtures often need upgrading. To be realistic, plan on adding $5,000 to $10,000 or more to the base price.

8. If possible, go with more and/or bigger windows that will make your home more livable and add to its value if you re-sell—it's an extra cost you'll recoup. On modular homes, the design staff can easily incorporate custom or larger windows into your home plans.

9. Upgrade the tub and shower stall for a good investment that will help the home keep and increase its value. Also, consider upgrading the fixtures. Bottom-of-the-line faucets and other fixtures lose their shine fast and need replacing after a couple of years.

10. Curb appeal not only gives you pride of ownership but is important in maintaining your home's value. Adding trim in a second color or upgrading the exterior is often worth the extra cost.

It's important to remember that, sooner or later, all homes sport a FOR SALE sign. If you keep that in mind when you buy, selling becomes easier and more profitable when you outgrow the house or get a job transfer.

Recommended Options or Upgrades to Consider

Even after you've purchased your home and have moved in, there are things you can do to increase your home-owning experience and make your manufactured home easier to sell when you decide to move:

- Go with a 4:12 pitch roof (roof angle drops four inches per foot). This gives you the look of a typical home with a pitched roof. You want to avoid the mobile home flat-roof silhouette, when possible. In fact, this is so important that many older stick-built homes with gravel or membrane flat or low-pitch roofs reroof by framing a new pitched roof over the old roof to improve curb appeal.

- Go with vinyl, fiber-cement, or other low-maintenance siding. Avoid cedar or other wood siding, which needs staining or painting every few years.

- Have a minimum of 200 amps electric service so you have enough to run current electronics and appliances.

- Upgrade the range/oven, refrigerator, and dishwasher. Get the make and model numbers from the home dealer or modular manufacturer, and compare with what you can buy elsewhere.

▪ Go with a gas water heater and furnace, if gas is available in your area. It's often cheaper than electric power or propane in most areas.

▪ Invest in upgraded molding packages for protection and resale.

▪ Use heavier six-panel door upgrades.

▪ Go with the best window package you can afford. Bigger and more windows add to the value and your enjoyment of the home.

▪ Upgrade the shower enclosures and fixtures. Better-quality baths last longer and add value. And in the long run they are more economical because they won't have to be replaced as soon.

▪ Before committing to factory air conditioning, compare their price to what you can obtain locally. Even if you don't plan on installing air conditioning, have the factory install the wiring so it can be added later. If the home has central heating, the duct work is likely already installed. Otherwise, that would become an upgrade.

▪ Upgrade the kitchen cabinets. This is an important item that adds to your home's value.

▪ Upgrade the light fixtures and ceiling fans, but check on the prices of factory versus what you can buy locally.

▪ Buy storm doors, which are often available on sale at home-improvement centers for less money, and install them yourself.

▪ Gas- or wood-burning stoves are a good option and add value and comfort to your home.

▪ Add skylights if feasible.

▪ Comparison-shop for furniture or decorating items like blinds and drapes before you buy them from the dealer or factory.

▪ Add inexpensive accessories like towel holders on your own and save money.

▪ Check factory-installed carpet prices; you may be able to save money locally with remnant sales and roll-end discounts.

The bottom line on buying a manufactured home is that, after you have visited a few dealers, it may seem that buying a manufactured home is lot like buying a used car. You have to wade through the gimmicks, canned sales pitches, and hype. Unfortunately, there are few shortcuts. The truth is, you have to do your homework and some comparison shopping to get the best deal. A recommended resource that can help you understand the industry and products is the third edition of Kevin Burnside's book, *Buying a Manufactured Home* (Cycle Publishing, 2008).

Finding a Lot and Obtaining the Necessary Permits

The real estate truism that location is everything is a good guide when you're shopping for a building lot. Location is the key to a home's holding or increasing its value. In fact, it's often better to have a smaller home in a good location than a larger home in a not-so-good location, such as near big-box stores, highway off-ramps, busy streets, bad schools, and so on. However, it's also important to take the long view of the area and factor in what the neighborhood might look like ten or twenty years from now.

The first step in shopping for a lot is to make a list of all the possible sites that are of interest. The more lots you have to choose from, the better. Once you've completed your list, start the process of elimination. The following tips will help you do that:

> **HOME-BUYING TIP**
>
> Before you talk to lot owners, make sure you're pre-approved for purchasing a lot and have construction loans for a house that will fit on the lot. Then, when an owner indicates interest in selling, you can move quickly with your offer.

- Check with the city or county planning authority to see what's planned for the area. If there's a master plan, study it carefully. The secluded lot you love now may have an industrial park next door in ten years, according to their plan.

- Look at the growth patterns for your area of interest. If all indications are that the area will increase in value, that's a plus. Also look for highways, off-ramps, or access roads that are planned for the area.

- Get a copy of any zoning and restrictive covenants (CC&Rs) for the development. Usually, better neighborhoods have more

restrictions on what you can build. Although sometimes annoy-
ing, these restrictions help neighborhoods maintain their value
and character.

■ Check out the cost of utilities. A cheaper lot that costs more to
run the utilities into may not be as good a deal as one that
has them stubbed to the property line. Running utility lines is
expensive and can run up site costs fast.

■ Make sure you line up all your building-site ducks in a row. Get
all the necessary building permits, utilities, impact statements,
and hookup fees nailed down. Then get the site-work subcontractors lined up and lock in their bid prices in writing, if the
dealer who sold you your home doesn't handle that.

Brent and Susan found a great deal on a lot next to a newly completed golf course that the local municipality was selling as surplus
property. A look at the CC&Rs revealed that homes had to be 1,200
square feet or more on the main floor, along with an attached two- or
three-car garage. The restrictions also limited their landscaping options
and required an underground sprinkling system to keep the lawn and
shrubs in good condition.

They planned on putting a modular home on the property, but
their plan fell short by 50 square feet—the minimum size of homes
allowed in the subdivision—and they counted on having a double carport rather than a garage. But they got in touch with the design people
at the factory, and increased the square footage by enlarging two bedrooms and redesigning the carport to create a garage. This change
stretched the loan they qualified for to the limit, but it would create a
better home that would increase in value.

Finding the Right Building Lot for Your Home

The best and easiest way to find a building lot is to contact a Realtor
who works in your area of interest. Many times a Realtor will know of
developers who are selling lots to builders or can check the MLS for
what's available. Another good source is the newspaper classifieds
under "building lots." Yet another approach is to talk with developers
who are subdividing a property into building lots. And if you've ex-
hausted these sources, you'll need to get a bit more aggressive and
drive around your area of interest to see if you can spot a lot that
might work for you.

If you see a vacant lot, note the addresses of the homes on both sides and then check with the county recorder office for who owns the lot. Sometimes homebuilders will buy a double lot when they build and keep one for an investment or for a family member to build on in the future. However, in the ebb and flow of human events, plans and circumstances can change quickly. A vacant lot that's not for sale today may suddenly sport a FOR SALE sign tomorrow.

It doesn't hurt to call the owners of vacant lots and ask if they would consider selling. Sometimes after they have thought it over, you'll get a call from the lot owner that results in a deal. This was the case for Randall and Sharon, when they couldn't find a lot for sale in the area in which they lived. What few lots were available were tied up by a builder for spec or custom home jobs, and the builder wasn't interested in selling.

> **HOME-BUYING TIP**
>
> If you're in no hurry to find a lot, you can create a database of lot owners and contact them every three months by e-mail or letter, letting them know you're interested in their property, should they decide to sell.

As a last resort, Sharon started driving through neighborhoods they liked, looking for vacant lots. She made a list of those that looked interesting and got the names and addresses of the owners from the county recorder's office. It wasn't long before she had a list of eight possibilities. Three of the lot owners lived out of state, and from their addresses on the tax records, Sharon tracked down their phone numbers. She then contacted them to see if any showed interest in selling.

Five of the lot owners showed no interest in selling, but one of the out-of-state owners did express interest. The couple had purchased the lot a few years earlier with plans to build on it, but a job transfer changed their plans and they simply kept the lot as an investment. However, their son was planning on going to college in the fall, so when Sharon indicated an interest in purchasing their lot, they began to think about selling it in order to have more money for his tuition.

Ron and Sharon offered the couple the appraised value for their lot and agreed to split the cost of a certified appraisal. The sellers accepted the offer and the deal closed three weeks later. A proactive approach such as this often works because many owners don't think of selling until someone contacts them and starts the wheels spinning.

Obtaining the Necessary Permits and Paying the Site Fees
If you've hired a general contractor, getting the building permits and estimates for site improvements, and lining up the subcontractors, is

part of the bid. But if you're doing your own paperwork and lining up everything for the factory crew when the home arrives, you'll have to get the building permits yourself.

Typically, you go down to your city's building department and get a building permit or permits, depending on the area. The clerk can walk you through what's needed in your city or county. You get an application packet to fill out and you submit the completed forms along with a set (you may need up to three) of house plans. You also may have to pay a nonrefundable deposit or application fee. Within a week or two (with luck) you get the paperwork back with a list of fees that, in most cases, must be paid before you will be issued a certificate of occupancy (C of O).

The list of fees you will have to pay is usually called the *building fee schedule*. These fees vary from city to city, and range from almost nothing to thousands of dollars. Some of the most common fees are for building, plan check, water connection, utilities connections, water usage, sewer hookup, environmental impact fees, and fees to offset city maintenance costs of roads and improvements. The list sometimes gets long and grim, with all sorts of creatively named fees, before you get to the bottom line. Depending on the area, your building lot along with permits and site fees can run from 50 percent to nearly equal the cost of your home itself.

The Resale Value of Manufactured Homes

Manufactured homes can appreciate nicely and be a good investment. If the site is chosen carefully and the landscaping is attractive, the home can appreciate in value similarly to a stick-built house in a similar neighborhood. However, as mentioned earlier, the condition of your neighbors' homes plays an important role in how well your home maintains its value when you decide to resell.

Typically, entry-level home buyers and retirees buy the majority of manufactured homes. However, their selling strategies can differ, depending on which group you're in and if your home is on rented space or you own the lot.

Resale Values in Entry-Level Subdivisions

If your home is located in a new subdivision that attracts entry-level buyers, chances are that when you're ready to sell and move up, many others who bought at the same time will be selling as well. Buyers who are roughly in the same age group tend to reach the point when they're ready to buy a bigger home at about the same time. This results in a bubble of homes for sale in the area, and this bubble depresses the home values until supply and demand even out. It pays to keep this in mind when you buy in a newer subdivision and plan on selling in four or five years.

Brent and DeAnn had this problem when they bought a three-bedroom home in a new subdivision of manufactured homes. It was an attractive community with great landscaping, a pool, and clubhouse. The homes were similar in price and attracted mainly young first-time home buyers who could afford the low down FHA financing.

The five years Brent and DeAnn lived in the home were great, but as their family and income grew, so did their desire to move to a bigger home closer to work. Three bedrooms were no longer enough with twins on the way. When Brent and DeAnn decided to put their home on the market, about a dozen other FOR SALE signs appeared around the community. Some owners who were under pressure to sell owing to job changes or otherwise had to slash their prices. This created a downward price spiral as Realtors and appraisers priced the homes based on what others had sold for the last few months.

> ### HOME-BUYING TIP
>
> When buying a home you may outgrow and want to sell in a few years, go for the most bedrooms you can afford at the time. A three- or four-bedroom home holds its value and sells better than a two-bedroom model.

Because Brent and DeAnn had put a lot of effort into making their home attractive with good curb appeal, they were able to sell at close to a breakeven price. Had they been willing to stay in their current home for a couple of more years, they could have built up some equity and sold for a profit. But, in their case, they just wanted out so they could move on with their lives, and they were willing to walk away from the closing with no profit on their investment.

Resale Values in Retirement Subdivisions

Communities that cater to retirees are usually more stable than those that attract first-time home buyers, and therefore the homes have greater resale value. They normally don't have a three- to five-year selling bubble that can depress prices, and homeowners in these communities often stay until they move into an assisted living facility, a nursing home, or die. In a stable market, this can result in a relatively even home market with the number of homes for sale roughly equaling the number of buyers. However, in some areas with a high population of seniors, such as in Florida and the Sunbelt, a slow market can create an oversupply that depresses values.

As with any other real estate deal, look at the area sales statistics: list price to sales price and days-on-market before you commit. That super good deal may not be so good if you want to sell and can't.

Resale of Kit and Panel Homes

As with any type of real estate, area is a prime consideration. If you choose the area carefully, your home will maintain or increase in value over the long term. True, a down market will depress home values across the board, but these markets will eventually change and values can go up dramatically in a short time.

Three considerations to keep in mind are:

1. Think "sell" when you buy. Assume that you'll want to move in a few years because of job change or need a bigger home.

2. Keep the loan as low as possible and be wary of adjustable rate mortgages (ARMs).

3. Improve the home with the goal of making curb appeal and improvements that add value.

Seven Steps You Can Take to Make This Chapter Work for You

1. Use the information in this chapter to help you decide what type of manufactured home fits your budget and needs.

2. Complete the Figure 7.1 worksheet, "What Your Home Will Cost," to make sure the totals are close to what the bank will loan you.

3. Speak with a mortgage lender and find out how much home you can afford, then get preapproved for a mortgage and ask the lender to write you a preapproval letter.

4. Before visiting a manufactured home dealer, use the tips in this chapter to get a better sense of what you're looking for.

5. Review the recommended options and upgrades listed in this chapter and decide what you need for your new home now and what you can add later.

6. Before shopping for a building lot, do your homework and make sure you know as much as possible about the area in which you're interested.

7. If you're a first-time homeowner, look for a site that will increase in value and be easy to sell in a few years when your needs change and you want to move into a bigger home.

 C H A P T E R 8

Purchasing Insurance for Your New Home

Your home is one of the most important, and expensive, assets you probably will ever have. Yet for many home buyers, purchasing the insurance to cover their investment is a back-burner consideration. Often, a call from their mortgage lender prior to closing, asking what homeowner insurer will be used, prompts a panicked call to the company that sells them auto insurance or an agency recommended by a friend or relative. In their haste, many home buyers neither know whether they're getting the best insurance deal or the best coverage.

But that situation is changing in a big way. In many areas with a history of high insurance claims, such as Florida, Mississippi and Texas, coverage is difficult or impossible to find and very expensive if you can get it. In these areas you may want to shop for insurance coverage along with qualifying for a mortgage first before going home shopping.

Typically, without homeowners insurance, banks won't make a mortgage loan. Because this coverage is so important, some states are revising their real estate purchase agreements to include a provision stating that offers are subject to the buyer's successfully obtaining a policy.

So what insurance policies does a homebuyer need? In addition to the required basic coverage for liability, fire, and theft, several other types of insurance play a role in a typical real estate closing. These can include earthquake insurance or flood insurance if the home is in a designated flood area, as well as mortgage life insurance, title insurance, and private mortgage insurance, all of which will be discussed in this chapter.

In this chapter you'll learn how to:

- Understand the basics of homeowners insurance.

- Be aware of the different types of homeowners policies available.

- Review the three basic components of homeowners insurance in order to determine whether you have adequate coverage.

- Distinguish between the two types of policies you need if you're buying a condo or co-op, and be aware of the other coverage options you may need.

- Understand the importance of preparing an inventory of your possessions and know how to go about it in the most efficient and effective way.

- Understand why title insurance is so important and what it insures you for.

- Be aware of the additional types of insurance available.

The Basics of Homeowners Insurance

A homeowners policy protects the homeowner if the home is damaged or destroyed in a variety of ways, as stated in the policy. A buyer is required to have homeowners insurance while there is a mortgage balance to be paid off. If you have a single-family home, your mortgage lender requires you to have an HO-3 policy—which offers the broadest coverage of any of the homeowners policies—in force during the entire term of the loan. In fact, homeowners insurance is so important that lenders on many loans require borrowers to make monthly payments into an escrow account to pay the premiums when they come due each year, just as they do real estate taxes. This is to ensure that the bank's investment—your home—is protected against loss.

Typically, a homeowners policy covers the home, its contents, and any liability if someone gets hurt on your property. It also covers water damage from plumbing failures inside the home, but not from damage caused by water from an outside source, such as a flood. For coverage of damage caused by exterior water, you need a separate flood insurance policy sold only by the U.S. government.

For condo, co-op, and townhouse owners, lenders require HO-6 policies, which cover the unit's interior, its contents, and any liability for injuries incurred in the unit. The building's exterior, grounds, and general liability are covered by a master policy that insures the whole complex. Figure 8-1 shows the different types of policies, depending on your situation.

As an example of the necessity of having homeowners insurance, Dale and Janelle found a renovated bungalow in an upscale but older area. They hired a professional inspector who gave the property a good report and their FHA loan closing went smoothly. However, during the move-in, Janelle turned on the tub and another faucet to flush the drains and got distracted for a few minutes, letting the water run. Later, to her horror, she found a foot of water in their finished base-

FIGURE 8-1
Different types of homeowner policies.

Policy Type	What It Covers
HO-1	Bare-bones policy. No longer available in most states.
HO-2 (broad)	Covers most perils. Also available for mobile homes.
HO-3	The most popular policy. Protects from all perils except those excluded in the find print. Typical exclusions are flood, earthquake, and war.
HO-4	Renter's policy. Protects possessions only against the same perils as HO-3.
HO-6	Policy for condo or co-op owners. Covers the same perils as HO-3. A master insurance policy covering the structure is included in your HOA fees.
HO-8	A policy for older homes. Reimburses you for replacement cost minus depreciation. This policy will not reimburse you for the costs of bringing the home up to code.
	Policy Options
Actual cash value	Will replace home and possessions minus deduction for depreciation.
Replacement cost.	Pays the cost of rebuilding /repairing the home and possessions.
Guaranteed or extended replacement costs	Gives you the highest level of protection. Pays whatever it costs to rebuild your home to what it was before the disaster. However, on an older home, you may need an Ordinance or Law rider to pay for any costs to bring home components up to code if the home is dated. This policy may not be available for older homes. Some companies will go only 20–25 percent over policy limits.

ment, as the water had backed up through the floor drain into the laundry room.

A plumber checked out the sewer line to the street and found that tree roots had invaded the sewer pipe and created a partial obstruction. The normal flow of water from the bathtub and a faucet in the sink would probably be too little to cause a problem, but two faucets turned on full force had overloaded the sewer line and caused a backup through the basement floor drain. The result was considerable damage, with the wallboard, carpets, and some furniture soaked. Luckily, Dale and Janelle had bought a good homeowners policy that paid for the damage, less their $500 deductible.

With so many variables that can go wrong in a house, homeowners insurance and even some other insurance options are a necessary investment.

Making Insurance Payments Through Your Mortgage Escrow

A homeowners policy can protect you from the double whammy of having your home damaged or destroyed while having a mortgage to pay off. Your lender, of course, is aware of this, and that's why many of them require you to pay into an escrow account so that, when the policy comes due, the bill can be paid from those funds that have already been collected.

HOME-BUYING TIP

Start shopping around for homeowners insurance right after you get a mortgage preapproval letter. You don't want the lender calling you for a binder ASAP and forcing you to buy insurance without shopping around.

The exception is with conventional mortgages. Most lenders let you take care of the insurance on your own if you have put 20 percent or more down on the purchase. They reason that with that much of your money down, their exposure to loss is minimal. An exception is FHA/VA insured programs, which require a monthly escrow until the loan is paid off.

Typically, a few days before closing, your lender will contact you for the name and contact information of your insurance provider, or ask you to furnish them with a *binder*—a written insurance commitment and price quote. You don't write a check to the insurance company for this coverage; it's charged to you as one of your loan costs when you close.

Texas Insurance

In Texas, insurers can sell three policies: HO-A, HO-B, and HO-C. These are standardized policies with three levels of coverage. HO-A is a barebones policy; HO-B provides replacement cost coverage, and HO-C provides the most comprehensive coverage and, of course, costs the most. Because the prices Texas insurers charge are not regulated, you'll need to shop around for quotes, the same as you would in other states whose insurance rates aren't governed by state agencies. For Texas insurance information, go to www.tdi.state.tx.us.

For example, when you're sitting at the closing table with the settlement statements (HUDs) spread out in front of you, look at the 900 section, "Items Required by Lender to be Paid in Advance" on the second page of the document. You'll see a line worded something similar to "Hazard insurance premium to ABC Insurance." If you follow this line across the page to the first column, you'll see the first year's insurance premium. It can be anywhere from hundreds of dollars to thousands, depending on how expensive insurance coverage is in your area.

This first year's premium is part of your closing costs, but there's more. If the mortgage company is handling your insurance payments, they'll need to set up the escrow account to receive money that you pay into it each month. Your monthly payment will include one-twelfth of the premium, so you'll have enough money in the account a year from now to pay the cost of the insurance.

For example, if your annual insurance bill is $835, it will add about $70 to your monthly mortgage payment. However, to get the escrow fund set up and make sure you'll have $835 in it by next year, the lender charges you two months, or $140, to get the fund established. This charge is also part of your closing costs and is found in section 1000 of the HUD's "Reserves Deposited with Lender," where you'll see a line worded something similar

When the mortgage company pays the homeowners insurance out of your escrow account, many homeowners forget to review the policies every year for any upgrades or changes that are required. It's an out-of-sight, out-of-mind situation. Remember, too, that you can change coverage and/or companies a month or two before renewal date if you are able to find a better deal.

to "Hazard Insurance 2mo(s) @ $70/month." If you follow this line across to the first column, you'll see a charge for $140.

Paying Your Homeowners Insurance on Your Own

Although most conventional loans with a 20 percent or more down payment allow you to pay homeowners insurance and taxes on your own, some lenders give you the option of paying them monthly as part of your loan payment (see above). This means less paperwork for you and you don't have to write big checks as these bills come due.

HOME-BUYING TIP

Insurance companies factor in your credit rating when quoting a price. They've found that, statistically, people who have a poor credit rating are more likely to file a claim. Protecting your credit score will yield you big bucks.

If you elect to handle the insurance on your own, you don't want to forget and let the coverage lapse. If you do, your former insurer will notify the mortgage company and the mortgage company will immediately add *single vendor coverage*, a policy that protects the mortgage company's interest only and is expensive, costing about double what a homeowners policy costs.

Since you get an annual bill from your insurance company, it's a good idea to review your coverage and make any changes before you write that renewal check. Many homeowners go for years without giving their policies a thought, then a disaster strikes and they find that they are covered for only a fraction of their loss. Your insurance agent should be on your speed dial and coverage should be changed or added whenever you:

- Add a liability, such as a trampoline or swimming pool.

- Remodel your home and contractors and subcontractors will be working on it, because if one of them gets hurt on your property, you want to be covered.

- Turn your home into a rental.

- Leave your home vacant while trying to sell it.

- Add to or remodel your home, making changes that increase its value.

- Note that area's home values have increased from the previous year.

Policy Options

Homeowners insurance evolved in the late 1950s, when the insurance industry needed a single comprehensive policy to cover not only the house but also the contents and liability. The result is a standard policy that has two parts: property coverage and personal liability.

General Coverage

The most common policy, *Homeowners 3 (HO-3)*, covers the house and other structures for everything except earthquakes, floods, and other exclusions (the fine print), depending on the policy and insurer. The HO-3 is the policy that most insurers require you carry on your house as a loan condition.

Typically, HO-3 policies cover loss from fire, lightning, windstorms, hurricane wind damage but not from rain or flooding, tornadoes, hail, explosions, vehicles, smoke, theft vandalism, falling objects, and damage from ice, snow, or sleet and freezing pipes. It does not cover flood or water damage from outside sources, earthquakes, neglect, intentional loss, earth movements, power failure, and damage caused by war. Personal liability is also covered if you or your property injures someone.

Before you hire a contractor or subcontractor, get proof that the operator has general liability and workers compensation coverage. If a worker is injured on your property, you could be held liable. Go to www.iii.org and click on "Home," then scroll down to "Homeowner Tips" and click on "Remodeling Your Home."

There is one exclusion that trips up many homeowners who suffer a loss and have older homes. If the building code has changed, increasing the subsequent repair or replacement costs, the homeowner pays the difference.For example, if you have a fire and your home's electrical system is an older sixty amp fuse system, you'll end up picking up the cost to upgrade the electric service and all the other upgrades needed to bring the home into compliance with current codes. That can put you into a catch-22 situation. The local building authority won't let you hook up utilities or occupy the property until it's restored to current code; the insurance company will write you a check for your loss but not the upgrades. That means you write a check for the upgrades or find a friendly lender who will give you a construction loan and then refinance that cost and your mortgage balance into a new loan. Owing to limits on what you can claim from losses on personal possessions, such as furs, jewelry, and hobby collections, you may want to add *supplemental coverage* to your policy to protect high-value or hard-to-replace possessions. For example, if you had a rare stamp collection, you would want to get an appraisal and then supplemental coverage for its value; otherwise, you may not be happy with the insurer's settlement check if a fire destroyed it.

One especially worthwhile supplemental item is coverage for living expenses should your home be destroyed or damaged and you're forced to move out for a while. This insurance covers hotel bills, restaurant meals, and other living expenses incurred during rebuilding. It doesn't take much damage to a home for you to be glad you added this option to your policy.

Replacement Coverage

Most insurance companies offer *replacement cost coverage*. For an additional 10 percent or so, insurers will pay what it costs to replace your home and belongings up to the amount of your coverage. See Figure 8-2.

For example, if your fifty-two-inch LCD TV that cost you $3,600 is damaged in a fire, you'll get the full cost covered. By comparison, under standard coverage you would get the replacement cost minus a steep depreciation curve that's common for electronics. In other words, you would be lucky to get 50 percent, or $1,800, or the TV. If your home burns when it's ten years old and you had a $50,000 tile roof that was under warranty for twenty years, you would get a $25,000 reimbursement for the roof under standard or actual cash value coverage.

If your mortgage balance is about the same as the home's value, you will want to go with *extended coverage,* which guarantees full replacement. Otherwise, if you have a loss, your check from the insurance company may be thousands of dollars less than your mortgage balance. In order to avoid a sticky situation, whereby you have a destroyed home and an insurance company replacement check for less than your mortgage, many mortgage lenders require you to carry the extended coverage upgrade.

The next step up in coverage is *extended replacement*. You insure the home for the appraised value, and the policy will pay up to 125 percent of that amount to cover unforeseen costs. Even better is *guaranteed replacement,* which doesn't have a preset limit. However, be-

	FIGURE 8-2					
	What your policy covers and doesn't cover.					

Possible Claim Claim	Basic HO-1	Broad HO-2	Special HO-3	Renters HO-4	Condo HO-6	Older Home HO-8
Fire or lightning	Yes	Yes	Yes	Yes	Yes	Yes
Windstorm or hail	Yes	Yes	Yes	Yes	Yes	Yes
Explosion	Yes	Yes	Yes	Yes	Yes	Yes
Riot or civil disturbance	Yes	Yes	Yes	Yes	Yes	Yes
Damage by aircraft	Yes	Yes	Yes	Yes	Yes	Yes
Damage by vehicles	Yes	Yes	Yes	Yes	Yes	Yes
Smoke damage	Yes	Yes	Yes	Yes	Yes	Yes
Vandalism	Yes	Yes	Yes	Yes	Yes	Yes
Theft	Yes	Yes	Yes	Yes	Yes	Yes
Volcanic eruption	Yes	Yes	Yes	Yes	Yes	Yes
Damage from snow, ice, or sleet	No	Yes	Yes	Yes	Yes	No
Falling objects	No	Yes	Yes	Yes	Yes	No
Interior water damage from household plumbing, heat/AC, or appliances	No	Yes	Yes	Yes	Yes	No
Pipes or appliances freezing	No	Yes	Yes	Yes	Yes	No
Electrical overload and damage to wiring.	No	Yes	Yes	Yes	Yes	No

Note: Additional and specific perils can be added to your policy such as earthquake, mudslides, and extra coverage for valuables.

cause of big losses in recent years, many insurance companies have dropped this latter policy. You may have to shop around to find it, but it's definitely worth considering.

One important caveat in insurance shopping is that you not base your assumption as to what a policy is from its label. For instance, "guaranteed replacement" can mean different things with different companies. Although you would assume "guaranteed" means that if the cost of rebuilding a home is higher than the policy amount, you would still be covered, that's not always true. The only way to tell what you're getting is to read the fine print. If you don't understand the legalese, seek out someone who does before you commit.

If you're buying an older home, chances are that some of the wiring, plumbing, heating/cooling systems, and structure may no longer meet newer building codes. As mentioned earlier, should fire damage your home, the insurer is required to replace what you had, but not what's required to comply with current codes in order to rebuild. The cost to bring the house up to current building codes is up to you. You can solve this potentially expensive problem by getting *ordinance and law coverage*, which is a rider to your homeowners policy that applies to the costs of upgrading your home to meet existing building codes. Keep in mind that this rider will pick up the tab only for bringing the damaged part of the house up to code. It will not pay for bringing the undamaged part of the structure up to code. In other words, you could be better off if the house burned completely down rather than be partially damaged.

HOME-BUYING TIP

When you buy an older home, always get a professional home inspection and ask the inspector to give you a list of what items or conditions don't meet local building codes.

Rick and Andrea found out about this little wrinkle in homeowners insurance when they bought a 1940s brick bungalow with the dream of restoring it. They loved the wood floors and trim, the brick construction, and the wide front porch. Still wired with old-style wiring through a thirty-amp fuse box, the home needed an electrical upgrade as a first priority. But Rick and Andrea, in their enthusiasm, focused on stripping and sanding the floors, restoring the wood trim, and dealing with interior decorating projects.

Sometime during the second week of their restoration efforts, debris got into an electrical receptacle because the outlet face plates had been removed. The old wiring sparked and ignited partially stripped wallpaper and engulfed the wall in flames. Fortunately, the fire department reacted quickly and damage was limited to the front part of the house. After getting together with the insurance adjuster and their agent, the couple was shocked to learn that it would cost them more than $12,000 out of their pocket to restore the house to the condition where they could move back in. Their insurance policy would pay to bring it up to "as was" condition but would not pay to bring it up to code. And the owners could not get a building permit unless the house incorporated the building code upgrades.

Three important lessons learned from this are:

1. If you're buying an older home, make sure the home inspector includes in his or her report a list of items that don't meet current building codes. Wiring and heating systems are often at the top of the list for potential problems.

2. Triage the list of improvements you plan on doing, with bringing the home up to code at the top of the list. Wiring, plumbing, and heating systems should be a priority, because problems here can end up costing you big bucks.

3. Keep all the contracts, material receipts, and other paperwork in a safe place so you can document any improvements you have made. Also, photos and video records can be worth thousands of dollars to you in case of disaster and you need to prove the work you've done.

The Importance of a Home Inventory

It's amazing how much expensive stuff we accumulate, and if there's a flood or fire, many homeowners would have a hard time verifying what they have and its value to an adjuster. Having an up-to-date home inventory will help you get your insurance claim settled faster and verify losses for your tax returns. As a home buyer, a great time to inventory your stuff and start an inventory record system is when you move in and unpack in your new home. With a digital camera or video recorder you can create a record and store it on a CD or USB memory device.

One couple, Rocky and Lisa, used their video recorder to document their possessions when they moved into their new home during the first week of December. Unfortunately, three days after Christmas their home caught fire from a cracked flue in their wood-burning stove that allowed hot gases to ignite the ceiling. The fire totally destroyed the home. The camera, with the video disk still in it, was one of the few items they saved. This video record saved Rocky and Lisa a lot of problems and tens of thousands of dollars. There's no way they could have remembered or proved everything they lost in the fire without it.

To create your own inventory, start by making a list on paper of your possessions, describing each item and noting where you bought it. Include the make, model, and serial number. Using a file folder is helpful for keeping sales receipts, purchase contracts, and appraisals. Most digital cameras now have the resolution to snap pictures of the labels on appliances, electronic equipment, and other large items. As you're moving into your new home, take pictures of all your valuable items, along with the tags showing the serial and model numbers. You can store enough digital photos to give you a complete inventory on an inexpensive two- to four-gigabyte secure digital (SD) card or a USB flash drive.

As you begin to document the items in your home, keep the following in mind:

- As you inventory items such as jewelry, art work, or rare collectibles, which may have increased in value since you got them, make a separate list to run past your insurance agent. You may have to update your coverage if they have increased in value.

- Take pictures of the entire room first and then narrow the shots down to individual items. Also photograph labels, tags, or anything that helps identify each item and its value.

- If you have a video recorder, walk through your home and describe the contents as you record. Also tape the outside of the home and note any upgrades you've done.

Regardless of how you compile an inventory record, keep it (or a duplicate) in a safe place off-site, in a safe deposit box or at a friend or relative's house or at your office. When you make a significant purchase, update the information while it's still fresh in your mind. If you ever have a loss, hand a copy of your USB or CD to the adjuster to document your claim and you will likely receive a faster and much bigger insurance check.

The Three Components of a Homeowners Policy

Before you settle on a homeowners policy, look at the three basic policy components—structure, personal property, and liability—to see if

---

Building Codes and Permits

Your city or county building codes handle fire or life-safety issues. In general, a building permit is required when you remodel or add to your home. A building inspector comes by at different stages of the work to make sure your improvements conform to the local building codes. Things can get sticky if you have made improvements that required a permit and you didn't get one. The insurance company can void its coverage if you have a fire or other problem.

Renovation without a permit can come back to haunt you when you sell and the mortgage lender asks for proof of compliance. Also, insurance companies are now rating states and cities on how well they enforce their building codes, and your insurance costs may depend on that rating. Check out www.codecheck.com for more information.

you have enough protection. Even if you aren't buying on the San Andreas fault or you don't collect antique firearms, you'll probably need to get additional coverage for peace of mind.

Structure

Many common problems that plague homeowners from time to time, such as earthquakes, floods, failed sump pumps, and backed-up sewers, aren't covered in basic policies. To get this additional coverage, you need to ask your agent to add an *endorsement*, or rider, to your policy. The extra cost of these riders is often more than worth it if you have a problem.

The higher a specific risk is for your area, the more important it is to add this coverage. For instance, coverage for sewer clogs is usually less than $100 a year, but it's a must, especially for older homes. A sewer backup is often expensive because it requires special cleanup procedures caused by the contamination. This is why Dale and Janelle had to call in a disaster cleanup company to handle their sewer backup problem mentioned at the start of the chapter. Removing raw sewer contamination added a couple of thousand dollars to their cleanup costs.

Personal Property

All HO-3 policies include coverage for the contents of your house, but often the amount isn't enough. Basic plans commonly pay 50 to 70 percent of the policy amount. For example, a $175,000 policy would likely give you anywhere from $87,000 to $122,000 for the contents. This may sound like a lot, but when you go through your home and total up everything you've got, it'll shock you. The value adds up fast when you total furniture, electronics, wardrobes, power tools, a stamp collection, and so on. If you have expensive items such gun or art collections, antiques, jewelry, and computer equipment, you may want to consider extra coverage based on their actual value.

Liability

Most policies have a $100,000 minimum liability that protects you in case somone is injured on your property. Whether that's enough depends on how much you have to lose if someone sues you. You can pay for more protection or add an umbrella policy that cover you for incidents away from home also.

For a home business office where clients come to you, your liability can skyrocket. Adding a $1 million umbrella policy for about $200 a year makes good sense.

Condo and Co-op Insurance

When you buy a condo or co-op, you'll likely pay for two policies. The homeowners association or co-op board buys a master policy that covers the common areas such as roof, basement, elevator, boiler, walkways, and infrastructure for liability and physical damage. The cost of this coverage is passed along to you as part of your monthly HOA fee or co-op maintenance fee.

A second policy, HO-6, is what you buy for insuring your personal possessions and any interior improvements you made to your unit. It also covers you for fire, theft, and other losses listed in your policy, as well as for liability and living expenses if you are forced from your unit because of an insured loss.

To insure your unit adequately, it's important to know what structural parts of your home are covered by the condo/co-op association policy and what aren't. Read the association's bylaws and/or get a copy of the policy. If you have questions, talk to a member of the association board or an insurance professional. For example, some associations insure the individual units as they were originally built, including the fixtures. In this case, the owner is responsible only for alterations to the original structure. In other words, if you remodel the kitchen or a bath, you are responsible for insuring those upgrades. Sometimes this includes not only improvements you make but also those made by previous owners. In other cases, the association is responsible only for insuring the bare walls, floors, and ceiling. The owner insures everything else.

Other coverage options you may be able to get depending on the area, association, or board are:

- *Unit assessment*, which reimburses your for your share of an assessment charged to all owners as a result of a covered loss. For instance, if fire damages the lobby, all the unit owners would equally share the repair costs, and if you have this coverage you wouldn't have to write a check.

- *Water backup*, which covers you from having to pay your share of the repair costs if sewers or drains back up and damage the property.

- ■ *Umbrella liability*, which is an inexpensive way to get more liability protection and broader coverage than included in a standard condo/co-op policy, but could give you more coverage for insuring rare art or stamp collections, etc.

- ■ *Flood or earthquake*, which if you live in an area prone to these disasters you'll need to buy. Note that these policies are separate. Flood coverage is available only from the federal government and is covered later in this chapter.

- ■ *Floater or endorsement*, which you should consider if you are the owner of expensive jewelry, furs, collectibles, or anything else that would be expensive to lose, because limits on standard policies are only a few thousand dollars.

When you're buying insurance, it's important to find an agent or company that specializes in condominiums or co-ops. They generally know what you need and may already be familiar with the community you're considering buying into. And when shopping for insurance, check with the insurer that underwrites coverage on the complex you're considering buying in—you may get a discount. Also get at least three quotes, since HO-6 costs can vary considerably.

Picking an Insurance Company and Getting the Best Deal

Many condo or co-op buyers don't take the time to shop for the best insurance deal. . The following are four things to look for when shopping for an HO-6 (condo or co-op) policy.

1. *Price.* Insurance policies and prices vary greatly from one company to another, so it definitely pays to shop around. Get at least three price quotes from different companies. Also, check with your state insurance department because it may publish a guide that shows what insurers charge in different parts of the state. Also, find out if you get a discount by going with the same company that has your HOA's master policy.

2. *Insurer stability.* It doesn't do you a lot of good if, when you submit the claim, you find the insurance company is bankrupt and can't pay. Do some homework and check with your state's insurance department for complaints and other information on insurers in your area.

3. *Service.* The insurance company and its representatives should answer your questions and handle claims fairly, efficiently, and

quickly. You can get a feel for this by talking to other customers who have used a particular company or agent. If you feel you're getting a run-around when you ask questions, find another company. It's important to find an agent who will take the time to look at your situation and tailor a policy to fit your needs.

4. *Availability.* Whether you buy from a local agent, directly from the company, or through the Internet, you should be able to contact the company or agent easily. If you can't, consider getting another company. Fast and easy claim service is one of the basic things you're paying for.

The Cost of a Homeowners Policy

Some of the factors that an insurance company uses to determine the cost of your premium on the homeowners insurance include the following:

- The square footage of the house and any additional structures.
- Building costs in your area.
- Your home's construction, materials, and features.
- The amount of crime in your neighborhood.
- The likelihood of damage from natural disasters such as earthquakes, hurricanes, hail, etc. (Keep in mind that where you live is a major component of your insurance costs.).
- The proximity of your home to a fire hydrant, source of water, and a fire station.
- Whether your community has a professional or volunteer fire service, as well as any other factors that can affect the time it takes to arrive and put out fires.
- Your home's current plumbing, heating, and electrical system.
- Your credit rating and claim history.

Get the best deal on your homeowners insurance you can. As mentioned earlier, compare quotes from different types of insurance companies. Some sell through their own agencies with the same name as the insurance company. Others sell through independent agents who offer policies from several different companies. You'll also find insurers who don't use agents and sell directly to consumers over the phone or through the Internet.

To save money, consider going with a higher deductible. The deductible is the amount of money you have to pay toward a loss before your insurance kicks in. The higher your deductible, the more money you can usually save on premiums. For instance, a $500 deductible may be the most common for a certain policy, but if you elect to increase that to $1,000 or $1,500, ask the agent how much that would save you. Sometimes the higher deductible is worth it, other times it isn't. And sometimes higher deductibles come with the territory. Buying a home on the Gulf Coast, in California's quake and fire area, or other problem-prone regions will certainly cost you a much larger deductible before coverage kicks in. Also, look into the possibility of making your home more disaster resistant. Find out from your insurance agent what steps you can take that will lower your premiums. Adding storm shutters or shatterproof glass, reinforcing the roof, and going with higher fire-rated shingles are some typical examples. Likewise, older homes can be retrofitted to make them better able to withstand earthquakes, floods, and wind damage. Consider modernizing the heating, plumbing, and electrical systems to reduce the risk of fire and water damage.

> When you shop for homeowners insurance, remember that you're insuring the home and not the land. You'll need to subtract the land value from the home's appraisal. Insurance agents should point this out, but many times they don't because it increases your premium and their profits.

You may also get a 5 to 15 percent discount when you buy your homeowners policy from the same company as handles your auto insurance. However, make certain this combined price is lower than buying separate coverage from different companies. Similarly, if applicable, check out senior citizen discounts, group coverage through your employer, and professional discounts. Some companies even give you a loyalty discount if you stay with them for so may years.

Other Types of Homeowners Insurance

In addition to the standard homeowner's policies, you may live in an area that has some additional or unusual perils, such as earthquakes, floods, wind, or fire. As a homeowner, it's up to you to assess your situation and discuss with your insurance agent what additional coverage you may want and is prudent for your area. Coverage and deductibles can vary from area to area depending on the potential for loss.

Earthquake Insurance

Standard homeowners, renters, and business insurance policies do not cover damage from earthquakes. However, coverage is available with an endorsement or as a separate policy through most companies. Unlike flood insurance, earthquake coverage is available from private insurance companies. California, however, has coverage available from the California Earthquake Authority (CEA).

Deductibles for earthquake insurance are most often 2 to 20 percent of a structure's replacement value rather than a set amount. For example, if it takes $250,000 to rebuild a home with a 2 percent deductible, you would be responsible for $5,000. Homeowners in high-risk states such as Washington, Nevada, and Utah face deductibles of 10 to 20 percent.

Premiums differ widely by location, insurer, and the type of structure. Generally, older buildings cost more to insure than newer ones. Wood frame structures have lower rates than brick buildings because they tend to better withstand quake stresses.

The cost of earthquake insurance is calculated on a per $1,000 basis. For instance, a frame house in the Pacific Northwest might cost between $1 to $3 dollars per $1,000, while on the East Coast it may cost less than fifty cents per $1,000.

HOME-BUYING TIP

In one case, a homeowner experienced a damaging flood when a new subdivision going in nearby rechanneled water from a heavy rainstorm. Flood water can damage homes from countless unsuspected sources. Flood insurance is often a cheap investment.

Flood Insurance

Homeowners policies don't cover flooding or water damage incurred from a source outside the structure. You can only get flood coverage from the federal government's National Flood Insurance Program (NFIP). It boils down to, if you don't have an NFIP policy, you don't have flood coverage.

Although you may live outside a Special Flood Hazard Area (SFHA) boundary—also called one-in-100 years flood elevation—the low cost of a NFIP policy may still be a good investment. Storm drains overflow and flood adjacent areas, canals break, and new developments may channel water to where it's never gone before, including your basement. In fact, according to NFIP figures, 25 percent of the over 600,000 claims paid out in the last three decades were to people outside flood zones, in low to moderate risk areas.

To find out if your home sits in a flood zone, contact your local building or planning department and ask to see the flood insurance rate map published by FEMA. If your zone designation begins with an A or V, you're in a flood plain. That means to obtain a mortgage, you'll need to add a flood insurance policy to your homeowners coverage. You can buy flood insurance in any community that has adopted a flood plain management program. Currently about 18,000 of the nation's 22,000 cities, towns, and counties have complied.

> For a wealth of information about flood insurance, go to www.floodsmart.gov/floodsmart. You can get rate data and a list of insurance agencies near you who sell NFIP policies.

Average yearly cost of flood insurance in high-risk areas for contents and dwelling can be as much as several thousand dollars a year depending on your home's value and location. In low or moderate risk areas, costs start at $119 a year. Coverage tops out at $250,000, with an additional $100,000 for contents. Sandbagging, pumping, and other preventive costs are also included. You can buy flood policies through local insurance agents, or the company that covers your homeowners policy can usually add this coverage.

Mortgage Life Insurance

Many people confuse mortgage life insurance with private mortgage insurance, or PMI. As you recall from Chapter 1, PMI is an insurance policy that mortgage lenders require on loans with less than 20 percent down to protect them from loss should the owner default.

Mortgage insurance policies can protect you should you become sick or disabled and be unable to make your mortgage payments. They can also pay off your mortgage if you die. Within a few days of closing on your mortgage, you'll likely get offers and brochures from your mortgage company or affiliates offering different types of mortgage insurance. These polices offer quite a few options and varying deductibles.

If this type of protection gives you a better night's sleep, get with your insurance agent and find out the cost of a policy that fits your situation. However, many financial experts question whether these polices are the best way to go. They maintain that for the cost, a term policy added to disability insurance would be cheaper. The best way to find out what's best for you is to compare quotes from several insurers, including the company that has your homeowners policy. Rates vary widely depending on age, area, and mortgage amount.

HOME-BUYING TIP

Before you commit to a mortgage insurance plan, check with your insurance agent to find out what a standard term policy in the amount of your mortgage would cost you. It may be cheaper than a decreasing term policy, which essentially starts at the value or your mortgage and decreases as you pay it off.

As for insurance that only pays off the mortgage if you die, you have two ways to go. One is a policy often called *decreasing term insurance*, where the coverage starts with your mortgage amount and the payoff decreases as the mortgage is paid off. However, many premium payments don't keep pace with the declining mortgage balance. The other option is a standard term life insurance policy. Many financial experts say that a standard term policy is not only cheaper but also has more flexibility. For example, mortgage insurance would pay off the loan balance automatically if you were to die; a regular term policy would pay the survivors. If the survivors didn't want to pay off the mortgage, they wouldn't have to.

The best way to shop for this type of coverage is to get quotes from several companies and compare the numbers and benefits. Start with your homeowner insurer; they may give you a multiple policy discount.

Title Insurance

In most states, home sellers are required to give you a title insurance policy that guarantees you're getting a good and clear title with no problems to the home you're buying. If title problems such as the forging of a deed, a lien from a divorce, a bankruptcy, or a boundary dispute anywhere along the chain of past homeowners pop up, the title company steps in and does whatever is necessary to take care of it. Your title insurance policy is good for as long as you own the home and, when you sell, you'll buy a policy for the new owners.

The purpose of a title company is threefold:

1. A title company researches the title history of the house you're buying and sells you the title insurance policy that covers you and the mortgage lender so they will make you a loan to buy the home.

2. In some states, the title company also handles and disburses escrow funds on behalf of the sellers, buyers, and mortgage companies.

3. In those states that don't require an attorney to close real estate transactions, title companies do the closings.

In the case of the third purpose, above, at closing, both buyers and sellers pay for title insurance, for different reasons. On the seller's side, a title insurance policy insures that the buyer has a good title. It's charged to the seller on the closing statements, or HUDs, and you'll find this charge in the 1100 section in the column labeled "Paid from Seller's Funds at Settlement." However, if the buyer is taking out a mortgage, the lender wants an *endorsement or secondary policy,* protecting the lender, too, in case title problems arise in the future. In this situation, the buyer pays for this cost, and it, too, is found in the 1100 section in the "Paid From Borrower's Funds at Settlement" column.

Usually, title insurance sits quietly in the background, forgotten by everyone, until a problem suddenly leaps out of nowhere and complicates everyone's life. Then it's a panic to find the title policy and what number to call.

Chuck and Kristen found out about title insurance when they thought they had bought a home on a half-acre along a river. What the seller didn't tell them was that the county had bought an easement (the right to use the strip of land) along the river for a parkway a few months previously. This reduced the back property line by thirty feet, and somehow the title search missed the easement.

> ### HOME-BUYING TIP
>
> A standard title insurance policy that most sellers offer gives you the minimum coverage in most states. As a homebuyer you want to put in your offer that the sellers furnish an American Land Title Association (ALTA) homeowner's policy or one with extended coverage that protects you from mechanics' liens, zoning issues, building permit violations, and encroachment of improvements. These policies cost about 10 percent more, but are well worth it.

Title Insurance Costs

Title insurance costs vary from state to state. Some states set the rates, others require the insurers to file their rates with a state agency, while still others have no regulation. In Iowa, home buyers purchase a title-warranty certificate from the Iowa Finance Authority. You get the same coverage as from a title company, but at a fraction of the cost. Ask your Realtor or mortgage lender what the norm is in your state.

When the owners were landscaping their backyard, a county parks employee came by to stake out the jogging trail, and told them they were encroaching on the future parkway. Understandably, the new homeowners were upset and they called their title company. Obviously, the title company made a mistake and the owners ended up with a fair settlement.

Typically, title insurance covers problems such as:

■ Forgery and impersonation.

■ Lack of competency, capacity, or legal authority of a party.

■ Deed not joined in by a necessary party, such as co-owner, heir, spouse, corporate officer, or business partner.

■ Undisclosed (recorded) prior mortgage, lien, easement, or use restriction.

■ Erroneous or inadequate legal descriptions.

■ Lack of right of access.

■ Deed not properly recorded.

■ Unrecorded matters such as adverse possession or prescriptive easement.

■ Erroneous or inadequate legal descriptions.

■ Deed to land with buildings encroaching on land of another.

■ Incorrect survey and location and dimensions of insured land.

■ Unrecorded mechanic's and estate tax liens.

- Preexisting violations of subdivision laws, zoning ordinances, or CC&Rs.

- Construction of improvement by a neighbor onto insured land.

As you can see, these are some heavy-duty problems that can ruin your day if they pop up unexpectedly.In one interesting example, Jack and Carolyn bought an older home in a small town, and the tax notice described the property dimensions as 110 feet by 140 feet. For over eighty years, everyone accepted those lot dimensions as indicated on the town plan. When they decided to build a fence and measured 110 feet from the lot's east corner, they found the 110-foot mark put them seven feet into their neighbors' front room. A messy situation.

Jack and Carolyn contacted the company that insured their title, which sent out a surveyor to check the property corners. As it turned out, the old town survey had a few problems. All the lot lines along the street had to be readjusted on the plan and new property descriptions worked up and recorded in the county recorder's office. It turned into a several thousand dollar project that the title insurance covered.

for more information on title insurance and rates, check out:

www.stewart.com

www.firstam.com

www.ifahome.com (in Iowa)

Private Mortgage Insurance

In addition to homeowners insurance and title insurance, the third important insurance product most homebuyers need is *private mortgage insurance* (PMI). As discussed in Chapter 2, this is a policy that protects the mortgage company from a buyer's defaulting on a mortgage. Were it not for this type of insurance, investors wouldn't invest the dollars needed for lenders to make low down-payment loans. Private mortgage insurers are usually separate companies from mortgage lenders and not a government agency.

PMI companies are the big elephants in the room during your application process. If they refuse to insure your transaction, the mortgage company won't make the loan and you get a denial letter.

If you put less than 20 percent down, you become a PMI customer and the cost is factored into your closing costs and monthly payment. The monthly premium is calculated on a sliding scale that depends on your down payment and credit score. For example, a $225,000 mortgage with 5 percent down might have a .70 percent monthly PMI premium, or $131.25. With 10 percent down, the PMI premium could drop to .50 percent or $93.75.

The PMI coverage is supposed to drop off when the loan is paid down 20 percent. But recently, with lower interest rates, many home-owners refinance when they can show they have 20 percent equity. If home values are going up, that can happen quickly. Also, on FHA-insured loans, the PMI doesn't drop off, so the strategy is to get into the house with an FHA loan and then refinance to a conventional 80 percent or less as soon as possible.

So how do you prove you have at least 20 percent equity? If you refinance, the appraiser's value is the magic number. But if you wait until you pay down the mortgage balance to 20 percent or more equity, it'll take you a long time. For instance, if you have a $225,000 loan at 6 percent, your monthly principal and interest payment is $1,348.99. To pay down the mortgage by 20 percent ($45,000) to $180,000 giving you an 80 percent balance, would take you eleven and a half years. If your PMI payment is $93.75 a month, that's $12,937.50 you would pay over eleven and a half years. So, it's in your best interests to either pay down the loan balance as quickly as you can or refinance as soon as possible.

Six Steps You Can Take to Make This Chapter Work for You

1. As soon as you get a mortgage preapproval letter, shop for and compare homeowner insurance plans, rates, and deductions.

2. Read your policies carefully so you know what is covered and what isn't.

3. If you're buying an older home, find out what components don't meet code. If the inspector finds problems, discuss your insurance options with your agent.

4. Decide if you need to add earthquake or flood insurance.

5. When moving into your new home, photo or video the house (inside and out) and your possessions in case you have to file a claim. Keep a copy in a safe place off site.

6. Discuss with your insurance agent if a mortgage insurance plan that insures you in case you can't make the payments or die is right for you.

■   ■   ■

After insurance, taxes are a big concern for home buyers. The next chapter explains how property and other taxes work.

Understanding the Tax Advantages and Implications of Home Ownership

One of the big reasons for buying a home is to gain the tax breaks that come with home ownership in the United States. Uncle Sam helps you pay your mortgage by allowing you to deduct from your income tax each year the interest on your loan and your annual property taxes. This savings even makes it possible for you to afford a bigger home than you could otherwise. Couple that incentive with an asset that increases in value (although a home's value can go down in the short term) over time and provides you a place to live and enjoy. Then add to that a shelter for $250,000 (for singles) or $500,000 (for couples) against any capital gains tax you might owe when you sell the house, and the advantages are hard to ignore.

Some people who prefer to rent feel that they are escaping having to pay property taxes. Actually, they aren't escaping them because the landlord includes them in the rent. If the building is reassessed and the taxes increase, the rent goes up either the following month or when the lease is next renewed. In this sense, landlords don't pay taxes, their tenants do—and the landlords still get the tax breaks. Now, that's a sweet deal for the landlord.

In addition to property taxes and mortgage interest, there are other tax advantages in buying and owning your own home, including the possibility of setting up a home office, improving your house to increase its value, and turning your home into an income-producing rental. There's a lot of exciting information in this chapter that can directly affect your checkbook balance.

In this chapter you'll learn how to:

- Tap your IRA or 401(k) for a penalty-free down payment on a home

- Deduct mortgage interest payments

- Deduct property taxes

- Take advantage of tax breaks by working from home

- Take advantage of tax breaks by owning rental property

- Protest your property taxes if you feel they are too high

- Take advantage of tax-deferred 1031 exchanges

The Tax Advantages of Buying and Owning Your Own Home

To get an idea of exactly how much you would save by buying a home, as compared to renting it, let's assume that a renter and a homeowner both make $60,000 a year. Now, suppose the renter pays $1,000 per month in rent and gets no tax breaks, and the homeowner is paying off a $140,000 loan with $1,100 a month payments. Real estate taxes are $1,500 and the mortgage interest paid that taxable year totals $9,756.

To keep it simple, assume that both the tenant and the homeowner are in the 25 percent income bracket. They both owe Uncle Sam (.25 x $60,000), or $15,000 in taxes. However, the homeowner can deduct $9,756 in interest, plus the $1,500 in property taxes, totaling $11,256. Subtracting that from the $60,000 income leaves $48,744. Multiply that adjusted income figure by a .25 tax bracket results in a tax bill of $12,186. That's a savings of $2,814, or $234 a month.

Effectively, the homeowner's after-tax monthly house payment ends up around $865, and after 360 payments he gets to keep the house, which has appreciated significantly. The renter, on the other hand, ends up with a stack of 360 rent receipts and a thank-you from the landlord for paying off his mortgage and giving him a tax break, too. Your tax situation may be a little different, but a useful rule-of-thumb is that you will save 15 to 20 percent of your monthly mortgage payment owing to tax breaks. However, speak with a tax professional to see exactly what you'll save and what mortgage payment option works best for you.

There are other advantages to owning a home, also.

Buying a Home Using Your 401(k) or IRA

You can tap into tax-deferred investment accounts with no penalty (for you or for family members) in order to come up with a down payment. Normally, if you withdraw funds from your 401(k) or IRA you would incur a tax penalty. But to help people buy a home, Congress—recognizing that one of the most difficult steps in purchasing a home is coming up with a down payment—provided an exception. Home buyers can now tap their retirement accounts without triggering stiff tax consequences.

One of the most flexible options allows a couple to jointly borrow up to 50 percent or $100,000, whichever is less, from their individual retirement accounts. They can do this tax- and penalty-free as long as the money is paid back. And you can use the loan not only for buying a home but also for home improvements and other related projects. If you use the funds to buy a primary residence, the payback is extended to ten years.

Even better, your loan from a 401(k) doesn't affect your loan-qualifying ratios. For instance, if you borrow $12,000 for a down payment, a lender normally would factor in the payments to determine how much home you can qualify for. But if the down payment loan comes from your 401(k), it doesn't affect your debt-to-income ratios.

You can also tap your IRA for up to $10,000 without penalty to help family members buy their first home, providing it's your first time using the home buyer

> **HOME-BUYING TIP**
>
> A great way for parents to help their kids buy a home is for the parents to borrow from their IRA. The loan is penalty free and the money can be a gift or loan, with payments spread over ten years.

penalty exclusion. For example, Eric and Amanda tapped their IRA when they helped their daughter buy her first home. Eric, a self-employed contractor, and Amanda, a legal secretary, together had a sizable IRA they could borrow from. When some past clients offered Eric a great deal on a home involved in an estate sale, he moved quickly by borrowing $10,000 from their IRA. It was a big convenience because he didn't have to tap into his business credit lines or qualify for a home equity loan.

Before you borrow from your IRA or 401(k) account, however, check with a tax professional to make sure you qualify for the exclusions.

Two types of tax breaks available to homeowners are credits and deductions. A *credit* allows you to deduct the amount directly from taxes owed. If you owe $3,000 in taxes and have a tax credit of $1,000, you would subtract it and write the government a check for $2,000.

A *deduction* allows you to enter a dollar amount in the appropriate schedule when calculating your taxes. For instance, let say you claim $9,600 for mortgage interest when itemizing your expenses on IRS Form 1040, Schedule A. You don't get a dollar-for-dollar return as you would a credit, but it and other deductions lower your taxable income and, as a result, you end up paying less tax. For more information, see www.irs.gov.

Mortgage Interest and Other Homeowner Deductions

Most often, homeowners are able to deduct the mortgage interest they have paid in the tax year claimed. This reduces their tax bills considerably. It's not a dollar-for-dollar reduction, but for most people it translates to a 10 to 25 percent savings. However, you must itemize these deductions on Schedule A, Form 1040, and not take the standard deduction, as many first-time homeowners did when they were tenants. See IRS publication 530.

Specifically, you can deduct the following mortgage interest and other lending-related homeowner costs.

- Interest on mortgages or loans secured by your home, up to $1 million.

- Interest on home equity or second mortgages and other loans secured by your home loans, up to $100,000.

- Points (pre-paid mortgage interest) you paid to buy down your interest rate.

- Private mortgage insurance (PMI) costs.

In addition, you can deduct some moving expenses, if you move closer to your job. The list of what you can and can't deduct regarding moving expenses is fairly involved, so check IRS Publication

521 and Form 3903 to total your deductions. You can download both of these in PDF format at www.irs.gov.

Other major tax deductions available to homeowners are property taxes, expenses incurred for having an office in your home, and costs involved in maintaining a rental property. These topics are discussed in the sections that follow.

Property Tax Deductions and How Property Taxes are Determined

After mortgage interest deductions, property taxes are the next big tax break for homeowners. Because there's much confusion and misunderstanding about how property taxes are levied, this section explains how the tax break is figured, and the next explains how to go about protesting your property taxes, should you view them as unfair.

How Property Taxes Are Set

For some reason, homeowners find property taxes a highly emotional subject, perhaps because it's a local tax that directly impacts all homeowners—plus, it's the biggest tax after federal income tax. One interesting thing about property taxes is their appearance of being applied arbitrarily. In addition, if the county is wrong in assessing your home, it's up to you to find out and correct that situation. So it behooves you to know how the system works so you don't overpay.

Understanding how property taxes work is fairly straightforward. Typically, counties go through four steps to arrive at how much you owe.

1. The assessor's office determines the value of all the properties in the county. It does this by appraisals, sales records, computer modeling, and building permits. The assessor then adds up all the real estate values in the county to get a grand total.

2. If your county uses the full-value approach, the assessor simply totals the appraised values for all the homes. But if the county uses an assessment ratio——one-half, for example—then you multiply the total value of all taxable properties by one-half.

3. Next, the county comes up with a tax rate. This is simply the budget the county needs to function in the coming year, divided by the value of all the real estate. For example, suppose the tax rate computes at .0076 and your house is assessed at

$250,000. Multiplying your house value by the .0076 tax rate gives you a $1,900 property tax bill. (This is why counties want to attract more development. It helps lower the tax rate and provide jobs—a double win for taxpayers.)

4. Finally, the county clerk mails out tax notices to the owners of all the properties in the county, with a deadline for receiving payment.

If, when you get your notice, you feel your taxes are too high, you can do two things. First, you can go to the budget hearing and challenge how the county spends the tax dollars. If enough people get upset, a referendum can be put on the ballot to impose a tax cap, as has happened in California, Texas, and some other states. Second, you can make sure your home's assessment is as low as possible. If the tax notice shows a value you think is too high, you can appeal to have it lowered. There's more about making such an appeal in the next section.

It's important to realize that when market values change, so does the assessed value of the homes in the area. For instance, if you were to add a garage or make an addition to your home, the assessed value would go up. Likewise, if you neglect your property or keep it in poor repair, the assessed value could go down. This is not a recommended way to lower your property taxes, however!

Contrary to what some homeowners think, the tax assessor does not create home values; the local real estate market does. For example, when home values were exploding a few years ago, valuations were also experiencing a steep increase. As higher sales prices became public record, appraisers, assessors, and Realtors used these comparable sales to establish value, and that created an upward spiral of house values. And as values spiraled higher, the tax revenues brought in as a result of those higher values also increased.

Why Have a Property Tax?

Property taxes are part of a well-balanced revenue system for government. It's a more stable source of money for the county to run its schools and other government services than sales and income taxes because it doesn't fluctuate as much when communities have recessions. Plus, when the county spends tax dollars on better schools, parks, and so on, property values in the area rise. In reality, some of the windfall benefits you receive are recaptured by the property tax.

Now that home prices are dropping in many locations, tax valuations and assessments should go down, too. But, that doesn't always happen. Many buyers are finding that county tax valuations have not always kept pace with current sales prices, so it becomes their problem to protest a too high county assessment.

Unfortunately, some previous home-owners didn't pay attention to their valuation notices and didn't protest an inaccurate tax assessment. Sometimes this oversight comes from homeowners whose mortgage companies collected property taxes as part of their monthly payment and then paid them when due. This creates an out-of-sight, out-of-mind situation and the county gets a windfall. And certainly the county isn't going to text-message anyone to tell them they are over-paying. The burden is on home buyers or current owners to scream foul if they think their property taxes are too high and take action to lower them.

HOME-BUYING TIP

When you're shopping for a home, don't put too much faith in the home values that county assessors come up with when determining your offering price. The assessments can greatly lag behind actual sales.

When you buy a home, your mortgage lender will usually require an escrow account for paying taxes and insurance if you put down less than 20 percent on the loan. You'll encounter this at the closing table, when going over the settlement statement, or HUDs.

The closing agent will point to a line labeled "County Taxes" (usually line 211). It will have two dates: the first date is January 1 because property taxes are billed from January 1, and the second date is the date you're closing on the house. You'll also notice two dollar amounts. The larger is the total property tax bill for the year and the smaller amount is the prorated amount that you receive as a credit.

Suppose, for example, that you're closing on March 27 and the property taxes for the year are $2,500. From January 1 to March 27 are eighty-six days that the seller has owned the house and owes taxes for those days. So, dividing $2,500 by 365 (bank days in a year) yields $6.85

Your county assessor's job is to keep track of ownership changes, maintain maps of parcel boundaries, keep descriptions of buildings, and keep property features up to date, in addition to keeping current on property values and trends so your property value reflects current market conditions.

a day, multiplied by 86 equals $589.04—the amount you're credited on the HUD because you'll have to pay the full year's taxes of $2,500 when the bill comes due later in the year. Incidently, the $2,500 tax bill minus the $589.04 of the seller's portion, or $1,910,96, is what you get to claim as a property tax deduction on your income taxes.

However, because the lender is paying your property taxes through an escrow account, the closing agent will usually charge you three months' tax payments to get the escrow fund started. In this case, it would be $2,500 divided by 12 (months), or $208.33 times 3 (months), or $624.99, that would show up in the HUDs 1000 section as a cost to you. This charge is considered part of your closing costs.

To take advantage of the property deduction on your income tax, you'll need to itemize these costs on Form 1040, Schedule A. If you haven't owned the home for a full tax year, your HUD settlement or closing statement will give you the prorated portion you can deduct, as explained above. As a new homeowner, it's important to keep the settlement statements handy, because you or your tax preparer will need them when filing. Should you lose this paperwork in the moving process (it happens all the time), contact your Realtor, title company, or closing attorney for copies.

When you close on your home, ask the title company for your property's tax parcel number (this is like a Social Security number for your property) and for the county's assessed value. If it's significantly higher than your purchase price, you may want to protest it. If you missed the time window the county gives you to protest, you'll need to wait until next year's appeal window rolls around.

Protesting Your Tax Assessment

When you buy a home, you get the tax rate that the previous owner was assessed. It may be low or high. Of course, if it's low you'll smile at your good fortune. But if it's higher than your purchase price, you'll want to appeal it.

In one instance, a buyer paid $390,000 for a home that the tax assessors showed on the tax notice as worth $475,000. Over the past year, values had dropped in the area, but county data hadn't caught up with the changes. And those adjustments could take a year or more to happen, which places the burden on you as the new home owner to appeal the assessment and get it lowered to the real value.

This advice is not limited to new home buyers, in fact. It is critical to anyone who owns a home, newly acquired or otherwise. Suppose your tax notice states the value of your house as $300,000. You feel this is high because you had an appraisal when you refinanced a couple of months ago and that was for $280,000. Then you happen to talk to your neighbor whose home is a bit larger, and his tax bill is $200 less than yours. You wonder how that can be.

It's easy, according to *Consumer Reports*, which has said that tax records show an error rate of 40 percent in estimating property taxes. Also, the National Taxpayer Union (www.nut.org) has announced that as many as 60 percent of all homeowners are overassessed on their home's value. That means you're most likely paying more property tax than you should.

Unfortunately to correct an overassessment and put some dollars back in your pocket, you need to prove to the county that it owes you the money. The good news is that it's not that hard if you follow a few easy steps. It's important to realize that an appeal is not a soapbox for you to complain about higher taxes, politics, or how the county is run. It's a tightly focused process that involves proving to an employee of the county assessor's office that your property is worth less than the present valuation. The person you talk to is not your enemy or a government pawn out to get you. Your job is to courteously and professionally present your case. You do that by sticking to the facts and letting your data work for you.

For a successful appeal you need to prove at least one of three things:

- *That items that affect the value are incorrect on your property record.* Get a copy of the assessor's record for your home. Check your county's Web site or call the assessor's office for a copy. Compare the assessor's record to your house. If there are discrepancies, highlight them or make a list of the ones that add value to your home but aren't there.

- *That you have evidence that similar properties in your area have sold for less than the assessment on your property.* To get this evidence, ask a Realtor to print out a list of recent (three months or less) sales of homes similar to yours in the area. Make sure the square footage, age, lot size, and amenities are as close to identical as possible. If you recently purchased the home, include your closing statement (HUDs).

■ *That other homeowners with similar homes (same square footage, age, lot size, and amenities) are paying less than you.* For example, if other homes in a subdivision with floor plans identical to yours are taxed less, then you have a case. To find this out, a title company, county recorder, or Realtor can give you a list of what other homes in your neighborhood are paying.

Once you've done your homework and gotten your data ducks in a row, you're ready to present your case. Figure 9-1 outlines the steps you'll need to take.

When you receive your assessment notice, read it for instructions about deadlines and filing procedures. They vary from state to state. If you don't understand them, call the assessor's office for help. A missed deadline or incorrect filing can result in an appeal dismissal.

The first step in the appeal process is usually an informal meeting with a staff member in the assessor's office, or you may be able to handle it by phone, mail, or e-mail. Information on the mechanics and deadlines for setting up an appointment should be included with your tax notice.

It's at this initial meeting that you submit the information you've put together to support your case. If the staff member feels you have a case, he or she may offer to look it over and get back to you with a ruling. When you get the ruling, if you don't feel it's fair, you can request a formal appeal to a local adjustment board.

At this second chance, you present your data again and ask for a reduction. Remember that the board is made up of people who are trying to be fair and equitable. You'll get better results if you keep your presentation focused and professional. Don't go off on tangents about how your aging mother needs a lifesaving operation or rant about why you think property taxes are too high.

The board will render a decision. Should you still disagree with the local board's decision, additional administrative or legal remedies are available that vary from state to state.

The Tax Advantages of Working at Home

Thanks to broadband technology and laptop computers, more people can work at home and leave the commuting to the rest of the world. To encourage this, Congress passed the Taxpayer Relief Act of 1997, which contained a modification of the IRS definition of "principal place of business."

FIGURE 9-1	
Typical steps to appeal your property taxes.	
Steps	**What You Need to Do**
Get a copy of your county's rules for protesting taxes. You usually get a copy with your tax notice.	Read the procedures carefully and note the dates you can request appointments.
Make sure the valuation notice values your property more than similar properties in your area. Get a copy of county's property record or data printout of your house.	Compare the property record with your home and look for discrepancies. Ask a Realtor to look up what similar properties have sold for in your neighborhood the last 3 months. If these sales are less than your valuation, press on.
Prepare your evidence.	Put together a list of similar properties that have sold or appraised for less than your home's valuation. Your comparisons must be accurate in terms of age, square footage, and amenities.
Set up a meeting.	Your tax notice gives you the phone numbers, e-mail addresses, or Web site to contact the assessor's office.
Show up at the meeting.	This step is an informal review of the data you have collected. Make sure the data are as accurate and complete as possible. Be calm and professional. The clerk is not your enemy.
The assessor's office gets back to you, but you still don't agree with their figures.	Ask for an appointment to present your case to the appeal board.
Appointment with the appeal board.	Present your data as you did before in the informal meeting and ask for a reduction.

Beginning in 1999, the new rules allowed those who don't have off-site office space to deduct the expenses for maintaining a home office. Contractors, sales reps, consultants, and others who perform services outside their office but need a home office can now benefit. However, you must use that office exclusively and regularly for business. You may also be entitled to a deduction if you use part of your home for business, such as maintaining paperwork or storing records.

One way of taking advantage of this rule is to convert or build a

---

Beware of Tax Scams

Around tax time, you'll probably get letters from firms offering to reduce your taxes for a percentage of the reduction. Many legitimate companies offer this service. Typically, they charge 30 to 50 percent of the savings. If you don't have time to protest your tax bill yourself, this can be a better way than not protesting at all. As usual, talk to three companies and get bids and references. But be wary of scammers who charge a fee upfront and promise to lower your taxes or get you a rebate. No one can predict if and what you can save without going through the appeal process. A legitimate company will not charge an upfront fee.

---

separate structure that's not attached to your house. Detached garages, carriage houses, sheds, small barns, and so on make great home-office conversions. For example, an architect converted a small barn into a studio that not only saved him a long commute but allowed him to work at home and save on expensive city rent.

HOME-BUYING TIP

If you have a business that you can run out of your home, you may want to factor that in when you shop for a new house. Look for an attic, basement, or outbuilding that can be converted into an office.

Depending on the percentage of your home you use for business, you should be able to deduct part of your utility bills, mortgage interest payments, repairs, depreciation, cost of an additional phone or DSL line, and office equipment, as well as other related expenses. You may also be able to depreciate computers, business machines, and office furniture.

However, it's important to clearly set aside the area you use for business. You can't put a filing cabinet in the family room that's used for watching TV and call it an office. The area must be used exclusively for business. If you decide to claim a home-office deduction, you should also keep meticulous records of all your expenses and be prepared to back them up if the IRS asks for proof.

Of course, there's a downside to creating a home office. Eventually you'll probably move, and if you've spent $20,000 to create a great home office, chance are you won't be able to add that to the price of the home. In some areas, it may even lower the value of your home. Also be aware that when you sell, the part of the home you used for an office may not apply to the personal-residence capital gains tax exclusion. Check with your tax adviser for the best way to handle home office deductions.

Before you draw up plans and get bids for that home office you saw in a magazine article, do some "what if" thinking. If you're planning on moving in a few years, will the home office add to the home's sales appeal? And if you're looking for a home and will need a home office, seek an extra bedroom that you can convert into an office and then restore to a bedroom without too much trouble or expense when you sell. Or, if you find a home with a killer home office, determine

> According the *Remodeling* magazine's 2007 "Cost vs. Value" report, the national average that homeowners recoup from the cost of adding a home office when they sell is 57 percent.

how much that office is adding to the home's asking price. Look at other homes that have sold in your area to get an idea of how much a home office contributes to a house's value.

In summary, Uncle Sam allows you the following additional tax deductions for having a home office:

- You can prorate your utilities by the square footage. That means your office square-footage versus the home's total square-footage. For example, suppose the office is 730 square feet and the home's total footage is 2,875. Dividing 730 square feet by 2,875 gives you 25 percent of the utilities and other expenses that are business related.

- You can prorate the cost of your homeowners insurance along with related riders and policies in proportion to how much applies to your home business—additional liability for when clients come to your home and coverage for business equipment and fixtures, for example.

> For more information on home office deductions, download IRS publication 587, "Business Use of Your Home," from www.irs.gov/pub/irs-pub/p587.pdf.

- Depreciation is allowed on the office portion of the home.

- Prorating property taxes is also allowed.

- Property maintenance costs for the office space can be prorated (but tricky, so consult a tax professional first).

■ Construction of an office on your lot or remodeling costs to add an office to your existing home. However, these improvements would be taxed differently from your home, so consult your tax adviser for how this would affect your situation.

The Tax Advantages of Owning Rental Property

The practice of renting out your extra space in the attic or basement is spreading to more affluent urban areas as well as prevalent in suburban neighborhoods. Empty-nesters, one-income families, widows, and widowers are taking in tenants to help pay the mortgage bills or generate extra cash.

HOME-BUYING TIP

If you're buying a home and a find a built-in rental appealing, ask your agent to check the MLS for similar homes with apartments. This is a simple search function for most MLS systems.

For example, when Sharee divorced, she ended up with the house and a $1,900 monthly mortgage payment. With little or no equity, and dropping home values in her area, selling was not an option. Nor did she want to ruin her credit for years to come with a short sale or foreclosure. But the home had a finished basement with an outside entrance, two bedrooms, a family room, full bath, and wet bar that Sharee converted into a kitchenette and rented for $800 a month.

Before you remodel or buy a home with an apartment, however, call your city or county zoning department. In most subdivisions, zoning laws limit houses to single-family occupancy, although that often doesn't apply to apartments for family members. However, when you rent to nonrelatives, you may violate zoning or local ordinances.

If your zoning prohibits renting to a nonrelative, you may be able to get the zoning board to approve a conditional or special-use permit. Usually, if your apartment and home have the required parking space and the neighbors don't object, it can be easy to get the change approved.

Getting a special-use permit entails going to the zoning department and filling out the paperwork. You may need to comply with restrictions on how utilities are set up as well as inspections for building code compliance. A hearing is also part of the process to give the neighbors a chance to protest.

Although it's tempting to shortcut the process and just rent out your apartment illegally, that can come back to bite you later on. True, some homeowners ignore zoning rules because the city or county is lax in enforcement, and they know they can get away with it. But administrations change and properties are eventually put up for sale. Lenders may want to see the special-use permit before they will refinance or finance a mortgage for new buyers. And you certainly don't want to have an insurance company deny a claim when your home is a pile of ashes and you've violated the policy terms.

Some homeowners add a basement or attic apartment when they build a new home. This gives them the option of creating space for parents or kids who may come home the second time around, or a rental in the future to add to the cash flow. Uncle Sam allows homeowners to deduct the following costs of turning part of a home into a rental space:

- You can prorate your utilities by the square footage, as above for office space.

- You can prorate the cost of your homeowners insurance along with related riders and policies, such as additional liability coverage.

- Depreciation is allowed on the rental part of the home.

- Prorating property taxes is also allowed.

- Property maintenance, such as exterior and interior painting and landscaping costs, can be prorated (but consult a tax professional first).

A disadvantage of creating a rental space in your home is the capital gains factor. When you sell a single-family home you have the first $250,000/$500,000 tax free, as explained in the next section of this chapter. But if you rent out the full basement, you may be able to claim only one-half the deduction because the other half is considered a business property.

Interestingly, you can get around this problem by converting the apartment back to being part of a single-family home before you sell. To qualify for the full exemption, the owners must occupy 100 percent of the house for two of the five years before they sell. However, this rule doesn't necessarily apply if a family member lives in the rental unit. So if you have an apartment or rental home and are intending to sell, look ahead and plan a way that will minimize the tax bite.

If you're buying a home with an apartment, added garage, or major remodeling job, you'll want to verify that building permits show the house is zoning compliant. You can get extended title insurance coverage that insures that previous owners have complied with all zoning and building permits.

HOME-BUYING TIP

Before you rent out your home or buy a home with an apartment, check with a tax professional to make sure it's in your best interests. Also see IRS publication 523, "Selling Your Home." In addition, for more tax information on renting out your home, check out IRS publication 527, "Residential Rental Property."

In one interesting case, homebuyers Brandon and Julie made an offer on a home with a basement apartment in a great neighborhood near a university. The basement apartment had been rented out for years, and several other homes on the street also had basement apartments. When the appraiser checked the zoning and found out that the basement apartment was illegal, she adjusted her appraisal down to the market value of a single-family home. Although the city's zoning department head said he hadn't and wouldn't enforce the zoning in this case, the department wouldn't approve the house for duplex zoning.

This created a sticky situation. As a single-family home, the appraisal came back $23,000 under the asking price. The sellers were upset because now the genie was out of the bottle and the home couldn't be sold as a duplex, lowering its value considerably. And no mortgage lender would finance an illegal duplex. Rather than walk away from the deal, the buyers offered to pay the appraised value for the home. The unhappy sellers struggled with the offer for a couple of days and finally accepted the grim reality that they had few options and signed the deal.

HOME-BUYING TIP

A duplex is a great way start building a real estate portfolio. Finance it as an owner-occupied dwelling and live in one side for a couple of years, then move up to another property and do the same again.

Brandon and Julie got a great deal on their "duplex" and plan on renting the basement. While they will have to sell the home down the road as a single family, that shouldn't present a problem because they bought it for its appraisal as a single-family dwelling. The lesson, here, is that before you buy a house with an apartment, check the zoning and verify existence of any other required permits. It can save you costly tax, insurance, and zoning headaches later on.

When You Sell: Capital Gains Taxes

Many people live in a house for enough years to see it appreciate in value—sometimes to appreciate a great deal, although the amount of appreciation varies with location and economic conditions. When you sell that house, the money from the sale goes, first, to pay any existing balance on your mortgage, Realtor fees, transfer taxes, and the like. But if the house's appreciation is great enough you come away with a capital gain, which is subject to federal income tax. After deducting any expenses you incurred to make the sale (including renovations), the first $250,000 per individual or $500,000 for a couple, is tax free. For a retiring couple whose house appreciated a great deal in the thirty years that they lived there, that can be a huge portion of the capital gain from the sale and a huge boost to their savings account.

For example, Ron and Laura took advantage of this exemption when they both retired and sold the home they had lived in for twenty-three years. They paid $62,000 for the home, and during those years it had appreciated to $387,000. When they sold it, they had paid off their mortgage and their capital gain was tax free because it was less than the $500,000 limit for a married couple.

Ron and Laura then bought a motor home with some of the proceeds of the sale and banked the rest. After closing on their home, they drove out of the title company's parking lot in their new RV and road off into the sunset. If they had been renters, there would have been no $387,000 check and no tax deductions from Uncle Sam along the way to help them make their monthly mortgage payments. They simply would have had a nice stack of 276 receipts to show for twenty-three years of monthly payments.

Tax-deferred Exchanges

For a first-time home buyer, a section on *tax-deferred exchanges*—whereby you can trade one real estate investment for another real estate investment and defer the capital gains taxes—may appear a little far out. But this underutilized financial tool can make a big difference in the following situations. For example, suppose you:

■ Want to keep your starter home for a rental when you move up to a larger house.

- Have rented part of your home and you want to sell, but some of the proceeds are subject to capital gains taxes.

- Want to trade your single-family home for a duplex or four-plex without paying capital gains taxes.

- There's a piece of land (or other real estate) you would like to trade your home for, but if the owner of that land sold, his capital gains tax would take a big cut of his proceeds.

The possibilities here are endless for creating win-win deals and deferring any capital gains obligation to a time when the tax bite may not be so painful. Unfortunately, paying capital gains taxes keeps many owners from selling their investment single-family homes and condos that they've owned for years and in which they have built up a lot of equity.

HOME-BUYING TIP

If you're a first-time home owner who wants to build a real estate portfolio, keep your first home as a rental when you move up. After you've built equity, you can use it to trade up to another dwelling that's larger, multifamily, or whatever else you want and you can defer the capital gains taxes at the same time.

But with a *1031 exchange*, owners can trade a home for raw land or an apartment building and defer their tax bite. A house the owners can't sell because of a slow market and have been forced to rent out can become part of a trade for real estate in another location that's more in tune with the seller's interests.

In any real estate market, there are property owners whose needs and interests change, and that change creates a constant flow of fresh, new opportunities. Some owners want to move up to bigger rental units, while others want to move down to something less demanding. A tax-deferred exchange is a great way to make either situation easier.

Although putting an exchange together is fairly straightforward, it may require the expertise of an exchange intermediary, accountant, and title/escrow company, depending on the number of properties involved and complexity. The exchange intermediary is the neutral party who handles the nuts and bolts of the exchange. To find one, check with Realtors, title, or escrow companies for referrals. You'll also need a title and/or escrow company to provide title work and handle the funding.

An exciting thing about 1031 exchanges is that you don't have to have two property owners who want to exchange straight across. You can bring in other buyers and sellers with their properties to add to the exchange pot, so that each participant ends up with a property he or she wants. For example, let's say you have a single-family rental (relinquished property) you want to trade for a vacant lot. You find a lot you want to buy, but the seller doesn't want your property. So you put together a purchase contact that is subject to your finding a buyer for your single-family house. When you find the buyer, everything goes into escrow and a three-way trade is completed. You get the lot you won't have to manage, the buyer you found gets a house, and the lot owner ends up with cash. Everyone meets his or her goals. Equities and costs are balanced by cash or proceeds from loans as needed from each party.

In this type of situation, everyone also gains by deferring the capital gains on the equity they've built up until a later time, when presumably the tax rates will drop or their situation changes to lessen the tax bite. When Norm and Sandy's jobs were transferred from Utah to Georgia, a slow market made selling their Utah home and a rental property difficult. So they decided to rent the houses, hired a rental company to manage the homes, and received rents that were close to their mortgage payments.

Five years later, when interest rates dropped, the market improved and home values increased sharply, Norm and Sandy decided to sell their Utah homes. Their strategy was to put the proceeds from the sales into a 1031 exchange escrow with a title company in Utah and find rental properties in Georgia. The money from the sale of the two Utah houses would go into escrow, to be used as a down payment for properties the owners hoped to find in Georgia.

Luckily, the tenants in one home wanted to buy the house and they were able to qualify for the mortgage payments, which were $80 a month less than their rent. The sale closed and the $87,000 profit went into the title company exchange department's escrow account. Meanwhile, the other home had a year's lease with six months to go, so that home couldn't go on the market until the lease was about up. While the paperwork for the rental sale was going forward, Norm and Sandy were looking for a property to make an offer on. The market was tight in Georgia and they didn't find anything they liked until two weeks after their home in Utah had closed. (The IRS allows forty-five days to identify an exchange property and up to 180 days to close the deal.) They made an offer on a three-bedroom condo in a good area for $265,000 and it was accepted. The $87,000 in escrow was used for a down payment and the balance was financed with a nonowner-occupied mortgage. The equity from one home was transferred to Georgia with no capital gains taxes due.

Norm and Sandy's other rental had six months to go on the lease. If the tenants couldn't or didn't want to buy it, the property would go on the market and the process would be repeated.

As you can see, the 1031 exchange is a great way to transfer equity from one area to another while deferring capital gains taxes. As a home buyer, if you're renting a home and want to buy it, but the owner is reluctant to sell it because of capital gains taxes, suggest that the landlord consult with a Realtor familiar with 1031 exchanges. Chances are this route will solve the owner's problem and get you the house.

> **HOME-BUYING TIP**
>
> A great read on 1031 exchanges is Jack Cummings's book, *The Tax-Free Exchange Loophole.*

The IRS requires the exchange to be real estate for real estate. That's a broad definition with a lot of opportunities. You can exchange a duplex for bare land, office building, warehouse, or wharf for a single-family home. Whether your trade is one property for ten or ten properties for one, the number doesn't matter. You can put as many exchange legs as needed into the deal to make it work, just so none of the properties is used as primary or secondary residences.

> A good Web site for learning more about 1031 exchanges is www.first am.com.

From the date of closing on the sale of the relinquished property (the one you just sold), you have forty-five days to find a replacement (one or more) and 180 days to close the deal. So, you need to insert a clause into all sale contracts in the deal that identifies them as part of a 1031 exchange. The IRS wants to see an easy-to-follow paper trail.

John and Angie went the exchange route when they decided that they no longer wanted the demands of being a landlord. They owned a duplex that had about $180,000 equity and didn't want to pay out a big part in taxes if they sold at that time. Although they didn't want to exchange it for more rental property, undeveloped land appeared to be a good way to go—low maintenance and no rent to collect or late-night plumbing problems to fix. They wanted care-free time to travel and not worry about problems back home.

Finding a buyer for their duplex was easy, and the sale closed with the proceeds going into escrow. About a week later, their Realtor found a five-acre parcel for sale that appeared to be in the path of eventual development and would make a perfect no-maintenance investment. Since the land cost $339,000, John and Angie needed about $160,000 to make a deal. They decided to take out a ten-year, low-interest equity line of credit on their home for the funds needed to complete the deal. The second leg of the 1031 exchange closed and everyone was happy.

As a result of the exchange, a young couple was able to buy a duplex that they had been searching for as their first home, and John and Angie didn't have to collect rents or do maintenance on their rental. Everyone won, and the tax man had to wait for another day to collect his due.

Putting together a 1031 exchange is straightforward and fun as you decide what type of real estate you find interesting. Figure 9-2 guides you through the process.

Six Steps You Can Take to Make This Chapter Work for You

1. If you look at your tax situation and find that renting is costing you big bucks, have a tax professional figure out how much you would save by buying a home.

2. If you're a first-time home buyer, look into using your IRA or 401(k) as a source of funds for a down payment. The tax code allows you to tap these funds penalty free to buy a home. They also allow parents or grandparents to tap theirs to help out family members with a down payment.

3. When you buy a home, look at the assessed value and property taxes. They may not be in line with current values and you may need to plan on protesting them as soon as possible. Call your county assessor to find out the when and how.

4. Consider creating a home office for convenience and tax savings. Before you leap, check with an appraiser or Realtor to find out how much it will increase the value of the home.

FIGURE 9-2
Typical steps to a 1031 tax-deferred exchange.

Steps	What's Involved
The property is listed for sale and a property exchange intermediary is lined up. The intermediary can be a title company or attorney who is experienced in exchanges.	Include a note in the listing and sale documents that the property is part of a 1031 exchange and all parties agree to participate.
A buyer for the property is found.	The intermediary prepares an assignment, giving the role of seller to the intermediary along with the other exchange paperwork that goes to the closing agent.
The sale is closed and equity funds are put in escrow.	Exchanger (seller) and buyer sign an assignment agreement which gives the intermediary the role of seller. The 45-day clock starts ticking for the exchanger to find and identify an exchange property.
The hunt for a replacement property is completed or well on its way by this time.	You have 45 days to find a property (180 days to close) and identify in writing by street address or legal description. This is forwarded to the intermediary.
The exchanger makes an offer on the property.	Included in the paperwork is a notice that the deal is part of a 1031 exchange with the required assignments. You need to create a clear paper trail for the IRS.
When there are multiple properties and legs to the exchange.	All the parts (legs) of the exchange are put into escrow and closed with each party getting its designated property at the same time. Closing and funding have to be within 180 days.
Tax forms are filed.	Exchangers file form 8824 with the IRS and any other state-required tax disclosure forms.

It's unfortunate, that when tax payments become part of a house payment, the tendency is to mail a monthly check and not think about it. As a result, it becomes an out-of-sight-out-of-mind situation and many homeowners don't check their tax assessment to make sure it's fair.

But, if you pay property taxes on your own, you develop a slightly different perspective. You feel the pain of writing a sizable check on or before November 30 every year and when the assessment goes up, the motivation is strong to challenge it. And you should according to the International Association of Assessing Officers (IAAO), more than half of the homeowners who protest their assessments get a reduction.

5. Look into converting an attic or basement into an income-producing rental that saves you on taxes, too. Check with your local zoning; if it isn't allowed you may be able to get a zoning variance if the neighbors don't object.

6. Consider buying a duplex or house and then keeping and renting it when you move up to a bigger home. Eventually, you can trade for other real estate using a 1031 tax-free exchange to defer any capital gains taxes.

CHAPTER 10

The Twenty Costliest Mistakes Homebuyers Make and How to Avoid them

No one likes to make mistakes. They're not only time-consuming but also in real estate they can cost you a lot of money. This chapter is a quick read to help you avoid the most common home-buying mistakes, based on many years of working with home buyers—especially first-timers.

Use this chapter as a checklist of what *not* to do when searching for your dream home and as a source of solutions when you encounter some sticky problems along the way.

Mistake #1: Attempting to Get the Best Deal by Waiting for Home Prices or Interest Rates to Bottom Out

Buyers frequently ask Realtors when the best time is to buy a home. Most experienced agents and mortgage lenders agree that you should buy a home:

- When you're tired of renting and want to own a home of your own.

- When your job is stable and your income will support the mortgage payments and other costs of home ownership.

Many home buyers who decide to wait for interest rates or house prices to hit bottom often end up paying more. It's difficult to know when rates will drop and for how long, or when house prices will bottom out and begin climbing again.

A few years ago, when interest rates dropped to within the 5 percent range, it triggered demand and home prices shot up overnight. Any gain you might realize by waiting for rates to go down even further would be more than offset by home prices going up. For example, let's say you find a good deal on a house priced at $275,000, but you decide to wait a bit, hoping that interest rates will drop even further before you make your move. Meanwhile, interest rates go up from 6 percent to 6.5 percent. That means a payment of $1,648.76 on $275,000 at 6 percent jumps $89.43 at 6.5 percent. To compensate for the increased interest you'll be paying, you would have to get the sellers to reduce their price another $10,000, which is unlikely. When you factor in the loss from not having the tax breaks of home ownership and the lost opportunity to build equity , that price drop for the house would need to be considerably greater to have made your wait worthwhile. And if home prices start to climb, the good deal you're waiting to get better is gone forever.

Typically, it's better to focus on house prices rather than interest rates when deciding when to buy. But in a market when home prices and interest rates (historically 6 percent or less) are both low, it's best to find your dream home and make an offer. The tax breaks, appreciation, and equity gained will more than offset your waiting for an interest rate to drop or home prices to bottom out.

Mistake #2: Failing to Get Your Ducks in a Row before Committing

Many home buyers looking for their first home, and owners moving up to newer homes as well, cause themselves unnecessary stress and financial loss because they haven't been organized about the process.

For example, when buyers moving from an apartment to a house forget or fail to factor in their lease expiration when they sign a purchase agreement, they can encounter a problem when they have to break their lease. Sometimes renters can get off the hook by forfeiting their deposit, but other times they get stuck with making both rent and mortgage payments until their lease expires. You can avoid this problem by confirming your lease expiration date with the landlord and keeping it in mind when you sign the purchase agreement and schedule the closing. In addition, it's important to read your lease carefully; if in doubt about the terms, speak to an attorney.

In one particular situation, first-time buyers made an offer on a house with a $1,000 deposit that was subject to mortgage approval only. When the buyers informed their landlord they were moving, he politely informed them they had three months left on their lease. They could move out, but he expected a check for $1,500 a month for the duration of the lease or he would enforce the terms in court. In the end, they were unable to cover both the down payment and the remaining lease payments, and as a result they lost both the house and their deposit. In a similar lease situation, rather than have the deal fall through, the sellers offered to pay the buyer's three months of remaining rent. They did this as a concession to get their home sold because of a slow market and they had to sell because of a job transfer.

If you happen to find a home that you can't live without and you have a lease, try negotiating with the seller to pick up some or all of the remaining months. Also, the landlord may be willing to cancel your lease if you're willing to forfeit the deposit. Yet another option is to extend the closing date on your new house until your lease expires. Keep in mind, however, that many sellers are reluctant to take their homes off the market for more than thirty days, lest they lose other buyers if your offer falls through.

There's also a flip side to consider: suppose your lease expires and you haven't found a house or you've got to move out before the closing. In this case, ask your landlord to extend the lease on a month-by-month basis, with a thirty-day notice before you move.

Other ways you can get your ducks lined up are:

- Getting an offer on an existing home before committing on a new home.

- Putting the money for a down payment and closing costs into your checking account so the lender can easily verify.

- Asking parents, if they are helping you with a down payment or closing costs, to put their money into their checking account so the lender can easily verify that those funds exist.

- Getting everyone agreed early on as to the possession date so you can line up a moving van for your move into the house; don't assume the sellers are on track—verify day and time the house will be vacant and you get the keys. It can get expensive keeping a moving van idle because of a misunderstanding.

Mistake #3: Buying a Home Before You've Sold Your Current One

If you own a home and sign a purchase or construction agreement on another one before you have sold your current home, things can get sticky. Some homeowners hope they'll be lucky and sell their house before the deadline. Should things not work out that way, it can be both frustrating and costly.

It's important to consider the consequences if your home doesn't sell. There are three common outcomes:

1. You sharply discount the price of your house to sell and then find you have less money for purchasing your new home.

2. You end up renting your house or working out a creative financing deal with risky buyers. These pressure-cooker deals have a 90 percent chance of ending in default.

3. You make an offer on the new house subject to sale of your other house. If the sellers are on the ball, they will require a clause in the agreement that binds you to an agreed-upon number of days to complete the sale if you have a buyer.

Sometimes the timing works out and you smoothly sell one house and buy another. People win the lottery, too. But for most home seller/buyer combos, the risks outweigh the rewards. Robert and Andrea found this out when they waited until their new home was sixty days from completion before they put their old home on the market, hoping to sell it right away.

Unfortunately, their old home needed some work to make it saleable, and Robert and Andrea were unwilling to put time or money into it because they were focused on their new home. But when their new home was finished and ready to close, their other home hadn't sold—or even had an offer. Without any other options, they rented the old house to cover the mortgage payments on it and qualify for their new house. A year later, their rental was still costing them about $210 a month because the rent didn't cover all their costs. To make matters worse, the home was going downhill fast because they had no money remaining (or desire) to do the maintenance; additionally, the loan balance on the rental house was about $20,000 more than its current market value which had dropped because of a slow market.

The best way to avoid this kind of situation is to sell your existing home first. If it sells before you have a new place, put everything you don't immediately need into storage and rent or stay with relatives until your new home is finished or you find that perfect home.

Mistake #4: Alienating the Sellers, Thereby Losing the Deal

Buyers often say and do things when dealing with sellers that can cost them the deal or cause the sellers to dig in their heels and cut off negotiations. You can use the following dos and don'ts as you look at homes and talk to sellers.

- *Don't* badmouth a home as you walk through it. Sellers (and their agents) are extremely sensitive to anyone's telling them their orange and black paint is bizarre, for example. True, you'll find some decorating that's over the edge, but it's best to withhold comments. You may find that this home turns out to be the one that best meets your needs, and sellers have long memories.

- *Don't* try to tear down the value of a home by pointing out its problems, in hopes of intimidating the sellers into lowering their price. This almost always backfires. If you like the home but feel it's overpriced, make a lower offer and explain specifically and respectfully how you arrived at your price. Negotiating a low offer always goes better when you focus on how the sellers will win and avoid hurting their egos.

- *Don't* discuss price, or try to negotiate by e-mail, phone, or text messaging. If you want to make an offer, fill out a purchase agreement and attach a mortgage preapproval letter and a serious deposit check. Sellers will often accept offers presented in this way that they would reject when kicking it around verbally.

- *Don't* ask sellers what would the lowest price would be that they would accept. This puts them on the defensive, makes you look like a predatory bargain hunter and hurts your credibility. Again, if you feel the price is too high, make a written offer and let them accept or counter with their lowest price. This gets the sales ball rolling, and many times the sellers will come around and accept market reality and a realistic price.

- *Don't* thrust lists of comparable sold or listed homes at sellers or their listing agent to try and justify a lower offer. Agents who use this tactic find it usually backfires. Keep in mind that buying and selling a home are emotional experiences. Sometimes you have to go slowly and let sellers vent their frustration with not getting what they think their home is worth before they settle down and get serious. In the end, most sellers come around, especially if they have to sell.

- *Don't* simply pull up in a seller's driveway and ask to see their home on the spot. Few sellers can maintain their homes in show condition all the time, so it's better to call and set up an appointment that gives them a couple of hours to get the house ready. You want to create positive feelings in case this home turns out to be your dream home.

- *Do* be punctual when you have an appointment to look at a home. If you get delayed, call the sellers and let them know you'll be late. Treat their time with respect and, if you make an offer, they will remember how you treated them. In a case of multiple offers, this can swing a deal in your favor.

Mistake #5: Neglecting to Get a Preapproval Letter

A branch manager at First American Title Company has estimated that about 30 percent of the transactions at her branch fall apart or are delayed before closing. The most common reason for this is the buyers' failure to be preapproved for a loan before making an offer. This mishap can result in lost time and embarrassment; it can also result in the forfeiture of earnest money.

You can prevent most of these problems by finding a mortgage lender before you start looking at homes. Go through the complete preapproval process and get a letter from your lender stating that you're good to go up to a certain mortgage amount. This means you have the funds in a checking or savings account for the down payment and closing and the lender can easily verify them.

Also attaching a preapproval letter to your offer gives you credibility and the sellers are often reluctant to pass up a bird-in-the-hand deal.

To recap why getting preapproved for a mortgage first is so important:

- You'll know exactly how much home you can afford, how much down payment you'll need, and what your estimated closing costs will be.

- You won't waste time looking at homes outside your price range.

- You'll be able to move quickly and make an offer when you do find your dream home. If you like a home, it's likely other buyers do, too, especially in prime areas.

- Your preapproval letter attached to your offer makes the seller take it seriously and can be the difference between acceptance and a counter or rejection.

For example, when Ryan and Brittany felt ready to buy their first home, they met with a lender they had chosen after talking to several possibilities. After checking their credit and employment, and verifying their source of down payment, the lender gave them a preapproval letter for $270,000. After two weeks of house hunting, Ryan and Brittany found their dream home. When their agent called to arrange a time to present the offer, she found out there was a competing offer that was $1,500 higher than theirs. The couple's agent, a real pro, pointed out to the sellers that her clients were loan approved and gave them the letter from the mortgage company. She stressed that her clients' offer was a bird-in-the-hand and that they could close in three weeks or less, subject only to the appraisal.

The agent with the competing offer didn't have a preapproval letter so that offer was subject to mortgage application and approval. Almost predictably, the sellers chose to go with the preapproved offer over a riskier one, despite its being less money. Obviously, the sellers didn't want to take their home off the market and wait a week or two to find out if the buyers had qualified. Timing and a sure-thing approach will often win out over a higher priced offer.

Mistake # 6: Failing to Have an Exit Strategy

Many first-time home buyers purchase a one-bedroom condo, a small two-bedroom home, or a PUD. They don't stop to think that in a few years their home will become too small, when the kids come along or their income increases and they want to move up.

It's important to think "sell" when you buy. In general, this means you should:

- Go with as many bedrooms and baths as you can afford.

- Shop carefully and buy in the best school district possible.

- Do some homework on the area and find out what future planning is on city drawing boards.

- Talk to people living in the neighborhood and find out the pros and cons of the region.

Nick, a first-time buyer, bought a one-bedroom condo after getting his first job out of college. Hearing that it's better to own than rent, he visited a new condo project and was smitten by the amenities and lifestyle image the development offered. He bought an apartment and lived there for two years. After getting married, he and his new wife lived in the condo for another two years before a baby came along. Suddenly, the one-bedroom condo became a tight fit.

When the bigger home became a priority for Nick and his family, they started looking. There were some nice homes they could afford, but they would have to sell the condo first. But when Nick spoke to a Realtor, he found out that quite a few units in the development were for sale at the time, and that finding a buyer could pose a challenge and take a while. He would probably have to discount the condo close to what he owned, or even less because other owners had dropped their prices to rock bottom. A year later, the condo still sported a FOR SALE sign and had no offers. Nick was seriously considering renting it if he didn't get an offer in the next couple of months.

As Nick learned the hard way, before you commit to buying a home of any sort, you have to think about how long you intend to live there. Remember that the average home buyer stays in a house about six years.

Mistake #7: Paying Little or No Attention to the Neighborhood

Both first-time and experienced home buyers can fall into the trap of not checking out the neighborhood when they see a house that pulls the right strings and pushes the right emotional buttons. They become so enamored with the house that they forget that there's more involved in their investment than simply the house and yard. Important questions that should be asked, but often overlooked are:

- Does the neighborhood attract gangs or other undesirable groups?

- Is there an active neighborhood crime-watch group?

- What is the age range of your neighbors? If you have kids, are there others in the area in the same age range?

- Does the neighborhood have a high turnover because many homes are rentals?

- How far away are the schools?

- Is public transportation close by?

No matter how much you like the house, if the neighborhood doesn't fit your lifestyle, you'll be selling before long and looking for a more compatible area. Juan and Rita experienced this when they bought a cute renovated bungalow in an older neighborhood. They soon found out that their neighborhood had several teens who occasionally raced up and down the street in their cars and that several homes were rentals with yards that were slowly going native.

Unfortunately, Juan and Rita didn't use a Realtor when they bought the house and had not shopped around. They had driven by the home, noticed a FOR SALE sign, and called the sellers. The sellers were an older couple who wanted to move to a warmer climate and so Juan and Rita offered them a good deal on the home. So focused were these buyers on the charming home that they didn't even think about the area, and lived to regret their decision.

To avoid making this mistake, spend some time in the neighborhood at different times of the day and evening, and talk to several would-be neighbors before you buy.

Mistake # 8: Buying the Wrong Type of House

How you can buy the wrong type of house seems hard to imagine, but it's a major reason many homeowners move. For instance, suppose you love the picturesque look of two-story homes, but you discover that having a family room in the basement is not what you want—a ranch with an open floor plan is what you really desire for family togetherness. Or perhaps you buy a home with the laundry room in the basement, and after a while you find that going up and down stairs is a real pain.

You need to look at how a house will function for your family before you make an offer. As you walk through a property, ask yourself the following questions:

- Is this home's floor plan really compatible with your family's lifestyle?

- Do you actually need a formal dining room or would a family room off the kitchen be a better choice?

- Do you need a den or extra bedroom that you can use as a home office?

Remember, the house has to fit only one family's lifestyle—yours. Sam and Becky made a lifestyle mistake when they found a charming two-story house in a great neighborhood near Sam's job. They loved the oak trim and crown molding, as well as a formal dining room and updated kitchen. Their three boys—ages five, nine, and twelve—were thrilled with the huge sycamores that dominated a quarter-acre back-yard.

The buyers made an offer with a thirty-day closing and the sellers accepted. A month later, the loan closed and Sam, Becky, and the kids moved into their new home. They were excited and spent the first couple of months settling in and exploring the area.

But then came time to register the kids for school, and Becky found out that the school was two miles away, which meant the kids would have to ride the bus. She also found out there were no families in the neighborhood with elementary-school-age kids for a possible car pool. The neighborhood consisted of mostly middle-aged couples and single homeowners that their family had little in common with. A few more months went by and Becky realized that the formal floor plan of a two-story wasn't her idea of a kid-friendly home. The boys wanted to be near the kitchen or wherever mom was, not downstairs in the family room or in the upstairs bedrooms.

A year later Sam and Becky put the home up for sale and started house hunting again. This time they determined to be wiser and do some homework before they jumped at a home with enticing curb appeal.

It's important to put some thought into what your family lifestyle is and to make a list of important things that you want in a home.

Don't be swayed by a cute restored bungalow just like the one you grew up in if a multilevel is a better fit with your lifestyle. Everyone once in a while, take a deep breath and do a reality check when you're out house shopping. Try to project what your needs will be in five to ten years from now. And don't let your emotions sway you if the floor plan doesn't fit your needs.

Mistake #9: Purchasing a New Home on Impulse

Many new home buyers fall into the trap of going through a model home in a new subdivision and the next thing they know they've committed to buy. The flash and tinsel of a model home can push some powerful emotional buttons. And, of course, that's what model homes are designed to do. The colors, lighting, furniture layout, scented candles, and soft music are all carefully planned to appeal to as many senses as possible and put you in a home-buying mood.

Also, new-home salespeople are trained to sell a lifestyle that's easy to buy into as well as to minimize buyer's remorse by frequent follow-up. They're good at keeping excitement levels up until the home is finished and the buyer is ready to close. This is not necessarily bad unless you buy more home than you can comfortably afford in a moment of weakness. It's important to take your time to shop and compare until you know what's available in your area in your price range. If you've been living in a one-bedroom apartment, anything over 900 square feet can look spacious. The impulse to fall for a larger home without setting a firm price limit beforehand can be irresistible.

On new construction, before you commit, check out the builder's reputation. Talk to three or four people who bought from that builder and listen to what they have to say. This is also a great way to see what your neighbors would be like. For instance, new home buyers Mike and Linda were seriously considering buying a home in a new subdivision. They loved the style and floor plans of the models and had even talked to the builder's lender and filled out an application. However, a little uneasy with the pressure and enticements from the salesperson and lender to commit, they decided to talk with several homeowners on one of the first streets built in the subdivision. They learned there were some unresolved drainage problems and no follow-through on parks and trails. In fact, several home buyers were considering legal action. In addition, many of the callbacks took several weeks to resolve, and then only after repeated calls. It didn't take long to realize that the builder didn't have a good reputation, and further checking revealed he had declared bankruptcy less than a year earlier.

That was enough for Mike and Linda to scratch the project off their list and move on. And it was lucky they did, because a couple of months later the development was featured on a local news channel because of problems homeowners who bought were having with the builder and developer.

Mistake #10: Investing in a Property That's Hard to Sell

Buying a property that will be difficult to sell later on is one of the biggest mistakes home buyers can make. It happens so often that you wonder what buyers were thinking (or not thinking) when they signed the purchase agreements. Three of the most common reasons buyers give as to why they bought a certain property is that they couldn't resist, it was such a good deal, or it was the biggest house they could find for the price.

Some buyers purchase properties to fix them up and live in or resell for a profit. This can work if you buy the properties cheap enough and you estimate the fix-up costs accurately. But many buyers who do this find that when they add the home's purchase price to the fix-up costs, they're at or above market value. If you want to go this route, you need to know the market in that area and be able to estimate fix-up costs accurately.

Days-on-market (DOM) is an important indicator to keep in mind, because it alerts you that a home may have problems. If a listing's DOM is over the area average, look for the reason. Sometimes a sale or two fails and the home was taken off the market during the *under contract* period, and this can run up the DOM meter; in most multiple listing systems, the DOM counter doesn't stop ticking until the sale closes.

Typical hard-to-sell properties include:

- Homes that back onto railroad tracks, freeways, industrial areas, high voltage power lines, frontage roads, or other obvious value killers.

- Homes that are overimproved for their area. A typical example would be a 900-square foot bungalow with an addition built on the back or side. Sometimes it's a well-planned addition that blends in; other times it's a tacky add-on.

- Homes in neighborhoods that have become run down owing to a high percentage of rentals or foreclosed properties (although if you're an investor, buying homes in these areas can eventually turn into good investments).

- Homes that stray too far from the architectural mainstream of what people are buying. Typical examples are round or hexagon homes, earth-covered homes, and conversions of other structures such as barns, silos, and sheds. These conversions can be quaint and even featured in a home magazine, but selling them and getting a return on your investment is not always easy.

- Homes that have site problems, such as steep slopes, gullies, little or no backyard, or lack of privacy from neighbors or street. Even the way a house sits on a lot can affect its value.

- Homes painted an unusual or unattractive color. Color can influence a home's value and cause it not to sell, especially in a slow market. As a buyer this can spell opportunity, though, if that's the only problem and you can make it a great deal. You can sometimes change an ugly duckling into a swan simply by changing a home's color scheme.

Mistake #11: Overextending Your Budget

A lender who prequalifies you for a loan may tell you that you're able to buy a $275,000 house. But keep in mind that buying for the full amount that you can qualify for may put you out of your financial comfort zone. A lender who offers to make you a loan that, when added to your other debt, consumes 50 percent or more of your income is not necessarily doing you a favor. Some families can handle that kind of debt load while others will go bankrupt fast.

Although lenders try to go with one-size-fits-all qualifying, it's up to you to look at your situation and lifestyle, and work the numbers to come up with a percent you can live with. Buying a smaller home now and moving up as your income increases and you build equity is a good approach. Also, avoid adjustable rate mortgages (ARMs) and low teaser rates that can increase your payments and boost your debt ratios higher than you anticipated.

However, there's another way to look at the amount of home you should buy. Some people claim that you should buy the most home you possibly can afford now. Then, as your income goes up and home values rise, you win, not only saving a move but also ending up with more equity and a home you'll enjoy more. This approach worked for many owners who bought during the last thirty years and have watched their homes' equity soar dramatically. Many of these home-owners say they struggled in the beginning, but as their incomes went up, the house payments took a smaller part of their paycheck.

For instance, Ross and Elaine were among those homeowners who bought their home in 1985 for $35,000, improved it over the years, and recently sold it for $396,000. According to Ross, their house pay-ment alone in the beginning took nearly 30 percent of their income. But by the time they sold it, it was nearly paid off and took less than 5 percent of their income.

Neither way is right or wrong; it depends on your values and prior-ities.

Mistake #12: Failing to Protect Yourself When You Make an Offer

Many home buyers, in the excitement of finding the home they've always wanted and writing an offer, forget to add contingencies that will protect them. A *contingency* is a clause added to an offer to make it subject to a certain event. Common contingencies or subject-tos include:

- Financing approval.

- Home inspection.

- Closing by a certain date.

- Replacing a roof, floor coverings, painting the home's inside or outside.

- Third-party approval, such as a bank in a short sale, parental approval, repair bids from contractors.

- Selling a current home by a certain date.

Although inserting contingencies in your offer may weaken it or make it less competitive, some are routinely needed to protect you from events that are out of your control. For example, one buyer's agent insisted on putting in a "subject to final loan approval" contin-gency in her client's offer, even though he had a mortgage preapproval letter. Unfortunately, two days before closing, the buyer lost his job owing to downsizing, and that eliminated any chance of closing on the loan. This saved the buyer from losing his $3,000 deposit.

Some especially important contingencies that protect you are:

■ Making your offer subject to a professional inspection. If you find problems, you have some leverage to get them fixed, or you can walk away and get your deposit back. You may want to add specific contingencies for mold, radon, rot behind stucco or siding, and other problems specific to your area.

■ Making your offer subject to final loan approval. Life is uncertain and sometimes things happen over which you have no control but that can prevent you from closing.

■ Adding a clause making the deal subject to your old home's closing. If you've made an offer on a new home, and your old home is sold but hasn't closed yet, this protects you should the buyers on your home run into problems that can domino and jeopardize your purchase.

■ Making the offer subject to the home appraisal for at least the sale price. If it comes in low, you'll have the option of negotiating a lower price or walking away and getting your deposit back.

Mistake #13: Getting Family, Relatives, and Friends Too Involved

Not involving your family or friends in your purchase of a home can sometimes be difficult. If mom and dad are putting up the down payment or co-signing the mortgage, then they'll be a big part of the deal regardless. But on the whole, getting too many opinions can be worse than getting no opinions at all. That's because, often, those whose opinions you seek will note your enthusiasm and support your decision, even if they think it's a bad one. Others who don't know what they're talking about will point out problems and badmouth a good house.

Greg and Linda found this out when they bought their first home. Naturally, they were excited and wanted to get as many friends and relatives involved as they could. Unfortunately, it didn't work out quite as they'd hoped. The more friends they took through the home, the more confused they got. Some loved it, others didn't. One uncle even told them that they were making a big mistake by moving into that neighborhood. After a week of being bombarded by mixed messages, the couple developed such a bad case of buyer's remorse that they called their agent and told him they were backing out. They couldn't stand the pressure and were willing to forfeit their $1,000 deposit.

So how do you avoid these situations?

- Rely on your agent, who is a professional and has an obligation to help you make the best deal possible. If a relative brings up a valid problem with the house, discuss it with your agent.

- Trust your research. You've undoubtedly looked at a dozen or so homes in your price range and have a good idea of values and neighborhoods. You know when you've made a good offer if you've followed the advice given in the last few chapters.

- When you've found a home you want to make an offer on, the last thing you want to do is involve Uncle Louie or your Cousin Joe, who happens to be a contractor. No matter how good they are, builders, remodelers, and contractors are not professional home inspectors. They may be skilled in their particular trade, but they're not trained to look for and find the problems a home inspector is.

- Involve family, relatives, and friends with a barbecue at your new house after you've moved in. They can see your new home with you in it already.

Mistake #14: Being Unable to Make a Decision

When you're searching for the right house, take your time to look at as many homes as you need to in order to get a good feel for the market. Once you've narrowed down your choices and have decided on a home, then it's time to move swiftly.

If you've been shopping around and have found your ideal home, it's likely other buyers have come to the same conclusion. In any market, the best homes in the best areas sell quickly, even in a slow market. So, act on your plans.

Todd and Alexis experienced hesitation when they were looking for their first home. After going through more than two dozen houses and not seeing anything that they liked, they were getting a little discouraged when their Realtor called about a home that had just come on the market. When they drove by, it was the home they were looking for—an updated three-bedroom cottage with newly painted yellow siding, full basement, and a detached double-car garage. Their agent wanted them to put together an offer immediately, because he didn't think it would remain on the market long.

But as much as they wanted the home, Todd and Alexis hesitated. They were scared to make a commitment and wanted to wait until the weekend, when their parents could go through the home. Unfortunately for them, the weekend walk-through never happened. Another couple also loved the home, quickly made an offer, and the FOR SALE sign soon sported a bright red "sold" sticker.

It's not uncommon for a home to sit on the market for weeks with no action, and suddenly two or three offers come in at the same time. It's almost spooky how often this happens, as most experienced Realtors will tell you. Fear of making a mistake is usually the culprit. The best way to work through this is to talk it over with your broker, lender, or someone who has bought a house before. Once you get your concerns out in the open, they often become easier to deal with.

Buyer's remorse is the real estate industry term for making an offer and then having all kinds of fears bounce around in your imagination. It not only applies to buying a home but also to buying cars, appliances, engagement rings, and many other financial commitments. It's important to realize that this is a normal reaction many buyers experience. The best way to cope with it is to review the reasons you made an offer and what your goals are. Talk to your agent or others who have gone through the home-buying experience.

Mistake #15: Neglecting to Get a Buyer's Broker Early On

Having a good Realtor on your side is the best thing you can do to find the home you're looking for and get the best deal. These agents know the market, the best neighborhoods, and what type of loan will best fit your situation. You'll save a lot of wheel spinning if you get an agent in the beginning.

The best part of working with an agent to find a house to buy is that it's free. You get professional help in sorting through the options, and the seller pays the agent's fee. Sellers are glad to pay a fee to get their home sold and avoid the hassle of handling multiple showings and providing selling details.

Typically, a buyer's agent represents you and looks out for your best interests. His or her access to the multiple listing service makes finding your dream home a lot easier. In one typical example, Max and Andrea were first-time home buyers who looked on their own for three months without success and were getting frustrated. Every weekend they circled ads, toured open houses, and called phone numbers on FOR SALE signs. The bewildering array of choices only added to the confusion. Finally, one of Andrea's co-workers suggested they talk to Carol, an agent she knew through her school's PTA.

The first thing Carol did when she met Max and Andrea was to ask them if they were working with a mortgage lender. When they said no, she arranged for them to meet with a lender and get the approval process started. Late the next day, the lender called Carol and told her that Max and Andrea looked pretty good. There were a couple of small credit problems he had to clear up, but that shouldn't be too difficult and they could buy a home around $260,000 with 10 percent down.

Carol met with the buyers and quickly determined what type of home, the number of bedrooms, and the amenities they wanted, along with areas with a reasonable commute. Carol found them fourteen homes that merited inspection. The first eight were nice but didn't click. The tenth home turned out to be a winner; it was exactly what the buyers were looking for. Max and Andrea quickly made an offer and Carol presented it to the sellers and their agent that evening. The offer was accepted, with a closing date scheduled in three weeks.

Although it's true that you can find a home on your own, going it without an agent limits you to about 15 percent of the market. Using a buyer's agent, however, can ensure you make the right moves and get the best deal.

Mistake #16: Failing to Get a Professional Home Inspection

Home inspections are critical for knowing what you're buying. Water damage, mold, electrical and plumbing problems, and problems that lurk in dark places are unknowns that an inspection can protect you from. In one case, Steve and Tiffany were so excited to find the charming brick bungalow on a tree-lined street. They drove the area often looking for one of the cute 1950s homes that lined the wide streets.

Their excitement soared as they walked through the home, noting all the wood trim and the spacious floor plan. It was exactly what they were looking for: a home where they could strip off the layers of paint and wallpaper and restore it to its former charm. They made an as-is offer that was accepted and a closing was scheduled in four weeks.Since these buyers were able to come up with 20 percent down, they opted to finance conventionally to avoid PMI costs. The appraisal came back at the sales price and all looked good for a smooth closing.

The sale closed and Steve and Tiffany started to move in. However, it didn't take long before problems started popping up. The gas company tagged the furnace because the service tech suspected it had a cracked chamber and the vent pipe was too close to a wood joist. Unfortunately, the couple had spent most of their money buying the home and didn't have funds for the major problems they encountered. Their Visa card took a hit for several thousand dollars as they replaced the furnace and upgraded the duct work.

Interestingly, Steve and Tiffany had erroneously felt that the bank's appraiser would find any problems and list them on the appraisal. In reality, an appraiser is interested only in the overall value of the home and is hired to ensure that value is in line with the sales price. Instead, these buyers should have hired a professional home inspector. The inspection report would have listed exactly what problems lurked under the rafters, joists, and in the dark places of the basement. They would also have found out the condition of the appliances, furnace, water heater, plumbing, electrical, and all the other important components of the home.

And if the inspection revealed problems, they could have used the inspection report to renegotiate the sale agreement or have walked away from the deal and gotten their deposit back. In reality, no buyers should buy a home without a professional home inspection. Never!

Mistake #17: Neglecting to Check Out the Homeowners Association Before Committing

In most states, HOAs have broad power to enforce the rules and collect fees and assessment. If you don't follow the rules or pay your monthly fees, the HOA can put a lien on your property and ultimately foreclose to collect back fees and assessments. But having a strong HOA is a double-edged sword. Strict rules can keep the project looking uniform and inviting, which maintains the community's value.

You may not like all the HOA rules, but changing them is not always easy. It usually entails getting like-minded owners together and electing a new board. If you can get a majority of the homeowners to go along with your proposal, that's great. If not, you can try again next election.

So you don't end up in a condo complex where you won't be happy living. Do the following homework before you buy:

- Get a copy of the CC&Rs and condo bylaws. Read them over carefully so you can decide whether you will be happy living there.

- Get a copy of the last several HOA meeting minutes so you know what the concerns are and what direction the community is heading.

- Get a financial statement. If major repairs are coming up and the board doesn't have reserves to handle them, you'll get hit with a hefty assessment.

- Speak to several neighbors and get the "lay of land."

- Check out the owners or neighbors above and on either side of the unit you're interested in. You don't want to move in next to a neighbor who likes to play bagpipes when he can't sleep.

- Walk around the complex and note the condition of the infrastructure. Is it well cared for or are there signs of deferred maintenance?

It's much cheaper to do a little homework and walk away from potential problems than to find out after you've moved in that you're not going to like living there.

Mistake #18: Assuming You Can't Afford to Buy a Home

It's amazing how many would-be home buyers assume they can't buy a home based on what they hear from friends, relatives, and the media, and don't to talk to a lender or Realtor for fear they'll be rejected. In reality, many prospective buyers have found a way to own their own home when they didn't think they could. They overcame their fear, spoke with a mortgage broker and lender, and found a way.

Some suggestions to help you get the ball rolling include:

- Realize the loan officer is on your side. If you can't qualify now, he or she can map out a plan of action that can get you headed in the right direction.

- Many people feel it takes years after a bankruptcy to get their credit back on track to buy a home. Not so. If you've paid your bills on time and corrected the problems that led to your bankruptcy, you may qualify after a year or two of discharge.

- Talk to an experienced Realtor who may know of homes for which you can work out a lease-option until you can qualify to buy.

- If you're divorced, your state housing authority may have programs for single parents. Check with an agent in your area for possibilities.

In one case, a home buyer had credit problems that prevented him from buying a home because a few late payments had damaged his credit. He contacted several homeowners with a plan that would allow him to buy their home if they would lease it to him for twelve months, by which time he would have cleared up his credit problems. He had to talk to about a dozen homeowners until he found one who had moved out of his house into a new one and was making payments on two homes.

After speaking to the buyer's mortgage lender and verifying that in a year he could qualify, the homeowner agreed to a lease-option. This created a win-win situation because the seller was relieved of making $1,900 a month in payments and the buyer was on his way to becoming a homeowner.

The bottom line is to not let doom and gloom convince you that you can't buy a home. Talk to lenders and Realtors and find out what it'll take to get you qualified and what other options are available.

Mistake #19: Failing to Take the Deadlines in Your Purchase Offer Seriously

Once you've made an offer on a home and the seller has accepted it, the clock starts ticking on certain deadlines written into the purchase offer. Many buyers rely on their agents or loan officers to keep track of the important dates, but if they mess up, you're the one who pays the price of a failed deal. To prevent this, review your purchase agreement and make a list of all the items with deadlines. Then cross each item off the list as it's completed.

These deadlines, which need to be met, include:

- Your final mortgage loan approval date.

- Your appraisal deadline.

- Various inspections such as home, mold, and radon, as well as any others needed based on your area.

- Property condition disclosures from the seller.

- Sending a repair addendum to the sellers concerning problems the home inspector found. Remember to note the time the sellers have to respond to your addendum and fix the problems detailed.

- Your homeowners and title insurance.

- Your settlement date, or the day you're scheduled to close on your mortgage loan.

Typically, you'll have about thirty days to closing, and during this time you'll need to arrange for the actions necessary to meet the deadlines indicated in your purchase agreement. If you miss these deadlines, the sellers can cancel your agreement and you're back to square one. Especially, meeting your deadlines can be critical if the sellers have a backup offer in the wings, particularly one that's for more money.

Mistake #20: Buying a Fixer-Upper or Investment Home Without Doing the Numbers

Some home buyers have the dream of buying a fixer-upper and restoring it to live-in condition or selling it for a profit. However, many who try this end up losing money or "getting chomped by the alligator," as it's called in the real estate industry. This is both unfortunate and unnecessary, because neophyte home buyers can avoid many of the financial alligators. Some of the bigger ones are:

- Failure to research or learn about area values, resulting in their overpaying for their home. As a result, they don't have enough money left to fund needed upgrades.

- Failure to accurately determine the cost of repairs and upgrades.

- Overconfidence in knowing what work on the home they can handle themselves and what they need to hire or contract out. This can easily wipe out any profit or equity anticipated.

- Lack of experience in determining what needs to be replaced and what can be fixed. Capable renovators tend to also be good scroungers for cheap materials they can use.

- Failure to work the numbers by adding the cost of the property to the estimated costs of renovation. The two numbers added together should be less than the market value of similar homes in the neighborhood. Failure to build their do-it-yourself skills so they can increase their profit margin. Many home-improvements centers host free classes on tiling, plumbing, and other basic skills.

- Neglecting to take the long view by keeping properties and letting their tenants pay off mortgage loans. Many buyers get impatient and try to flip properties for a quick buck rather than keeping them, building equity, and taking advantage of the tax breaks.

APPENDIX A

Tips and Traps for Single Home Buyers

Not surprisingly, the National Association of Realtors (NAR) reports that nearly 30 percent of 2006 home sales were to single buyers. What's interesting is that single females accounted for about 21 percent, compared to 9 percent for single men. Furthermore, more women (15.5 million) than men (11.8 million) live alone. Among them, women were more likely than men to own their homes (56 percent versus 47 percent).

This is undoubtedly because both men and women are choosing to pursue education, careers, and job opportunities and they have the income to buy. Also, buying a home was considered a good financial move for singles until the credit meltdown starting in late 2006 made qualifying a lot more difficult.

In light of the ongoing real estate recession and increasing unemployment numbers, it's likely the number of singles buying homes will decline significantly until the economy picks up steam again. Still, there's good opportunity to buy homes for steep discounts and single buyers shouldn't hesitate to stay in the market. Paying rent is still a deadend street in any economy.

Buying a home as a single person is not much different from buying one as a couple: it boils down to one income qualifying for the mortgage versus two incomes which means you'll likely have to buy a smaller home. In fact, some couples have to go this route, too. It's not that uncommon for either the husband or the wife to qualify individually for the mortgage because one has great credit and the other doesn't.

The key to a smooth and successful deal as a single buyer is to pick the right people to guide you through the process. Assuming you're a first-time home buyer, you need to assemble a team of professionals that have been discussed in earlier chapters such as:

1. A mortgage lender to put the financing together.

2. A Realtor who can guide you through the buying process.

3. An insurance agent for homeowners insurance and, if needed, flood, earthquake, or other disaster policies.

4. A professional home inspector.

If you feel hesitant to become a homeowner because this is your first time or you've heard a few horror stories, consider the following tips to make it easier:

- Go with the best area you can afford. If possible, pick an area (or condo complex) that has other single homeowners.

- Even though you're single, look for an area with good schools. You may want to sell and move up to a bigger home in the future, and homes in good school boundaries tend to increase or hold their values better.

- Hire a home inspector who encourages you to come along on the inspection. He or she can point out to you how a house works and important pointers on maintaining it.

- Get friends and relatives involved in helping you decorate the home and making it your own.

- Don't let negative people discourage you from pursuing your dream of home ownership.

- Once you savor the freedom to indulge your creative decorating talents and get the pet you've always wanted, you'll never look back.

 APPENDIX B

Tips on Selling Your Home

Buying and selling a home are often intertwined actions. For example, when sellers close on one home they often immediately become buyers and close on their new home. If you can work out the timing right, that's great. You've made your life a lot easier and have saved a double move. But it does not always work out so smoothly.

To help you put together a double close, here are some tips on selling your home faster and for the most money possible.

First Impressions Count

When most people sell their car, they clean it meticulously inside, out-side, and under the hood, or they send it to a detail shop. They intu-itively understand that you can't sell a car that doesn't look sharp. There's lots of competition out there and buyers are discriminating. Yet it's amazing how many people put their homes on the market with nowhere near the thought and planning they would put into selling their cars. It's as if they suddenly decided to sell, so they ran down to the home center, bought a FOR SALE sign, and planted it on their front lawn—end of process. You can do that and your home may sell, but it'll likely cost you time and result in a lower offer, just as would trying to sell that 2001 Honda without prepping it first.

Just as first impressions are important for getting that first date, the same is true with your selling your house. With good curb appeal, the sale is half made, whereas if buyers drive by your home and don't like what they see, it's off to the next house; they won't even glance back through their rearview mirror. Here are some tips on how to bring up the curb appeal on your home so that buyers will be excited to see what's inside:

- Walk across the street from your home and pretend you're a buyer. What do you see that detracts from good curb appeal? Take lots of photos and look them over carefully. Note the problem areas and make a list of those things that need correcting.

- Trees should frame your house, not block a buyer's view, so if necessary, clear out trees and shrubs that obscure the front view or detract from it. Of course, if you have 100-year-old sycamores, cutting them down may not be a good idea; older trees that line a street can make a neighborhood more appealing, and mature trees in a yard have intrinsic value.

- Trim foundation shrubs to only 3 or 4 feet high. Don't let the shrubs grow so tall that they block the front windows.

- Check the walkway to the front door, the porch, steps, and railings. The entry is a critical part of a home's curb appeal; it should be welcoming not only to prospective buyers but also allow those buyers to envision welcoming their friends later on.

- Because the entrance to your home is another important impression-making item, be sure the front door is freshly painted or stained and the fixtures are free of tarnish. If the front door has seen better days, replace it with one that complements your house style. Don't forget the porch light and the door bell, either—they are important fixtures.

- A roof in good condition creates a positive first-time impression. If shingles are missing, cracked, or weathered, you've got a problem. Buyers will wonder what else is wrong, and whether there are leaks. Reshingling or replacing the roof is a good investment. If you fix it, the higher offers you'll receive for your house will likely more than equal the cost of having made the repair.

When buyers are impressed with your home's curb appeal, they'll walk through the front door with a feeling of "I could enjoy living here." To keep this feeling and build more excitement, make it easy for them to envision themselves living in the home:

- Remove all excess furniture as well as trophies, family pictures, and other personal items, as well as anything else that may distract a buyer from focusing on the positive aspects of your home.

■ Repair holes and dings in the walls, and then give them a fresh coat of paint.

■ Make the kitchen look inviting by cleaning, refurbishing, or replacing kitchen cabinets and counters.

■ Upgrade the baths by cleaning and resealing the caulking around tubs and showers. Replace the lights over sinks if needed, and hang a new shower curtain to spice up a drab bathroom.

■ Make sure all the floor coverings are in good condition and, if necessary, replace worn carpets and refinish wood floors that show traffic wear.

■ Give the home a thorough cleaning. If you don't have time, hire a cleaning service to make your home sparkle.

Remember that you're competing with other homes in the area for a limited number of buyers; a successful sale depends on your home's standing out from the others.

Agents and appraisers will price your home by comparing it to what similar homes have sold for in the area in the last ninety days. True, you may think you have the nicest home in the neighborhood, but your "extras" may not add to value, so always make it more competitive. An experienced agent or appraiser can tell you what extras add value and which ones don't.

Finally, here are seven mistakes to avoid in selling your home:

1. Don't price your home according to what you need to get out of it; rather, go with market data. Your home will sit on the market and may eventually sell, but probably for less than if you had priced it based on its market value in the first place.

2. Don't add the cost of upgrades to the home's value. Buyers expect a good roof and a home in good condition for the price. If you try to add the cost of a new roof, appliances, new carpets, or other upgrades, you'll price your home out of the market.

3. Don't list with the agent who quotes you the highest price. Instead, interview two or three agents and go with the one with the best track record in your area.

4. Don't make the mistake of being unaware of the average selling time for similar homes in your area. If you haven't gotten any offers within this time frame, bite the bullet and lower your price. You might also look at your home carefully and see if you can figure out what's turning off buyers. Then have a frank discussion with your agent as to what you can do to correct any problems.

5. Don't take the lazy approach and offer a carpet, painting, or redecorating allowance. Do what's necessary to make your home attractive with neutral colors. Buyers often make low offers on homes that need work, but they want the allowances, too. It's a no-win situation for you as a seller because you end up attracting the bottom-feeders looking for good deals.

6. Don't neglect to get a professional home inspection before you put your home on the market, because you'll be setting yourself up for problems down the road. By getting the inspection upfront, you know what repairs are needed. Use the inspection as a sales tool to show that the home is in good condition, and have the receipts and work orders to prove that you've corrected any problems.

7. Don't get emotional and immediately reject a low offer, because you could be losing a potential sale. Many buyers come in with low offers to see what you'll do. They feel they have to try to get a super good deal—it's an ego thing. But if you don't take it personally and you handle it professionally, you can often turn a low offer into a sale. Stay calm and work up a counteroffer you can live with.

APPENDIX C

Web Resources

Home Shopping and Buying Web Sites

www.Realtor.com
www.hud.gov/buying/comq.cfm
www.hud.gov/buying/booklet.pdf
www.Homeseekers.com
www.Cyberhomes.com
www.Realestatebook.com
www.Owners.com
www.Zillow.com

Credit Scoring Sites

www.myfico.com
www.experian.com
www.equifax.com
www.transunion.com
www.mycreditfile.com

Closing Documents (HUD-1) and Good Faith Estimates

www.hud.gov/offices/adm/
    hudclips/forms/files/1a.pdf

www.hud.gov/content/releases/
    pr08–033.pdf
www.hud.gov/buying/booklet.pdf

Financial Calculators

www.hsh.com/calculators.html
www.mortgage-minder.com
www.calculated.com

Secondary Mortgage Markets

www.fanniemae.com
www.freddiemac.com
www.ginniemae.com

Government Loan Programs

www.hud.gov
www.rurdev.usda.gov
www.va.gov

State and Local Loan Programs

www.hud.gov/local/index.cfm

Internet Mortgage Lenders

www.countrywide.com
www.e-loan.com
www.wellsfargo.com

Home Inspectors

www.ashi.com
www.nibi.com
www.inspecthomes.org
www.hif-assoc.org

Homeowners Insurance

www.iii.org/individuals/homei
www.geico.com/getaquote/
    homeowners
www.statefarm.com
www.pueblo.gsa.gov/cic_text/
    housing/12ways/12ways.htm
www.libertymutual.com

Flood Insurance

www.fema.gov/nfip

Title Insurance

www.firstam.com
www.stewart.com
In Iowa only: www.ifahome.com

Information on Modular and Manufactured Homes

www.manufacturedhomesource.com
www.modularhomeplace.com
www.manufacturedhousing.org
www.mhoaa.us
www.modularhousing.com

Tax Information

www.irs.gov and irs.gov/faqs/
    faq3–6.html
www.orps.state.ny.us/pamphlet/
    taxworks.htm
www.bankrate.com/brm/itax/
    news/20030806a1.asp
www.wwwebtax.com/
    deductions_taxes/taxes.htm
www.realestateabc.com/taxes/
    deductible2.htm

Glossary

Addendum. An addition or modification to a purchase agreement. Sometimes called a rider or amendment.

Adjustable Rate Mortgage (ARM). A mortgage with a payment that goes up or down according to the performance of an economic index such as the one-year Treasury Bill. Payments can adjust every six months, one year, two years, etc., depending on the plan. The margin (stays constant) is added to the index rate to come up with the interest rate you'll pay for the next adjustment period.

Agency. The relationship between a buyer or seller and a real estate broker.

Allowance. The amount of money a contractor allows for appliances, upgrades, or options.

Amortization. When a loan's monthly payments include principal and interest and will pay to zero in x number of years, it's called an amortized loan. A printout that shows how much goes to principal and interest each month is an amortization schedule.

Annual percentage rate (APR). The APR interest rate is calculated by adding the closing costs to the loan amount and recalculating keeping the payment and term the same.

Application fees. Fees that you pay a lender up front for a credit report, appraisal, and sometimes for locking in an interest rate.

Appraisal. The opinion of a licensed appraiser on what a property is worth in the current market. Appraisers are licensed in most states.

Appreciation. When a home's value increases.

Balloon mortgage. A mortgage that typically has payments of a 30-year mortgage, but with the full balance due much sooner, in 1, 5, or 10 years, for example.

Bid. A written proposal from a contractor to build a house according to the specifications you agree on for a certain price. Also, subcontractors can submit bids for certain parts of the construction.

Building permit. A document issued by the city or county building department granting permission to build the house according to the specs you've submitted.

Buydown. Typically, a lender will give you a lower interest rate for a fee. For instance, 1 percent of the loan amount could buy down the interest rate 1/6 of 1 percent, depending on the market. Builders can advertise a lower interest because they've agreed to pay the lender for the buy-down.

Buyer's market. Market conditions that favor the buyer. There are more homes for sale than there are buyers. The opposite is a *seller's market*.

Callback. A return visit by the contractor to repair or replace items he has found to be unsatisfactory or that require service under the warranty.

Cap. On a variable interest loan it's the maximum rate a loan can go during the life of the loan.

CC&R. Covenants, conditions, and restrictions are recorded rules that govern what you can and can't do with your property.

Change order. Written authorization for the contractor to make changes or additions to the original contract along with any additional costs incurred.

Closing costs. Fees paid at closing to the lender. They typically total 3–4% of the loan amount.

Closing statement. Also known as a *settlement statement* or *HUD*.

Condominium. A dwelling of two or more units where the homeowners own the interior space of their unit but own everything else in common with the other owners.

Conforming loan. One that meets with *Fannie Mae* or *Freddie Mac* underwriting standards.

Conventional mortgage. A mortgage that is not insured by a government agency. Quasi-government corporations like *Fannie Mae* and *Freddie Mac,* as well as banks, pension funds, and investors, buy these loans as investments.

Co-op building. An apartment building that is owned by a corporation that sells shares to people who want to lease an apartment. Owning shares entitles you to lease a certain apartment, and you pay a monthly assessment, which includes your share of operating costs and taxes.

Cost-plus contract. You agree to pay the contractor the cost of materials and labor plus a certain percentage for profit and overhead. This is also known as a time and materials contract.

Counteroffer. When you make a written offer on a property, the sellers can accept, reject, or counter your offer with the price and/or terms they will agree to in writing. Sometimes, the counter, counteroffer process goes back and forth several times until the parties reach agreement.

Curb appeal. The impression a house gives when a buyer drives by to assess the property.

Depreciation. When a home's value decreases.

Desktop underwriting. Automated underwriting.

Draw. A payment to the contractor at certain stages of construction to pay for work done to that point. The draw schedule should be outlined in the contract.

Dual agency. This is when a real estate agent represents both the buyer and seller in a real estate transaction.

Due on sale clause. Nearly every mortgage has a clause that requires the mortgage to be paid off when the home is sold without paying off the mortgage.

Earnest money. When you make an offer, you give the sellers or their agent a deposit to show good faith so they'll take the home off the market for a specified period of time.

Easement. A right given by a landowner to a third party to make use of the land for a specific purpose. Typical easements are for utilities, sewers, water mains, or access to another property. Easements are recorded in the county recorder's office.

Encroachment. A neighbor's fence, driveway, structure, or whatever encroaches on your lot. Many times the property owner doesn't even realize it until a survey is completed.

Equity. The difference between your mortgage balance and the current market value of your home.

Fannie Mae. Federal National Mortgage Association.

Freddie Mac. Federal Home Loan Mortgage Corporation.

Ginnie Mae. Government National Mortgage Association.

Good Faith Estimate. Lenders are required to give you in writing a breakdown of all your closing costs and loan fees along with an APR quote within 3 days of your application.

Hazard insurance. Insurance that covers the property against damage and liability.

Home inspection. Usually refers to an inspection performed by a licensed home inspector.

Homeowners association. A corporation formed to handle the affairs of a subdivision, condo, or *PUD* project. All the property owners are members of the association. Officers are elected by the members to enforce the rules, collect fees, and pay the bills.

Home warranty. An insurance policy that insures electrical, plumbing, heating, and appliances in a home for one year. Also, a warranty the builder or a third party issues insuring new construction against defects.

Index. On a *variable rate loan,* it's the base interest rate the lender adds the margin rate to in order to calculate the interest you'll pay for the next period.

Late charge. A penalty applied to a mortgage payment that arrives after the 10- to 15-day grace period. A typical late charge is 4 percent of the payment.

Lease with option to buy. A lease where the tenant has the right to buy the property for an agreed upon amount within a certain time period. Sometimes part of the monthly payment is applied to the purchase price if the tenant buys the property as agreed upon.

Leverage. Using mostly borrowed money to buy a property. The buyers have from nothing to only a small percentage of their own money in the deal.

Lien. The legal claim that is recorded and attaches to property.

Lien release. A document that voids the legal rights of the contractor, subcontractors, and suppliers to place a *lien* against your property. You should never close new construction until you have lien releases from all subcontractors and suppliers verifying they have been paid in full for labor and materials.

Limited Agency Consent Agreement. The agent agrees in writing to represent both parties and not disclose anything that would hurt either party's bargaining position.

Loan commitment. A document that a mortgage provider gives you that states you have been approved for a loan at a certain interest for a certain length of time. It may also have conditions that you need to meet for final approval. A commitment is good for a limited time, usually 30–60 days.

Loan origination fee. A one-time fee charged by the lender to do the loan. It's usually .5 to 1 percent of the loan amount.

Loan-to-value ratio (LTV). The percent the bank loans you to the value (sales price) of the home. If you borrow 80 percent or put

20 percent down, the LTV would be 80 percent. A 10 percent down payment would give you a 90 percent LTV, and so on.

Lock-in. The interest rate the bank offers and you agree to for a certain period of time, usually 30–60 days. Depending on the market, you may lock in a rate at the time of application; other times you may let it float hoping it will go down before closing.

Maintenance fee. The monthly fee you pay to the *homeowners association* for taking care of the grounds, structures, or whatever else is included in the association agreement.

Mechanic's lien. A *lien* obtained by an unpaid subcontractor or supplier that attaches to your home. Legally, your home can be sold to pay the subcontractor or supplier.

MLS. Realtor's Multiple Listing Service.

Mortgage broker. A person or company that brings together a lender and homebuyer and processes the mortgage application.

Mortgagee. The entity that lends money secured by property (lender).

Mortgagor. The one who borrows money secured by the property (borrower).

Negative equity. A situation where you owe more on the house than it's worth on the current market.

Nonconforming loan. A loan that doesn't meet with Fannie Mae or Freddie Mac underwriting standards.

Option. A buyer pays a fee to tie up a property for an agreed on price and length of time. At the end of the time period, the buyer either performs or loses the option fee.

Personal property. Property that is not attached to a dwelling and/or not included in the sale. Examples are refrigerators, furniture, and artwork.

PITI. An acronym for principal, interest, taxes, and insurance when referring to a mortgage payment.

Planned Unit Development (PUD). A community that has a homeowners association that handles common areas. PUDs are typically single-family homes or connected units with a private lot.

Plans and specifications. Drawings for the project, along with a list of the products, materials, quantities, and finishes to be used in the project.

Points. Each point equals 1 percent of the loan amount. Points are usually used to *buy down* an interest rate. What a point is worth can change daily in response to the financial market.

Prepaid interest. Usually interest paid from the day of closing to the end of the month. Your first mortgage payment will then start on the first of the following month. This is so everyone's mortgage payment is due on the first of the month, not a month from the day they close. Also see *points.*

Prepayment penalty. A fee the mortgage company charges you to pay off a loan early. It can be a flat fee or a percentage of the loan amount.

Prequalifying for a loan. A commitment from a bank that you qualify for a loan subject to certain conditions.

Private mortgage insurance (PMI). An insurance premium you pay to protect the bank against default if your loan is more than 80 percent of the purchase price.

PUD. See *Planned Unit Development.*

Punch list. When the home is just about completed, you do a walk through with the contractor or foreman and make a list of problems and items to be fixed or completed. Preferably, these items will be completed before you close.

Real estate owned (REO). Homes that lenders have foreclosed on and now own.

Realtor. Someone who is a member of the National Association of Realtors and the appropriate state and local boards.

Regulation Z. Also known as the Truth in Lending Act. It requires lenders to provide a written good faith estimate or a breakdown of the closing costs a buyer pays to get the loan.

Reserve. Money set aside by a condo, co-op, or homeowners association for future improvements and repairs.

RV. Recreational vehicle.

Secondary market. The wholesale mortgage industry.

Seller's market. Market conditions that favor the seller, in which there are more homebuyers than homes for sale on the market. The opposite is a *buyer's market.*

Settlement statement. Also known as a *closing statement* or *HUD.* It's a breakdown of all the costs and fees you pay to get a mortgage.

Short sale. Lenders agreeing to take less than the balance owed on a mortgage so that they don't have to foreclose.

Subcontractor. A person or company hired by the contractor to perform specialized work such as framing, sheet rocking, plumbing, or electrical. Sometimes referred to as a trade contractor.

Title company. A company that insures property against defects in the title. It may also close the loan and prepare closing documents.

Title insurance. An insurance policy that insures your property against problems arising from defects in the title such as *liens,* forgeries, and *easements.*

Town houses. Condominium units that are typically built side by side rather than as multistory units.

Transaction brokerage. A transaction broker working with a consumer without establishing an agency relationship.

Truth in Lending Act. See *Regulation Z.*

Variable interest rate. A mortgage that has an interest rate that goes up or down according to the performance of a financial index. A popular index is the Treasury Bill Index.

Warehousing the loan. Banks and other money sources buying or making mortgage loans for their own portfolios.

Zoning. Local cities' and counties' laws that govern how land is used and what and where certain structures can be built. These laws are often called zoning ordinances.

Suggested Reading

Bandy, Arlene. *Surviving Homeowner Associations.* New Bern, NC: Trafford Publishing, 2005.

Burnside, Kevin. *Buying a Manufactured Home.* San Francisco: Van Der Plas Publications, 2002.

Davis, Sid. *The First-Time Homeowner's Survival Guide.* New York: AMACOM, 2007.

Glink, Alice R.. *100 Questions Every First-Time Home Buyer Should Ask.* New York: Times Business, 2000.

Greenwald, Joni, Harriet Graves, Shannon Keegan, and Ryan Shacklett. *Homeowner Associations: A Nightmare or Dream Come True.* Denver: Cassie Publications, 1998.

Irwin, Robert. *Tips and Traps When Buying a Condo, Co-op or Townhouse.* New York: McGraw-Hill, 2000.

———. *Tips and Traps When Buying a Home.* New York: McGraw-Hill, 2009.

Ramsey, Tracey. *Saving the Deal, How to Avoid Financing Fiascoes and Other Real Estate Deal Killers.* New York, AMACOM, 2008.

Treganowan, Jeff and Susan. *The Ultimate New-home Buying Guide.* North Conway, NH: Maple Leaf Press, 2001.

Watkins, A. M.. *Manufactured Houses, Finding and Buying Your Dream Home for Less.* Chicago: Real Estate Education Co., 1994.

Webb, Martha. *Finding Home, Buying the House That's Right for You.* New York: Three Rivers Press, 1998.

Index

Index